① word list   ③ Silent Reading
② Oral reading ④ Listening

Diagnostic Teaching of Reading

③ Qualitative:
① WR miscue analysis: (During graded word lists + IRI oral selections)
  * Used to determine reading skill strengths + weaknesses
  * Used to set up inst. groups or indi. inst. planning

wds. Isolation | wds. in context

  ① Tend to read wds. more accurately (more info. to aid in decoding wds)

(ie) *If student makes same mistake w/ both, probably is failing use semantic + syntactic info. provided by text. Read to focus may focus too much on phonic & structure.

  * Don't worry about planning skill lessons for miscues that don't change meaning of passages.

② Comprehension Question analysis → higher order questions
  (a) main idea = central theme (b) detail = info. stated in material
  (c) inference (higher order) = not directly stated/implied (bk. ground)
  (d) Sequence = order of events (e) cause + effect =
  (f) vocabulary = meaning of wd. or phrase

MISCUES (any deviation from the text.)
COUNT AGAINST:
① Circle Omission: to (the) school
W9-AWD-011
out & write in was pronounced
mc (b) mispronunciation: Sound out
Concern (non-word) = insert / cross out / spell phonetically
③ Repetitions: (Stahling Procedure) underline
④ Insertion: (A) write in wd. in
⑤ Prompts: "P" = teacher prompt
⑥ Reversals: that the said crossout (see substitution)

DO NOT COUNT:
① Self-correct: "C" or "✓" code twice
② Dialect: "D"
③ Hesitations: Slashes
④ Phrasing: circle missed punctuation

$$\text{Word Recognition Formula:} = \frac{\# \text{ of wds.} - \text{miscues}}{\# \text{ of wds}}$$

(ie) $\frac{50-1}{50} = 98\%$

$$\text{Comprehension Formula:} \frac{\# \text{ of Questions} - \text{Quest. missed}}{\# \text{ of Questions}}$$

(ie) $\frac{10-1.5}{10} = 85\%$ $(+, -, \frac{1}{2})$

SCORING = Use Predetermined Criteria (Betts Criteria)
  (a) Scoring aid = wds. - proper nouns + special wds.

WORKSHEETS (2)
① Wk. sheet for Word Recogn. Tally Chart:
  (a) Consolidate counts of types of miscues from oral passages.
  (b) View common + types of errors
    (A) all miscues of type except self-corrected
    (mc) meaning change (also goes in A column)
    (sc) Self-correct

Totals should equal
Summary of Quant. Analysis = Types of miscues in context (Row totals)

* # of mc will never be larger than # in A.

② Worksheet for Qualitative Analysis of Uncorrected miscues in context
  (a) mispro. (b) subst (c) Insertion (d) Omission (e) reversal (f) No SC   use for + Summary of Qualt. Analysis
① expected response = (none for Insertions) ③ Syntactic = fits in sentence
② unexpected = (what actually said) ④ Semantic = meaning disturbed:
  has close text to # of miscues
  does not fit sentence

WorkSheets (Cont.)

③ Summary of Quantitative Analysis: ③

(a) __IND RL__: highest level at which no more than 2 errors.

(b) __INST RL__: highest level no more than 4 errors

(c) FRust R-L: lowest level w/5 or more errors.

Comp. Skills Analysis Chart

℗ Skill	# of Qu	# of errors	% of errors
1. main idea	11	0	0
2. c + a	14	6	42.8

Formula → $\dfrac{\text{\# of errors}}{\text{total \# of questions}} = \%\ of\ errors$

④ Summary of Qualitative Analysis ④

Single Cons. (s)

Cons. blends (st)

Single vowels (a)

vowel
diagraphs (ea) (2 letters give single sound)

Consonant diagraphs (sh)

Diphthongs (oi)(aw)

→ will be a part of what is in each lesson

→ strategies don't always work for every situation

(walker Ch. 4)

③ 4 Elements of Diagnostic Teaching

① CDA = Continuous Diagnostic Assessment | have lessons relate to one another / greater for transfer.

Brief; Approx 5 min.
- Listening to student read + talking to them afterwards about what they read.
- helps to update you knowledge of student as a reader

② SAS = Strategy + Skill Instruction   ℗ kwl
- introduce new idea or new reading strategies (Ch. 9)
- ideas behind the strategy (students must know)
- comes after IRI

③ GCR = Guided Contextual Reading
- helping student apply a teaching strategy as they read.
- done w/ interaction
  (must teach idea + transfer) - extended reading

④ PRW = Personalized Reading + Writing
- invest in literacy (broad sense)
- doing things which are meaningful to student
- relevant to student

Diagnostic Teaching of Reading: Techniques for Instruction and Assessment

SECOND EDITION

BARBARA J. WALKER

Eastern Montana College

Merrill, an imprint of
Macmillan Publishing Company
New York

Maxwell Macmillan Canada
Toronto

Maxwell Macmillan International
New York   Oxford   Singapore   Sydney

Editor: Linda James Scharp
Production Editor: Jonathan Lawrence
Art Coordinator: Vincent A. Smith
Text Designer: Debra A. Fargo
Production Buyer: Pamela D. Bennett

This book was set in Garamond by Clarinda Company and was printed and bound by R.R. Donnelley & Sons Company. The cover was printed by New England Book Components.

Macmillan Publishing Company
866 Third Avenue
New York, NY 10022

Macmillan Publishing Company is part of the
Maxwell Communication Group of Companies.

Maxwell Macmillan Canada, Inc.
1200 Eglington Avenue East, Suite 200
Don Mills, Ontario M3C 3N1

Library of Congress Cataloging-in-Publication Data
Walker, Barbara J., 1946–
    Diagnostic teaching of reading : techniques for instruction and assessment / Barbara J. Walker.— 2nd ed.
        p.   cm.
    Includes bibliographical references and index.
    ISBN 0–02–424305–1
    1. Reading—Remedial teaching.   2. Individualized reading instruction.   3. Reading—Ability testing.   4. Reading comprehension. I. Title.
    LB1050.5.W35   1992   91–524
    428.4'07—dc20   CIP

Printing: 4 5 6 7 8 9   Year: 4 5

To Lorrin, Sharon and Chris

Preface

As our national diversity grows, teachers must increasingly celebrate our likenesses, empathetically discuss our differences, and resolve that there is not one best way to teach all children to read. The Great Debate has continued but the conclusions have been the same. "No one approach is so distinctly better in all situations and respects than the others that it should be considered the one best method and the one to be used exclusively" (Bond & Dykstra, 1967, p. 123). However, we have increasingly expanded our concepts of the instructional process. At the core of this knowledge has been the continued assertion that effective instruction is executed by effective teachers. This book provides a tool for teachers to understand the various instructional frameworks underlying diagnostic teaching techniques.

Embodied within this book is the strong belief that as a nation of readers our strengths lie in our individual differences. These individual differences need to be nurtured within our instructional programs, building upon the unique strengths that each student possesses. Furthermore, effective teachers use these strengths to expand students' conceptual knowledge, creating intelligent citizens.

Teachers are often keen observers and reflective thinkers. This book promotes the idea that teachers can make sophisticated diagnostic judgments and identify appropriate instructional techniques. This text delineates the process of diagnostic teaching so that teachers can make sophisticated diagnostic judgments and identify appropriate instructional techniques. This text delineates the process of diagnostic teaching so that teachers can make informed instructional decisions leading to a renewal of teachers' decision-making power.

THE REVISION

This new edition reflects my growing commitment to diagnostic teaching as a means to assess readers' growth and select instructional procedures that optimize learning. The following changes were made:

1. In Chapter 1, I have expanded the explanation of the interactive model and described how readers *become* "at risk."
2. I have added 10 new techniques to reflect the growing whole language movement. I understand that for an increasing number of teachers the whole language philosophy is reflected in techniques used in classroom practice. The added techniques will aid teachers in implementing the whole language philosophy.

3. The chapters are reorganized with the theoretical chapters on diagnostic teaching appearing at the beginning and the two chapters dealing with techniques appearing at the end of the book.
4. For each technique, I have designated the predominant focus of instruction according to the categories in Chapter 8, "Selecting Techniques."
5. In Chapter 8 on "Selecting Techniques," I have added a chart that classifies techniques according to the source of information (reader-based or text-based) that is stressed during implementation.
6. I have also reorganized Chapter 8 to coordinate with the diagnostic teaching session. Teachers use techniques for different purposes and therefore change the emphasis they place on them. This section explains that shift in emphasis.
7. In Chapter 6, "Formulating Hypotheses," I have added a section on how to analyze the data gathered from the diagnostic questions in Chapter 5. I have explained how this information correlates to the charts in Chapter 8, "Selecting Techniques."

HOW THE TEXT DEVELOPED

This book grew out of a need encountered in translating theory and test results into practice that would effectively help the problem reader. When I began writing diagnostic evaluations, I used the traditional battery of tests, and from these tests I made an educated guess about how a particular problem reader would respond to instruction. I sent my report (based on both normative test data and criterion-referenced tests) to the parents, who in turn took the report to the school. BUT NOTHING CHANGED. I was not really communicating with my clients because I had not told them how to *teach* the problem reader. They did not know how to translate the test data into effective instruction.

Then I began using teaching lessons during the diagnostic evaluations. Working with graduate interns in the reading clinic, I would suggest a certain technique to use during assessment, but they would be unable to implement the suggestion until I had personally explained the steps. Missing in the reading field was a simple, straightforward, written explanation of how to implement specific teaching techniques. So I began to write down step-by-step procedures to guide them. Chapter 9 was born.

Then one astute graduate student asked, "How do you know what will work?" What I had learned to do as a clinician was intuitively to measure the sparkles in the clients' eyes. When I analyzed why specific techniques had worked with certain students, the decision-making cycle of diagnostic teaching moved from intuitive to instructable. This book is the outcome of that transformation.

WHO WILL USE THE BOOK

This book can be used in a reading practicum and in reading clinic experiences. It also supplements coursework in diagnosis and remediation of reading difficulties. Furthermore, school psychologists, learning specialists, and remedial reading teachers will find it a useful reference. The instructional techniques were written in a step-by-step fashion so that classroom teachers and practicum students can readily follow the prescribed procedures. My goal is to increase communication between the practitioner and diagnostic specialists as well as the practicum student and the college professor.

HOW THE BOOK IS ORGANIZED

Chapter 1 presents the decision-making process of diagnostic teaching. It presents some common initial diagnostic decisions and lays the groundwork for the rest of the text. Chapter 2 describes the influence on diagnostic decisions. Factors impacting the student's reading performance are the reader, the text, the task, the technique, and the context. Chapter 3 presents strategies for effective diagnostic teaching, while Chapter 4 develops a framework for a diagnostic teaching session.

Chapter 5 explains how to gather diagnostic data, while Chapter 6 shows how to formulate hypotheses using the collected data. Chapter 7 provides the procedures for using teaching (rather than testing) as a method of reading evaluation.

Chapter 8 classifies the diagnostic teaching techniques using several methods: the targeted skill taught, the strategy taught, the instructional framework implemented, the type of text used, the response mode used, the structure of instruction selected, and the cognitive processing emphasized.

Chapter 9 presents a simple description and procedures for 60 techniques. Following each description is an explanation of when that approach is most effective in teaching reading. It describes the view of reading underlying the technique and provides a checklist for the diagnostic teacher to assess its effectiveness with a particular student.

ACKNOWLEDGMENTS

This text represents a point of view developed over years of clinical experience. There are several people whom I would like to acknowledge as inspiration to me. First, I want to thank Darrell D. Ray, Oklahoma State University, who has been my mentor and advisor. At the cornerstone of this text is his strong belief that children who experience reading difficulty need instruction that uses their strengths and is continually adjusted to meet their changing needs. I thank him for initiating my quest to understand individual differences in learning to read. Also, I want to thank my knowledgeable friends who read parts of the text and offered suggestions, criticisms, and support for my efforts. I am especially grateful for the ideas and comments of Claudia Dybdahl, University of Alaska, regarding qualitative assessment and William Powell, University of Florida, regarding quantitative assessment and classifying techniques. Their professional critique of my initial ideas set the course for the view of assessment in the text.

Equally important have been the number of undergraduate and graduate students in the Reading Clinic at Eastern Montana College who enthusiastically implemented the techniques in this book. Several students contributed in unique ways to the development of this text. I am especially indebted to Laurie Markle for working on the diagnostic teaching format, to Jean Muir for collecting the initial references, and to Vance Dols and Rilla Hardgrove for editing the first draft of the text.

Special thanks are extended to my reviewers for their thorough critiques of the first edition: Tim Blair, Texas A&M University; Jill Fitzgerald, University of North Carolina; Jean Dreher, University of Maryland; Ann Marshall Huston, Lynchburg College; Donald O'Brien, SUNY at Buffalo; Robert Panchyshyn, Western Kentucky University; William R. Powell, University of Florida; Robert Rude, Rhode Island College; and Amy J. Thorleifson, Seattle University. I also appreciate the useful suggestions for the second edition provided by the following reviewers: Lawrence Erickson, Southern Illinois University; Joan Gipe, University of New Orleans; Paul Hollingsworth, Brigham Young University; Bonnie Konopak, Louisiana State University; Harry Miller, Northeast Louisiana University; and Lynne Weisenbach, University of Indianapolis. I have also appreciated the astute judgment of the staff at Merrill, an imprint of Macmillan Publishing Company, especially Jeff Johnston for his encouragement and perspective as I labored with the initial drafts; Linda Scharp, editor; and Linda Bayma and Jonathan Lawrence for their untiring efforts to keep the project moving at all times. I am especially thankful for the editorial work of Jeanne Zingale and Rita Francis.

I owe a great deal to each of the eager students who willingly let me test my ideas about instruction. I am especially indebted to my own two children, Chris and Sharon, who let me teach them in different ways. They were very patient children as they shared their mother with the reading profession. Last, I would like to thank my husband, Lorrin, and my good friend, Marleen Moulden. They have listened to my ideas about instruction, offered counsel, and shared my belief in children throughout the writing of this text.

Adjusting instruction to meet the changing needs of students in our classrooms and clinics is a challenging and rewarding task. This text is designed to facilitate that decision-making process.

Contents

What Is Diagnostic Teaching?

I nstruction that fits the needs of the problem reader improves reading performance and promotes fluent reading with comprehension. This book explains the process of identifying instructional alternatives that fit the problem reader. Diagnostic teaching uses instruction to understand how a student solves the reading problem. While teaching, the instructor assesses how the problem reader approaches the reading event. Using this information, she establishes the instructional conditions necessary for the problem reader to learn. Diagnostic teaching, then, is the process of using assessment and instruction at the same time to establish the instructional conditions that produce optimal learning.

In *Becoming a Nation of Readers,* Jeanne Chall states:

> The underlying causes of the reading difficulties of individuals are not always easy to detect . . . [But research and clinical practice] indicate that the best treatment is *excellent instruction,* which in turn seems to heighten interest and hope as well as improve reading skills and uses of reading. Thus *concern for individual needs,* as well as improved instruction . . . will be needed if we are truly to become a nation of readers. (pp. 124–125, emphasis added)

The diagnostic teacher identifies specific instructional alternatives for problem readers that result in improved reading performance. As a reader begins to experience successful reading, he attributes his reading improvement to effective reading strategies. This attribution, in turn, increases his use of these strategies. The diagnostic teacher's task is to monitor this improvement and identify the instructional modifications that produced it. Therefore, she formulates her diagnostic hypotheses by observing those instructional conditions that improve reading. This process is outlined in Figure 1–1. The decision-making cycle of diagnostic teaching begins in the midst of a *reading event* where the teacher can observe the reader's strategies for constructing meaning. From these observations she constructs various types of assessment activities. She uses the information from these activities and her observations within the reading event to *formulate diagnostic hypotheses* and select instructional techniques that will advance the student's reading. As she *teaches the diagnostic lesson,* the teacher adjusts her original plan to ensure comprehension. After the lesson, she *assesses the growth* the reader made as well as *evaluates* the effectiveness of the adjustments she made. Using this information she either *establishes the conditions* for learning or *recycles,* that is reformulates or makes new hypotheses. In this decision-making cycle the diagnostic teacher shifts between assessment and instruction to create evaluations that emerge from and immediately

Figure 1–1
The Decision-
Making Cycle of
Diagnostic
Teaching

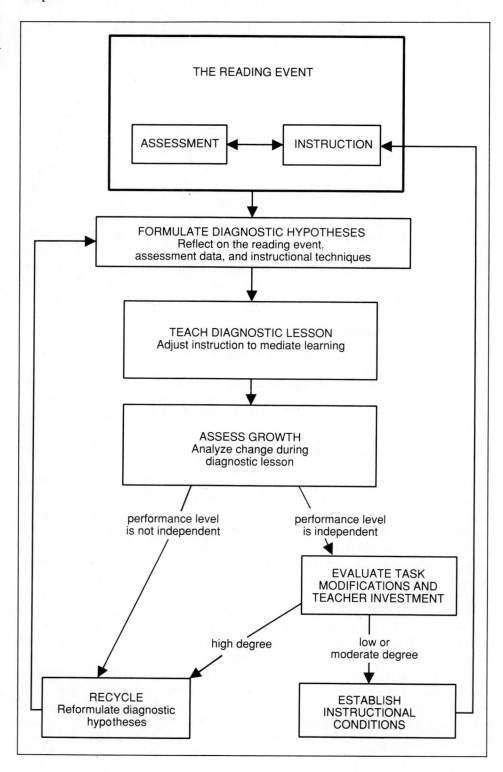

influence instruction within the reading event. Diagnostic teaching, then, allows the teacher to "manipulate in a planned way any of the factors that are suspected to be contributing or inhibiting reading achievement" (Wixson & Lipson, 1986, p. 143).

Diagnostic teaching is the process of using assessment and instruction at the same time *to identify the instructional modifications that enable problem readers to become independent learners.*

Thus, "diagnosis is nothing more than the application of a straightforward, common sense, problem-solving approach to the study of children who have difficulties in reading" (Harris & Sippay 1985, p. 230). The diagnostic teacher is thus an active problem solver. She is much more than a test giver. She is first and foremost a teacher. As she teaches, she explores how a particular student solves the reading problem. She knows that his reading is affected not only by the skills he knows but also by the strategies he uses. Thinking about what the student already knows and does when he learns, the diagnostic teacher selects techniques that will teach the needed skills and strategies in the most efficient way. Rather than looking for the causes of reading disabilities, "the focus of diagnostic teaching is . . . on the here and now of what the child can and cannot do . . . and on matching this information with appropriate opportunities for learning" (Harris, 1977, p. 25).

INTERACTIVE READING PROCESS

The diagnostic teacher makes decisions based on her understanding of how reading occurs. In this book, the theory of reading acquisition is based on an interactive view of reading. This view holds that reading involves using both information from the letters and words in the text and information that the reader already knows to construct meaning. Efficient reading "requires readers—real live readers with ideas and attitudes of their own—to interpret what the author is saying" (Langer, 1982, p. 41). The reader is an active learner who interprets what he reads using what the text says (text-based information) and what he knows (reader-based information). In other words, the reader uses these two sources of information at the same time to interpret text. These information sources are strategically combined as the student reads. Effective readers use the following strategies:

1. Effective readers coordinate the reading process combining both the text and personal knowledge. While reading, such readers construct a tentative model of meaning based on inferences about the author's intended meaning. They shift between using what they know (reader-based inferencing) and what the text says (text-based inferencing) to construct their model of meaning (Pearson & Johnson, 1978).
2. Effective readers elaborate what they read (McNeil, 1987). They think about how the text they are reading relates to what they know. Thus they make connections that help them remember and interpret what they read. These new connections become part of what readers know.

3. Effective readers monitor their understanding to see if it makes sense (Baker & Brown, 1984). If it does not make sense, effective readers check their purposes for reading to see if they were on the right track, check their own knowledge and compare it to what they are reading, and vary their strategies to remove difficulties in interpreting text.

4. Effective readers use the context of the situation to focus understanding. This focus, or perspective, influences the construction of a "successful text." Such readers ask, "What's the right text for this context?" (Harste, Woodward, & Burke, 1984, p. 201). The readers' perceptions and presuppositions about the context of the reading event affect their comprehension.

Reading is an interactive process in which readers shift between sources of information (what they know and what the text says), elaborate meaning and strategies, check their interpretation (revising when appropriate), and use the setting to focus their interpretation.

The following scenario illustrates this active process when encountering an unknown word. A text has a picture of a baseball diamond with a figure running toward second base at the top of a page and the following sentence at the bottom of the page: "The girl hit the home run." From the picture of the baseball diamond, Bobbie guesses that the story is about a boy. However, when the sentence about a girl is read, the graphic cue *g* instead of *b* cues the reader that the story is about a girl rather than a boy. The initial hypothesis, that the story is about a boy, is based on previous experience with similar situations and stories *(combine sources of information).*

The reader selects cues from the text and measures them against his own background knowledge and important textual information. If the response is confirmed, or fits, reading continues. For example, when the expected response for the baseball story could not be confirmed because the word *girl* does not look like *boy,* the reader asked himself, "What word is like *boy* that begins with a *g?* " In other words, he wanted to know what word semantically and graphically fits *(monitor meaning).*

Our experiences and the language used to describe them build our schema, or our personal world view. By watching television, playing in the neighborhood, and listening to storybooks, children develop a schema that the game of baseball is played by both males and females; however, when they read about baseball, the stars or characters are mostly boys *(use situational context).* In the baseball story example, the expected response of *boy* was revised according to grapho-phonic information, and the resulting sentence was read, "The girl hit the home run." This information caused the reader to refine the schema that "stories about baseball usually have boys for heroes" to be more inclusive, namely that "stories about baseball usually have boys for heroes, but sometimes they have girls *(elaborate).*"

This interactive model can provide a framework for analyzing the behaviors of problem readers. As Bobbie did in the previous example, readers consider many factors within any given reading event to make sense of what they are reading. Such factors include the reader's topic knowledge, strategy deployment, and purposes for reading, as well as the text and the setting. Thus, a reading problem, rather than being a static deficit within the reader, is a set of strengths and weaknesses impacted by interactions among these factors and classroom instruction (Wixson & Lipson, 1986).

Although readers use their strengths to solve problems in text interpretation, sometimes these strengths result in compensatory behaviors that inhibit rather than enhance the reader's construction of meaning. While effective readers combine sources of information, problem readers vary in their use of these strategies. The point of view of this text is that problem readers often experience a deficit in either a skill or strategy that causes them to shift away from one information source. They compensate by using their strength and thus eliminate a need to use their deficient knowledge source (Stanovich, 1980). This overreliance on their strength often results in inefficient reading. It is the diagnostic teacher's role to use these strengths to show students how to use their weaker information source when text interpretation breaks down.

For example, readers who easily learn to decode words and recall text-based information often develop the idea that reading is simply repeating a string of words from the text. They become bound by the text and do not combine both the text and their experiences. This behavior is often coupled with the likelihood that the student will be placed in a text that is difficult for him (Gambrell, Wilson, & Gantt, 1981) and asked to read fewer authentic texts or stories (Juel, 1988). While effective readers elaborate both the content and their strategies, problem readers often read in texts demanding for them where they cannot readily elaborate either the content or their strategy deployment. For example, if Bobbie could not read the words *baseball* or *hit,* the sentence would have been difficult to read and Bobbie would have allocated most of his resources to constructing meaning. Bobbie's elaboration of the content (sometimes *girls* can be baseball heroes) and his strategies (when the word that I said doesn't look like the text, I can think of another word that fits) would have been minimal. After an extended period of failing to combine sources of information or elaborate their strategies, these readers become accustomed to understanding only bits and pieces of what they are reading and passively reading words. They also stop checking their interpretation or actively constructing meaning (Walker, 1990b). For instance, if Bobbie had an extended period of time reading difficult text, then he might have continued to read the story miscalling *boy* for *girl* and therefore misconstruing a major character in the story. Habitual passive reading fails to build an expectation that reading is a strategic process where readers combine their resources to make sense of text. While effective readers readily monitor their understanding, problem readers passively read text, amplifying their reading difficulty. If readers continually fail to construct appropriate meaning when reading, they alter how they perceive themselves within the context of a reading event (Paris & Oka, 1989). They attribute their continued failure to an ability (a fixed characteristic) that they do not possess rather than to a strategic process that they can acquire (Schunk & Rice, 1987). This attitude reinforces the belief that if they try to read they will fail, and if they fail again they are admitting their lack of ability. Knowing they have facilities in other academic situations, for instance in mathematics, these problem readers reduce their effort and cease to try. This allows them to attribute failure to "not having tried" rather than to their lack of ability. Effective readers can choose among different strategies as they read, while problem readers perceive an unfamiliar reading situation as failure, thus decreasing their motivation.

Rather than actively constructing meaning, problem readers perpetually read with one or more of the following characteristics. They (a) overrely on a single information source (usually a strength), (b) read difficult text restricting elaboration of content and strategies, (c) read without monitoring meaning, resulting in passive reading, or (d) define the context of reading as a failure situation.

INSTRUCTIONAL PROCESS

The goal of diagnostic teaching is to establish appropriate learning opportunities for problem readers. If the students use effective strategies and make adjustments for themselves, a simple lesson framework of readiness, active reading, and reacting is sufficient. Problem readers, however, have difficulty making adjustments and employing effective strategies. Inefficient readers often need to be shown exactly how to use effective reading strategies. They need instruction modified during the lesson framework. The diagnostic teacher, as a result, continually assesses what and how problem readers are learning and makes instructional adjustments to ensure successful reading. The process of adjusting instruction to ensure learning is called *mediating learning.*

The diagnostic teacher mediates learning, which means she adjusts instruction to ensure successful text interpretation.

The diagnostic teacher specifically selects activities that will directly mediate learning for each problem reader. She establishes what the student already knows and adjusts instruction to overlap his present knowledge with new information. Furthermore, she evaluates how the student learned what he knows to establish strategy strengths. The diagnostic teacher mediates learning by "starting with adjustments that permit students to demonstrate strengths" (Wilson & Cleland, 1985, p. 112). Then the diagnostic teacher shows the student how to incorporate non-preferred strategies into how he solves the reading problem. A problem reader often relies heavily on his strengths. Initially, the diagnostic teacher selects a technique that allows him to demonstrate these strengths. As the student experiences success with the new reading task, the diagnostic teacher selects techniques that have a more integrated instructional approach. This allows the diagnostic teacher to use learner strengths (what he already knows and does) to show him how to use his weaker information source when reading.

Diagnostic teaching techniques were developed from different views of reading and learning. The three major views are these:

☐ **Bottom-Up View.** Simply stated, the bottom-up view of reading focuses on text-based processing as the major instructional concern of teachers. Learning to read is viewed as a series of associations or subskills that are reinforced until they become automatic. Letters are linked to form words, words are linked to form sentences, and sentences are linked to form ideas; that is, the parts of reading are put together to form the whole. This is viewed as bottom-up processing, in which processing text shapes the learner's response.

☐ **Top-Down View.** The top-down view of reading focuses on the reader-based processing as the major instructional concern of teachers. The reader is viewed as an active problem solver who guesses what the author is saying. Then he samples textual information to check his guesses. Ideas about what the author is saying are verified through a minimal amount of textual cues; that is, reading is viewed as negotiating meaning between an author and a reader. This is viewed as a top-down process, in which the reader's ideas create his response.

☐ **Interactive View.** The interactive view of reading focuses on the active-constructive nature of reading as the major instructional concern of teachers. The reader is viewed as using both reader-based (top-down) processing and text-based (bottom-up) processing to form a model of meaning. Although he is active, his guesses are formed on the basis of what the text says and what he already knows about this information; that is, reading is viewed as constructing meaning. This is viewed as an interactive process where the reader strategically shifts between the text and what he already knows to construct his response.

The techniques from differing points of view can be matched to the learner strengths. The diagnostic teacher selects instructional techniques that allow students to use their strengths. Then she uses these strengths to show the students how to solve their reading problems. Finally, the diagnostic teacher leads problem readers to more integrated reading by selecting techniques that have a more interactive approach to reading. This sequence allows the diagnostic teacher to use learner strengths to show problem readers how to use their weaker information source.

ASSESSMENT PROCESS

In diagnostic teaching, assessment is continuous. As the student learns, diagnostic information is immediately incorporated into the lesson. The teacher thus attacks the problem as she teaches, not after she has gathered the facts.

During a diagnostic teaching lesson, for example, the teacher discovered at midpoint in the story that a student could not sequence the events. Rather than continue trying to teach using the instructional format of predict, read to find out, and summarize, she introduced a story map (see "Story Map" in Chapter 9), a visual arrangement of the sequence of events that are related to the problem. The information from the beginning of the story was reviewed and placed on the map. The instructional format was changed to summarize what was on the map, make a prediction, and read to find out what happened next. The final step became to add to the story map, tell how the new information fits into the story, and how it fits with the previous prediction. The lesson format changed because the teacher assessed the difficulty during the lesson and changed the instructional conditions or format. This modification increased student learning.

The assessment, however, includes much more than whether the student's learning increased. Because the diagnostic teacher collects data as she teaches, she also analyzes how she modifies her initial plan in order to mediate learning. Assessment during diagnostic teaching allows the teacher to alter her instruction systematically providing support for student learning. After the lesson, she assesses the amount and type of support (teacher investment) the students needed to make a change in their reading behavior. Likewise, the diagnostic teacher can orchestrate reading tasks in a variety of ways such as introducing graphic aids (story maps) or asking students to read aloud. These changes are made to foster strategic reading. Again, the teacher records the adjustments (task modifications) she devises during the diagnostic lesson. Diagnostic teaching means that assessment occurs during the lesson. Thus, the information derived is both practical and valid because it is gained through authentic literacy activities. Furthermore, diagnostic teaching is efficient because learning does not stop in order to test. Learning becomes an integral part of the assessment process.

Diagnostic teaching means that assessment is continuous as the student is learning. The diagnostic teacher adjusts instruction as she teaches, not after she has gathered the facts.

To lead students to more efficient reading, the diagnostic teacher looks for recurring patterns among the variables of the reading event (see Chapter 2 for further discussion) and uses this information when she establishes the optimal instructional conditions. As she teaches, the diagnostic teacher assesses student performance and changes her instruction in order to mediate learning, thus showing students how to use what they already know to solve new reading problems. This leads readers to more efficient strategy use.

As materials and activities are adjusted to the needs of the problem reader, the diagnostic teacher maintains a close match between the text and the student's reading level. Although this attitude permeates all instruction, the degree that the diagnostic teacher uses continuous assessment is not practical for the classroom teacher. The classroom teacher cannot continuously assess and modify her instruction in 25 different directions at once. The classroom teacher makes some adjustments, but the majority of the time she teaches to an instructional group as a whole. At every instructional point, however, the diagnostic teacher assesses how the problem reader is learning from her instruction and adjusts her instruction. Assessment becomes an integral part of diagnostic teaching.

DIAGNOSTIC TEACHING PROCESS

Diagnostic teaching is a dynamic process in which decisions about what the reader needs change as the student learns. Initial diagnostic information can be gathered through screening or from classroom instruction. This initial information is then expanded through informal assessment (see Chapter 5). The informal assessment allows the diagnostic teacher to identify the major presenting problem and a placement level that is moderately difficult for the student. From this information the diagnostic teacher makes tentative decisions about placement and instruction.

As she teaches, the diagnostic teacher also analyzes the effects of the variables of the reading event (see Chapter 2) to help her formulate her hypotheses. She gathers further data about the strategies that the student uses to understand the text (see Chapter 5). After the lesson, she reflects on the information she has gathered, the reading event where instruction occurred, and her roles (see Chapter 3) during instruction to formulate and refine her diagnostic hypotheses. Reflecting on this information, the diagnostic teacher selects techniques (see Chapter 8) to adjust instruction in order to mediate learning for the problem reader.

The diagnostic teacher again instructs a lesson, using her new plan. At this point the diagnostic teacher may choose to cycle back through the process and instruct a new lesson; or she can continue to the next step, which assesses the reader's growth during instruction. To establish the amount of the reader's change, the diagnostic teacher assesses the reader's growth that resulted from the instructional adjustment (see Chapter 7 for the format to assess growth). Then, she establishes optimal conditions for a reader as dictated by these results. The decision-making cycle of the diagnostic teacher illustrated in Figure 1–1 is thus complete.

SUMMARY

The process of diagnostic teaching uses instruction to understand how the problem reader approaches the reading event. The goal of diagnostic teaching is to identify instructional alternatives that create improved reading performance for the problem reader. Instruction is viewed as mediating learning, where the teacher focuses on how the learner solves the reading problem by gathering data as she teaches. Furthermore, she views reading as an interactive process where the reader uses what he knows to interpret what the text says. Therefore, the diagnostic teacher uses the student's strengths (knowledge and strategies) to lead the student to integrate new information as well as new strategies into his reading repertoire. She then assesses reading growth due to her instruction. She bases her decisions regarding the next steps in a student's instruction on this assessment as well as on reflection on the success she has achieved by the adjustments she has made. These decisions become increasingly more refined as the diagnostic teacher considers the reading event, evaluates the strategies of the problem reader, and matches those with appropriate techniques.

The Reading Event

Diagnostic teaching establishes those instructional conditions that will result in improved reading of more difficult text. The diagnostic teacher (unlike the regular classroom teacher, who focuses on a progression of skill development in graded text) bases his decision making on the patterns of interactions during the reading event (see Figure 2–1). Those patterns that recur are considered the most representative of the student's reading behavior. From these patterns, the diagnostic teacher predicts what instructional circumstances will positively affect a student's reading behavior; the ultimate goal of assessment, therefore, is to identify optimum instructional conditions for the individual reader.

During instruction, the diagnostic teacher analyzes five variables of the reading event—reader, text, task, technique, and context—and evaluates their effect on the reader's performance. The variables do not act in isolation but affect one another during the course of instruction. Rather than limiting the effects of the variables, the diagnostic teacher evaluates how changing any one of them affects a reader's response.

Through repeated instructional opportunities, the teacher evaluates the interactions of these five variables. During the lesson he evaluates the diagnostic task (*what* he asks the *reader* to do) and the technique (*how* he asks her to complete the task). He evaluates *what is read* and how it affects reading performance. In this way he assesses how the text affects reading performance. The diagnostic teacher evaluates the reader's performance to assess her approach to the instructional event. Equally important, he evaluates the *context* where instruction occurs. The context of the instructional event affects the student's perception of the task as well as her use of prior knowledge related to the text content. As shown in Figure 2–2, these five variables influence reading performance during any given reading event and continuously interact as instruction occurs. This chapter elaborates on each variable.

TASK

Students are often mystified when trying to figure out what task they are to complete during an instructional lesson. In fact, many teachers evaluate precisely that: the rapidity with which students can figure out the task. It is not unusual that after reading a paragraph and being asked literal questions, students ask for a second chance, now that they know what the teacher wants for an answer.

Figure 2 – 1
The Decision-
Making Cycle of
Diagnostic
Teaching

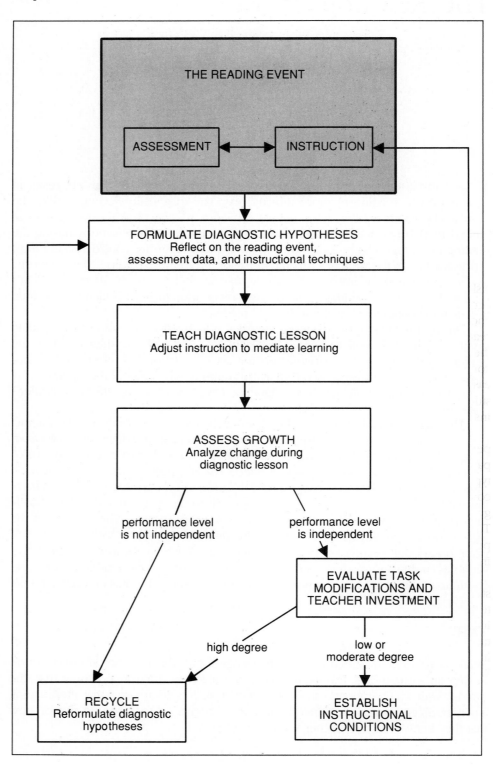

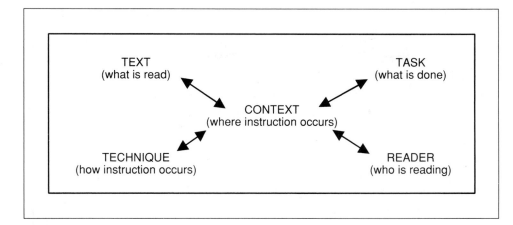

Figure 2-2
The Reading
Event

To demystify reading tasks, the diagnostic teacher creates authentic, functional tasks in his classroom. These activities "allow children to experience literacy as it occurs in the world outside of school" (Rowe & Harste, 1986). Teachers need to choose activities that will show children the variety of functions that reading can serve: reading for pleasure, reading for information, or reading to remember. Tasks are therefore understood in terms of the context in which they are embedded. If learners complete authentic tasks that are familiar and functional, they will generate responses easily. However, if the task is contrived to teach an isolated part of reading, then students must define the task as well as its function. Thus, contrived tasks make instruction less effective for the problem reader.

Therefore, the kind of task students are asked to do affects their reading performance. For instance, students who are repeatedly asked one type of question pay more attention to that type of information (Reynolds, 1980). In other words, the type of questions asked narrows a reader's purpose for reading and therefore limits comprehension. For example, a description of a room was read by two groups; one group pretended to be potential home buyers and the other pretended to be burglars. The two groups remembered different information because their purpose or task perception was different (Pichert, 1979). The reader's purpose or task perception influences responses to teacher-generated questions.

As the diagnostic teacher varies the task demands and questioning strategies, students' performances also change. In one study, when students were given formal, text-based questions and assignments, they tended to report more story elements and interpret the text objectively. But when these same students were given questions and task assignments that were more personal, they included fewer story elements and interpreted the stories in light of their prior experiences (Newell, Suszynski, & Weingart, 1989).

Reading comprehension can be assessed using two formats. The teacher can use direct questions: "How did Johnny solve his problem?" Or he can ask students to retell the story: "Tell me this story in your own words." However, the kind of information required and the organization of the response make these tasks quite different. Direct questioning asks for information from the text that relates specifically to the stem of the question. An oral retelling, however, asks students to organize a response according to what they think is important.

The types of questions asked also change the task. Sometimes the diagnostic teacher uses a series of direct, literal questions: "Who were the characters? What did they do? What was the outcome?" Answering these questions is different from answering questions about the overall theme: "What was the author trying to tell you in this story? Do you think the author has a reason for including this character?" These questions require different kinds of reasoning (Fitzgerald, 1989; Johnston & Pearson, 1982). The first group of questions requires a factual recall of stated information. The second group requires that readers use inferential thinking about the author's intended meaning. The readers have to use several parts of the text to construct a rationale for their answers. Still other questions ask students to respond personally to information in the text: "Have you had similar experiences to Jack's? Did you feel the same?"

Besides the reasoning requirements, the order in which the teacher asks the questions can also change the task. Questions can probe a logical sequence of story development, or they can require nothing more than a random recall of unrelated facts. These two tasks are different. Questions that probe a logical sequence of story events cause students to think about story development and, therefore, increase the comprehension of the story (Beck, Omanson, & McKeown, 1982). Unrelated literal questions, however, are harder to answer because there is no relationship among the answers. Furthermore, asking students to relate story comprehension to their own experiences can prompt them to associate what was read with what they already know and thereby increase comprehension (Johnston, 1983).

The questions that the diagnostic teacher asks change the task, making it harder or easier to understand stories. If the teacher probes to clarify a response, he influences comprehension and changes the original task demands. This change often increases comprehension. When incomplete responses are unprobed, valuable information about comprehension is lost. When possible, the diagnostic teacher probes the students' responses and records the task modifications that increase reader performance.

In addition to the task demands placed on the reader during story discussion, the diagnostic teacher uses either silent or oral reading during the diagnostic lesson. Sometimes oral reading is performed to prove a prediction; thus students are reading material that has been previously read. Therefore, they use meaning to facilitate their oral reading. At other times, however, the oral reading occurs on an initial reading of the passage. This places an additional demand on the processing of information (Allington, 1984b). In this instance, readers must attend not only to meaning but also to oral production of the text.

Finally, the task changes if the readers can refer to the text for answers. The difference in the responses when the text is available and when it is not becomes a task condition. Consequently, different task conditions result in various instructional conditions that can be modified by the diagnostic teacher.

In summary, the task can vary during reading instruction. It can be the oral or silent reading of sentences, paragraphs, or stories. After students read the story, the task can vary from answering direct questions to elaborate, unaided recall of textual information. Sometimes these responses require students to locate the answer in the text, while at other times the text is not used to answer questions. Questioning can also vary from literal teacher-generated questions to nonliteral student-generated questions. Furthermore, responses to these questions can require different kinds of reasoning; they vary from factual recall to personal application. As these tasks change, an equally important variation is the perceived purpose of the task by the reader. Altering any of these conditions changes the nature of the information obtained during a diagnostic lesson. It is the diagnostic teacher's responsibility to analyze the major task features of the diagnostic lesson and vary them (when necessary) to enhance reading performance. The following list provides task considerations that establish what the child is asked to do and can be used to focus reflective thinking about the reading event.

What the teacher asks students to do affects the kind of information he has about them. Many a beginning teacher evaluates only oral reading and believes that his students have no reading problem. If he had asked questions after silent reading, he would have found that the students did not comprehend what they read silently. They did not know how to think about what they were reading. The diagnostic teacher thinks about what he asks students to do when they read. Then he formulates tentative decisions about the students' reading performances.

- ☐ Purpose for the task
- ☐ Task segment
  Sentences, paragraphs, stories, etc.
- ☐ Question type
  Literal, nonliteral, main idea, vocabulary
- ☐ Production requirements
  One-word response, retelling, finding answer in text
- ☐ Reasoning requirements of task
  Factual recall, inference, application
- ☐ Oral or silent reading
- ☐ Availability of text

TEXT

Traditionally, variation in student performance is attributed to the readability level of the text. However, the influence that the text has on reading performance is much more complex. The diagnostic teacher, therefore, systematically evaluates what the student is reading. He thinks about the possible textual characteristics that affect reading performance (Graves, 1986; Wixson & Lipson, 1986). He thinks about the content, length, and complexity of the passage, as well as its coherence, words, and structure. The length of the passage, for example, can affect both error rate and comprehension performance. Many short passages have an extremely heavy information load, requiring an extraordinary amount of comprehension in a short span. Longer passages, on the other hand, often contain examples, diagrams, and explanations that aid comprehension. For some students, however, reading a long passage orally often reduces comprehension and accuracy because of the attention demanded by oral production over a long period of time. Other students' strategies improve as they read longer passages (Hric, Wixson, Kunji, & Bosky, 1988). The diagnostic teacher thinks about how passage length, amount of information, and use of examples affect reading performance.

Reading performance also changes when reading narrative or expository text. Each of these textual formats requires a different kind of reading strategy. Narrative text is organized using characters who have problems that are solved. The story line is developed through the actions, consequences, and events that occur in solving the problem. Expository texts are organized around main ideas, key vocabulary used to relate those ideas, and the supporting details that explain the main idea. Since each of these formats is organized differently, readers are not the same in their experience with them, which increases the variability of their performance (Garner, Alexander, Slater, Hare, Smith, & Reis, 1986).

The way the text is written, moreover, influences what is remembered. Authors who logically organize the text using the formats for narrative or expository text facilitate reader performance. If a text follows a logical organization, it is easier to comprehend and remember (Hare, Rabinowitz, & Schieble, 1989; Stein & Trabasso, 1982). Thus the style the author uses will affect reader performance. High quality literature provides students with authentic experiences that allow them to personally identify with characters in the stories (Routman, 1988). When expository text is written in a more engaging style (more like a novel), it is also more easily remembered (Slater, 1986). Logical organization and engaging style affect reading performance.

The content likewise affects reading performance. Students differ in what they already know about the topic they are reading. The more students use what they already know about a particular content, the more they will remember when they read the text (Pearson, Hansen, & Gordon, 1979). The diagnostic teacher analyzes the content of the text and how much prior knowledge students need to know before they read the text. For example, the sentence "She wore a parka" requires more prior knowledge on the part of the reader than "She wore a parka to protect her from the cold wind." The diagnostic teacher evaluates the effect that text content and required prior knowledge have on reader performance.

Sentence structure also affects reading performance. Some texts are constructed of simple sentences that require the reader to infer causality. For example, "The dog ran. The chair fell" requires that the reader infer that the dog ran when the chair fell. Other texts are constructed with more complex sentences that reveal causality and facilitate comprehension. The wording "The dog ran because the chair fell" describes the relationship between the dog running and the chair falling (Beck, McKeown, Omanson, & Pople, 1984). Sometimes the simple sentences do not tell a story. If the sentences are combined to form a well-structured story, they are easier to understand (Brennan, Bridge, & Winograd, 1986).

The predictability of the sentences also affects reading performance. If the text contains repeated language patterns, the child can predict a word by using the pattern of the language (Routman, 1988). For example, the language pattern in the following paragraph allows readers to use a minimal amount of visual cues to guess the words: "There was an old fisherman who swallowed a shark. He swallowed the shark to catch the piranha. He swallowed the piranha to catch the crayfish. He swallowed the crayfish to catch the gnat. He swallowed the gnat as he yawned on the shore."

In addition to predictable patterns, other word choices affect recognition and comprehension of text. Some texts have words that are easy to read but do not convey the exact meaning (Graves, 1986). For example, "This boy had that" uses easy words, but it does not describe the exact meaning of the story. In another text, the words may be harder to read but more precise in conveying the intended meaning of the text: "The tall boy had the ice cream cone." This sentence uses harder words, but the meaning is clearer because the words are more precise.

During initial reading instruction, word choices are highly related to reading performance. For children who have profited from instruction in synthetic phonics, a text that is decodable is easier to read ("The pig went to dig a hole") than a text that consists primarily of sight words ("The children have gone to the house") (Barr, 1974–1975). As children apply the rules of the phonetic system to a text that has a high percentage of sight words, the error pattern will reveal a different set of problems than might appear if the text contained decodable words that followed the rules they had been taught (Juel, 1984) (see Chapter 5).

The diagnostic teacher thinks about the words in the text. He evaluates whether the words can be easily decoded using phonic rules. If the students were taught to read using a sight word approach (see "Sight Word Approach" in Chapter 9), the diagnostic teacher evaluates whether the words are the words that they have been taught in the program. If so, students can use this knowledge to read the unfamiliar text. They figure out a word by thinking, "What word do I already know that starts with a *b?*" If the words are unknown, the diagnostic teacher checks to see if the new words have similar letter patterns to the words that the students already know. If the new words have the same pattern as the known words, students can figure out a word by thinking, "What word do I already know that looks like this word?" However, if the word has not been taught and does not have a similar pattern, students will stumble over words, substituting words that make sense but do not look like the words in the story. Therefore, the diagnostic teacher evaluates the words in the text to assess their influence on student performance.

The text can help or hinder reading performance. The kind of text that is read will affect the information the teacher gathers about students' reading. For example, an informal reading inventory placed a student at the sixth-grade reading level; however, this same student had difficulty when she read the 10-page story in the sixth-grade reader. Three text characteristics had changed. The content had changed from information about sunflowers to a story about a boy who was cleaning his room. The text length had changed from short paragraphs to a long story. The text format had changed from expository to narrative.

A reflective teacher looks closely at the kind of text he has asked students to read. He asks himself, "Are there features of the text that affect students' reading?" Then he asks, "Have these same features affected the reading before?" In other words, "Is this a consistent problem?"

In conclusion, a variety of textual characteristics affect student reading performance. Passage length, content, and complexity affect student performance. Equally important is the density of information and the elaboration of information by the use of examples, pictures, diagrams, and headings. Through their word choices, authors can require an extensive background knowledge or coherently organize the text to develop word meanings. Furthermore, an engaging style (whether the text is expository or narrative) facilitates comprehension of the text. In other words, the diagnostic teacher examines the text to evaluate these features that affect student reading performance:

- ☐ Passage length
- ☐ Passage type
  Informational or narrative
- ☐ Type of content
- ☐ Organizational structure
  Headings, diagrams, etc.
- ☐ Background knowledge required of reader
- ☐ Grammatical complexity
- ☐ Word choices
  Decodability, distinctive meanings
- ☐ Density of information
- ☐ Elaboration or use of examples
- ☐ Coherence or unity of text
- ☐ Engaging style

READER

Bringing to the task and the text their own knowledge and strategies, learners perform in distinctively different ways; therefore, the diagnostic teacher observes students' interactions within the reading event to assess learner differences. Readers differ not only on *what* they already know (knowledge-based differences) but also on *how* they integrate new information into what they already know (strategy-based differences). Initially, the diagnostic teacher evaluates knowledge-based differences. He establishes reading levels for instruction. He matches the readability of the text with the level of reading performance for the students. Concurrently, he finds out what the readers already know about the task of reading and the content that he is to teach. As the instruction begins, the diagnostic teacher looks for patterns within the reading event to analyze skill knowledge. Word identification skills (e.g., sight word knowledge, phonic knowledge, and context use), vocabulary knowledge, and fluency are evaluated in relation to overall reading. Comprehension skills (e.g., identifying the main idea or problem, the key details or events, and the theme or the resolution) are also evaluated during instruction.

Equally important to skill knowledge is the general knowledge the students possess. Some students have a rich variety of experiences and are able to talk about their experiences. Talking about experiences indicates that students are organizing and classifying their worlds of experience. When they read, they use their prior experiences and the words they know to express them. Other students have limited experiences or limited word knowledge, which provides difficulty when reading (Harris & Sipay, 1985). Therefore, students' knowledge of the world and the words they use to describe their experiences influence comprehension and word identification (Barr & Sadow, 1985).

These knowledge-based differences are accentuated by differences in problem-solving strategies. Students differ in the strategies they use for solving the reading problem. Some students select meaning cues, while others select graphic cues. Some students rely heavily on their background knowledge, while others use only the text to form hypotheses while they are reading. Some students revise and monitor their model of meaning readily, while others need concrete facts before they revise their models (Spiro & Myers, 1984). These problem-solving strategies are observed by evaluating the pattern of verbal responses and word identification errors as the students read and answer questions. Looking for these consistent patterns, the diagnostic teacher notices students' selection strategies (the way they find cues and use sources of information), monitoring strategies (the way they check their understanding), and organizational strategies (the way they relate new information to what they already know). Initially, the diagnostic teacher notices whether or not the readers explore a range of clues to enhance comprehension and remedy word identification errors. To repair mistakes, students can use the overall meaning ("Oops, that doesn't make sense") or the way the word fits into the sentence ("That doesn't sound like a sentence"). Sometimes students use what the word looks like or sounds like ("Oops, I didn't say what those letters say") to restore comprehension. Efficient readers select appropriate cues and flexibly use sources of information; however, inefficient readers often use only a single source of information to remedy errors when reading.

Readers also differ in their monitoring strategies, or when and how they check their understanding. Students' strategies for monitoring word identification and comprehension are evaluated through oral reading and story discussions. Young and less skilled readers monitor their reading less frequently (August, Flavell, & Clift, 1984; Paris & Myers, 1981). They tend to read a string of words without checking to see if they make sense. When their understanding breaks down, students differ in their persistence to regain meaning. Many poor readers tend to give up when encountering repeated mistakes, while good readers persist in employing a variety of strategies to solve problems.

Finally, readers differ in the way they organize responses. During a discussion, some students answer literal-level questions with exact, text-based responses, while others answer questions by relying heavily on the overall theme of the story and inferring facts about the story rather than recalling specific information (Pearson & Spiro, 1980). Retellings can also indicate students' ability to organize and elaborate verbal responses. In an oral retelling, the brevity or elaboration of the story theme is noted to indicate a preference for generalizing or using specific facts.

Through instructional interactions, the teacher notes students' attribution patterns. Attribution patterns are the reasons and expectations that students have for participating in a reading event. They formulate these reasons from past experiences and their personal coping strategies. *Attribution patterns* stem from readers' beliefs and concepts related to the task and topic, the emotional support needed during instruction, and the reasons they formulated for their past success or failure in reading. From these, readers create expectations that impact their interpretations. Readers from various cultures and subcultures hold beliefs about the content and the task that determine the levels of importance of information and how they group this information into categories (Lipson, 1983). For example, women from Greece and America were asked to make up stories about pictures (Tannen, 1982). The women from Greece told an interesting story concentrating on character and ethics as if they were seasoned storytellers. On the other hand, the American women told a detailed story with logically sequenced events as if they were being tested on their ability to recall facts. The two groups of women approached the task differently because of the attributions they made about the task. They therefore recalled quite different information.

Students also respond differently to the type of feedback and prompting that the teacher uses. Some students need specific feedback that tells them what they did wrong and how to do the problem the "right" (expected) way. In other words, they prefer a high degree of teacher guidance. Other students prefer a simple acknowledgment that they are on the right track. They prefer to work out their mistakes on their own. Therefore, students also differ in the number of exact examples they need to incorporate a skill or a strategy. Some students rapidly understand a single example and transfer the new strategy to other situations, while other students need a series of examples and teacher guidance over a period of time before they understand how to apply the new strategies.

The teacher also notes the students' need for "sense making." Some students like to work practice examples and actually love workbook exercises, despite their lack of a substantial purpose in the instructional program. Such students believe the teacher is right. There are other students, however, who have a high need for activities to be purposeful. They use sense making to check their reading. They need reasons for doing the work they are asked to complete.

Finally, the diagnostic teacher evaluates how the students respond to their own successes and failures. Some readers persist when confronted with a difficult task, while others give up easily and are more likely to attribute failure to a lack of ability (an attribute not subject to control). When these readers are successful, they attribute success to luck or an easy task (Bristow, 1985).

How readers approach the reading event affects the kind of information a teacher has about them. A teacher makes many diagnostic decisions about differences among the learners in his classroom based on what his students know, how they learn, and their attributions. Although this is appropriate, a teacher should evaluate how the other variables of the reading event affect the reading patterns that the readers use. He asks, "Is what I am observing an attribute that I always see in these readers, or has something in the reading event affected their performance?" Therefore, to assess the readers, he looks for a consistent pattern of responses over different reading events.

In conclusion, readers differ not only on what they already know as evaluated by level of performance, skill knowledge, and content knowledge, but also on the strategies they possess. These strategy-based differences include patterns of organizing knowledge, cue and strategy selection, and monitoring and shifting of these strategies. Students also have different attribution patterns. The attributions developed within their own culture affect their reading as well as their personal needs. Some students need a high degree of structure, teacher direction, and frequent feedback; others prefer little structure, self-directed learning with minimal feedback, and tasks that make sense. By evaluating the following patterns of reading performance, the diagnostic teacher detects the strategies readers use when reading.

☐ Knowledge-based patterns
　Level of performance
　Skill proficiencies and deficiencies
　　Print and meaning processing
　Language proficiencies and deficiencies
　　Word and world knowledge
☐ Strategy-based patterns
　Strategies used and needed
　　Selection—source of information
　　　Text or prior knowledge
　　Monitoring—active or passive
　　Elaboration and level of response
　　　One word or embellished
　　　Literal or nonliteral
☐ Attribution patterns
　Need for structure and feedback
　Need for human sense
　Attribution of success or failure
　Attributions from culture

TECHNIQUE

A key to effective instructional decision making is an analysis of the intervention, or the techniques, that the diagnostic teacher employs. During the lesson, the diagnostic teacher thinks about how the readers will best profit from instruction. Subsequently, he analyzes how various techniques approach instruction so that he can match readers' strategies with the most efficient instructional techniques. There are several considerations when analyzing instructional techniques.

Initially, the diagnostic teacher must decide whether a technique is to introduce a skill/strategy in isolation or to help the student learn more about reading stories (Pearson & Johnson, 1978). Some techniques incorporate strategy instruction as they teach skills, while other techniques focus only on the skills (Samuels, 1980). Question-answer relationships (see Chapter 9) is a technique developed to teach the skill of answering comprehension questions. Students learn to analyze questions as to the source of information needed to answer the question. The sources are explained as "right there," "think and search," and "on my own." Students are not only taught the skill of answering comprehension questions that are both literal and nonliteral, but they are also shown when it is most efficient to use the various skills. They are given strategies for using the skill. On the other hand, a typical synthetic phonics lesson (see Chapter 9) is different. It teaches the skill of blending sounds together to form words. However, students are not taught how that skill is used as a flexible strategy when errors occur as they read.

Techniques also differ in their function within the instructional framework and the texts appropriate for the instructional format. Some techniques develop prerequisite knowledge in order to understand the content of the story. Techniques that introduce vocabulary and develop background knowledge are used prior to reading, while other techniques focus on developing active reading during the actual reading of the text. Techniques like the directed reading-thinking activity, reciprocal questioning procedure, and reciprocal teaching (see chapters 8 and 9) are used during the reading of the story to promote active comprehension. Furthermore, after a story is read, techniques can extend the comprehension of the story (see "Story Map" in Chapter 9) or reinforce word identification and fluency (see "Repeated Readings" in Chapter 9).

Techniques also differ in the mode of response that readers are asked to use. Some techniques ask students to discuss verbally what they learn when reading. By sharing their thoughts through a discussion, students select what is important to reconstruct the story. They actually construct an answer rather than merely recall events. Other techniques ask students to write about what they have read, which facilitates meaning construction. Again students must decide what is important, as well as how they will communicate what they learned. Readers vary in their ability and preference for response modes. Some students like to discuss what they have learned and share ideas and thoughts. Other students, however, prefer to write what they are thinking so that they can revise their understanding before communicating what they think. The diagnostic teacher selects a response mode that will mediate learning for a particular student.

As discussed in Chapter 1, techniques also differ according to what source of information is emphasized during instruction. Some techniques ask students to use their prior knowledge or reader-based inferencing. In using these techniques, the diagnostic teacher helps students focus on what they know to figure out what the text may say. In other words, they use a top-down approach. Message Writing (see Chapter 9) is an approach that begins by using what students know and then helps them construct rules for word and sentence analysis. In this approach, the students use what they want to say (reader-based inferencing) to figure out unknown words as they write. Other techniques, however, ask the student to use the information in the text. In using these techniques, the diagnostic teacher helps the student focus mainly on the text to figure out the meaning. For example, in the Synthetic Phonics approach (see Chapter 9), the student is asked to decode words letter by letter, focusing on the text to figure out the words. After the word is decoded, the student is asked to think about what it might mean. In these approaches, the students are continually asked to refer to the text when problems in print processing occur.

Techniques also differ in the nature of the structure that is provided by the diagnostic teacher during implementation. Some techniques require that the teacher present the information in a rather nondirective format and simply provide thoughtful questions and support for reading. These techniques rely on students to construct their own rules for the consistency of language. When using these techniques, the diagnostic teacher immerses students in contextual reading and then facilitates their inquiry. It is assumed that students will be able to discover the consistency and meaning of the text on their own. The language experience approach (see Chapter 9), where students read stories that they have dictated to the teacher, is based on an implicit, nondirective approach to learning. This technique allows students to learn to read by using their own language structures.

Other techniques require that the teacher direct learning by modeling how the skill/strategy is to be used when reading text. Furthermore, students are directed in how to incorporate this skill/strategy into their reading. Reciprocal teaching (see Chapter 9) is a technique that uses explicit instruction. Students are shown how to summarize, ask good questions, clarify difficult parts, and predict what will be discussed. First the teacher models the strategy; then the students lead the discussion with the teacher offering encouragement and talking about when it is best to use the strategies.

Not only do techniques differ in their function as exemplified by their instructional frameworks, they also differ in the cognitive demands placed on learners by the instructional sequence. Some techniques present reading tasks as a whole and show students how the parts are organized within the whole. They often use visualization rather than words to develop understanding. The predictable language approach (see Chapter 9) is an example of a technique that introduces the story as a whole. Children read along with the teacher to develop the predictable pattern. After the story has been read as a whole several times, students are asked to identify individual words.

How the teacher directs the reading event affects the information he gathers. Techniques vary in the demands placed on learners. For example, a teacher explicitly tells a student to look at the sounds of letters and blend the sounds together to form words; however, the student prefers to create her own rules, and thinking about sounds is her weakness. The ineffective teacher continues to teach the letter sounds, providing a high degree of feedback about her errors and finally concluding that she is passive and a nonreader.

However, the effective diagnostic teacher probes further. He changes the technique to include predictable stories that have phonetically consistent words. When the student self-corrects, the teacher asks, "How did you figure that out?" The student then tells him her reasons for phonics: "I thought about other words that looked like this word and then I substituted the sounds. You see hopping *looks like* popping. *Words that look alike at the end usually sound alike." The diagnostic teacher changed the technique from explicit instruction in letter sounds to implicit instruction in a text that requires students to create their own rules for phonics. The reflective teacher thinks about how he is directing instruction. He asks himself, "Are there other ways to present this task so that this student can learn more efficiently?"*

Other techniques present the parts of the reading task in a sequential, step-by-step progression that leads to the formation of the whole. These techniques emphasize verbalizing the separate parts, logically structuring these parts into a whole, and explicitly stating rules for organizing the parts into a whole. Synthetic phonics is an example of a technique that is sequential in nature. The synthetic phonics approach begins by teaching the sounds of letters. These sounds are then blended to form words, and finally rules for the different sound combinations are given.

Although there seems to be an either/or situation in evaluating techniques, in reality the techniques can be placed upon a continuum of instructional features. For example, a technique is neither an explicit nor an implicit technique; rather, each technique falls along a continuum with a tendency to approach instruction from a more or less explicit or implicit structure. The relative significance of its approach depends on the learner's task knowledge and task independence as well as the teacher's execution.

In conclusion, teaching techniques vary in the way the diagnostic teacher presents instruction. Techniques are designed to teach skills or strategies or both. The techniques can be more appropriately placed either before, during, or after instruction. Some techniques are more appropriate for narrative text while others are better for expository material. Techniques also vary in the amount of teacher direction necessary for their implementation. Some techniques present information as a whole (simultaneously) and then show the parts (sequentially), while other techniques present information in separate parts (sequentially) and then show how the parts fit into the whole (simultaneously). The diagnostic teacher evaluates the instructional features of each technique as well as the students' responses to the techniques. These features include the following:

☐ Skill instruction
   Word identification, fluency,
   vocabulary, comprehension, or study skills
☐ Strategy instruction
   Predict, monitor, elaborate
☐ Instructional framework
   Before, during, or after reading
☐ Type of text
   Narrative or expository
☐ Mode of response
   Discussion or writing
☐ Source of information
   Reader-based or text-based
☐ Instructional structure
   Implicit or explicit
☐ Instructional sequence
   Simultaneous or successive (sequential)

He then selects the most efficient technique to mediate learning for his students.

CONTEXT

Context plays a key role in influencing the learning that occurs during the instructional event. How teachers and students exchange information about what they are reading affects meaning construction. In one study, for example, children's story retellings were more complete when conveyed to a peer who had not read the story than when told to a teacher who had read the story (Harste, Burke, & Woodward, 1982). Likewise, when inner-city children were interviewed in a testing situation, they were unable to draw logical relationships in conversation. But when these same children were interviewed in a social situation, they were expressive and logical (Labov, 1972). Students' perception of the context, whether it is assessment or discussion, affects their responses. A fifth grader explained this very simply: "It is like school has a big circle around it. Once I walk into this circle, I don't talk. Outside this circle, I talk a lot. I talk with my friends about the ideas I have. But in school, I don't talk about the ideas that I have" (S. R. Walker, personal communication, February 17, 1982).

This example illustrates the status of schooling. Schooling has become a culture of its own where students are taught formal rules within well-structured problems. Unfortunately, problem solving, particularly when reading, is a complex, dynamic activity that depends heavily on the context in which it is situated. Both in reading and oral discussion a simple sentence can have various meanings depending on the context. For example, the sentence, "The ball hit the dish" could mean a cat was playing with a ball of yarn, and the ball hit the cat's dish. However, in a biography of Pelé, a Brazilian soccer player, it could mean the soccer ball hit a satellite dish when he was playing in the neighborhood streets. The meaning depends on the context. Thus, knowledge is reconstructed within each experience as the learner reflects on how a particular context affects his interpretation. As students read and resolve ambiguities in a variety of literacy contexts, they refine and generalize their knowledge and strategies. As a result, knowledge and strategies are constantly evolving with each new situation.

Often, however, instruction does not focus on an exchange of ideas about the content read and the strategies used to derive meaning from texts. Much of the time teachers ask questions to assess learning rather than discuss ideas (Durkin, 1978-1979). Continual random assessment after reading a story can inhibit an exchange of relevant information. By focusing on irrelevant facts without connecting them to the reader's knowledge, the teacher inhibits reading comprehension and reinforces a context of interrogation rather than discussion (Beck et al., 1984). This stifled context does not allow students to participate in authentic reading tasks like discussions that occur in the real world.

In discussions and assessment the diagnostic teacher analyzes his own dialogue as well as the students' responses. He is aware of the silent time between responses and the scaffolds, or prompts, he uses to promote meaning construction within the social context (Bloome & Green, 1984). He thinks about how he formed his questions and how they influence the response. If students are unable to respond to questions, the diagnostic teacher rephrases his question. For example, he can suggest they look together for the page in the text where it talks about the topic. Then he can ask students to read the page orally. And finally, he can rephrase the question using words directly from the text and show students how to find the answer. This type of prompting engages students in a meaning search to find information that was forgotten.

At other times the diagnostic teacher can ask students if they have had similar experiences. This can prompt an elaboration of information from the text with background knowledge. If students cannot construct meaning, the teacher thinks about how he can help them correct their errors. He asks himself, "Do I need to explain what the word means or do I need to reread the text with expression?" These on-the-spot analyses allow the teacher to rephrase questions and segment the task to ensure successful task completion (Cioffi & Carney, 1983).

Likewise the teacher decides at what strategic points during the lesson framework he needs to provide assistance to increase comprehension. If he provides assistance before the lesson, students might read the story with ease; however, they might profit more from talking about reading strategies as they read the story. If he intervenes at the appropriate instructional points during the reading event, he is able to support story comprehension and build more appropriate student-teacher discussion. In this situation, the diagnostic teacher evaluates his presentation as well as students' responses. These analyses can foster an engaging and dynamic relationship between the diagnostic teacher and his students.

Readers who are prompted with "Does that make sense?" increasingly think about the meaning of the text as they read. They become fluent oral readers who correct their own mistakes. However, those students who are given the word or told to sound it out do not develop a meaning base for reading. They continue to focus on the words in the text without thinking about their meaning (Rasinski & Deford, 1988). This leads to less fluent reading and narrow strategies for correcting oral reading errors.

Teachers differ not only on how they support learning but also on when they prompt students. Sometimes teachers interrupt at the point of error and prompt with a word-level prompt. At other times teachers wait until the end of the sentence and then say, "Try that again; that didn't make sense" (Allington, 1980). Allowing students to read to the end of the sentence rather than interrupting at the point of error facilitates more active reading strategies and communicates to readers that they can think through problems when they read (Cazden, 1981). When teachers interrupt students at the point of error and focus on accuracy rather than meaning, they encourage a helpless approach to problems. Many times this focus is projected in teachers' expectations for students. If teachers expect failure and little effort, then their language, wait time, and prompting can convey this expectation to the readers. Consequently, the readers respond according to the teachers' expectations (Bloome & Green, 1984). They slowly change their perceptions of the literacy context and begin to judge themselves as unable to read. This contributes to their associating the context of reading events with failure.

Often school reinforces this definition. When teachers focus on skill weaknesses and repeatedly evaluate these skills using criterion-referenced tests, they reinforce the reader's association of reading with failure. Likewise, when teachers use norm-referenced evaluations, they reward students who learn easily and quickly rather than assist problem readers who may require adjustments in their learning (Raffini, 1988).

Although the problem readers try hard, they do not meet the standard created by other rapid learners in the classroom. Over time, they change their perceptions of the context and view literacy events as experiences to avoid because their efforts do not result in positive evaluations by their teachers.

A key to reversing students' association of reading with failure is an instructional context where students discuss the strategies they use to construct meaning (Walker, 1990b). Discussing how they interpret text increases the likelihood that the students will define the context of the discussion as a place to refine and elaborate their knowledge and strategies.

The context of the reading event is a powerful influence on readers' performances. The situational context affects the information the teacher gathers about students' reading. For example, an informal assessment that used only factual questions after silent reading placed a student at the third-grade level; however, this same student was able to answer inferential questions at the eighth-grade level. When she discussed the same story with her peers, she recalled 80% of the facts as she needed them to support her interpretation. In this case, the context had changed from silent reading and answering factual questions in a relatively sterile context to silent reading and discussing the story in an interactive instructional group.

The diagnostic teacher thinks about how he negotiates meaning within a social-interactive context that requires collaboration among group members. As the teacher becomes a sympathetic partner in understanding text rather than an assessor of students' deficits, he increases reading behavior through an instructional context that focuses on meaning. As an active listener responding creatively and consistently within the reading event, he carefully analyzes his own behavior and its effect on reading performance.

In conclusion, the context (or where instruction takes place) influences diagnostic decision making. The context can vary by who is a member of the instructional group and the students' perception of his membership in that group. Teacher expectations and scaffolding also influence the context. The time allowed on the task, the wait time during instruction, and the timing of teacher assistance are influential factors in reading performance. The diagnostic teacher evaluates all these factors in the following list in order to make diagnostic decisions.

- ☐ Learning situation
  Focus on constructing meaning and collaboration
- ☐ Previous learning situations
- ☐ Teacher expectation
- ☐ Teacher dialogue
- ☐ Wait time
- ☐ Time allowed on task
- ☐ Point of intervention during lesson

SUMMARY

In summary, five interrelated variables establish the parameters of diagnostic teaching, which occurs in an interactive learning situation rather than a static, product-oriented situation. By evaluating these five variables, the diagnostic teacher identifies the instructional conditions for optimal learning. Reading instruction and assessment are redirected to the interrelationship of the variables rather than just student deficits.

Roles of Diagnostic Teaching

Effective diagnostic teaching involves making instructional decisions before, during, and after the reading event. At the core of decision making is the effective teacher who reflects on her instruction. As she teaches, the diagnostic teacher continually identifies those instructional modifications that enable problem readers to become independent learners. She thinks about her role within the context of the reading event (see Figure 3–1). This chapter delineates five roles of effective diagnostic teaching: reflecting, planning, mediating, enabling, and responding. These roles are supported by eight instructional guidelines that focus diagnostic teaching and encourage students to realize their individual potential as learners. As the effective teacher assumes these roles, she views problem readers from different perspectives. As she reflects on her decision making, therefore, she considers each of these roles and its influence on her instruction.

The first role of effective diagnostic teaching is reflecting. Central to diagnostic teaching is the teacher who reflects on the interactions during the reading event. She checks the instructional decisions she makes with her personal assumptions about reading and cross-checks her lesson plans with students' learning. As she is teaching, she analyzes how she modifies instruction and the language she uses to mediate learning. Teaching as reflecting means that every interaction is analyzed so that appropriate instructional adjustments can be made.

The second role of diagnostic teaching is planning. As the diagnostic teacher plans her lesson, she thinks about the *whole act of reading* and selects experiences for students to share their ideas in a group. She teaches not only reading skills but also how those skills fit together when reading. As she plans her lessons, she selects activities that will not only stimulate learning, but *ensure success*. To do so she uses familiar and interesting stories. At the end of the lesson the diagnostic teacher encourages students to evaluate their experiences focusing their attention on their developing strengths. Teaching as planning means that the diagnostic teacher focuses on the whole act of reading, ensuring success for each child.

The third role of diagnostic teaching is mediating. The effective diagnostic teacher *encourages active reading* by asking questions that not only lead students through the story but relate the events and key ideas to what students already know. As she teaches, the diagnostic teacher actively aids students in sense-making, phasing in to support reading and phasing out to promote self-directed learning (Singer, 1989). During the lesson, the diagnostic teacher *assesses while she instructs* so she can modify her instruction to meet students' changing instructional needs. Teaching as mediating

Figure 3–1
The Decision-
Making Cycle of
Diagnostic
Teaching

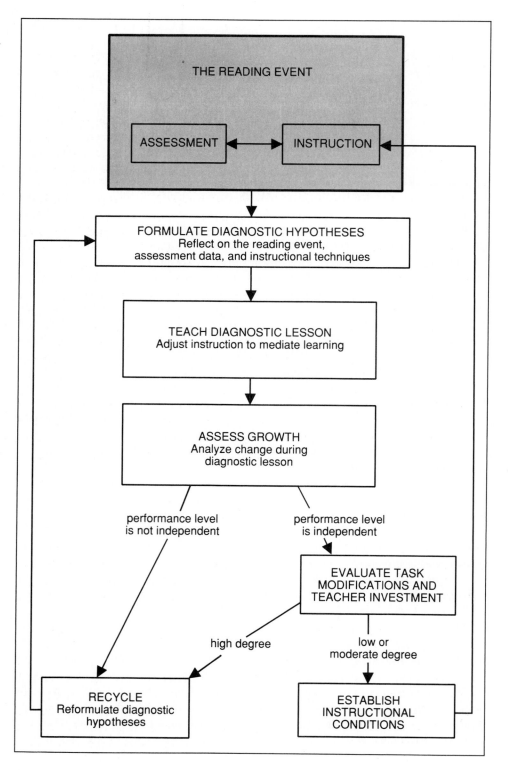

means that the diagnostic teacher uses students' present strategies to lead them to more active reading strategies.

The fourth role of effective diagnostic teaching is enabling. She helps her students develop a *concept of themselves as readers.* Immersing her students in relevant and successful reading experiences, she attributes their success to the effective strategies they use. As she plans lessons, she thinks about how to *build students' control* over their learning. She plans lessons where she models her own internal thinking, asks students to share in thinking through the problem, and actively listens and encourages students to tell her how they solve the reading problem. Teaching as enabling means that the diagnostic teacher provides students with the resources to understand themselves as readers, thinkers, and problem solvers.

In the fifth role, the diagnostic teacher views teaching as responding to individual human needs. An effective diagnostic teacher *accepts the individual differences* among her students. She knows that the experiences of her students vary widely and plans her instruction to account for the differences in what her students already know. She thinks about the different ways her students solve problems and plans lessons that use their problem-solving strengths. In accepting their individual differences, the effective teacher *fosters a reality-oriented environment* by accepting individuality but expecting all students to read. She uses laughter to develop a relaxed atmosphere where students learn to cope with their mistakes and produce intelligent ideas. She also reacts personally to literacy, sharing her personal change in interpretations. Teaching as a human response means that the diagnostic teacher discusses individuality and making mistakes as human conditions.

These roles and the instructional guidelines they represent work together to create an instructional environment where all students learn. This model fosters instructional interactions that focus on the whole reading event, giving students self-control of their own learning and creating a coherent learning experience for them. Figure 3–2 suggests the interrelation between the roles and guidelines discussed in this chapter.

REFLECTING

The reflective diagnostic teacher considers and selects among alternatives and, at the same time, anticipates the consequences of differing decisions before, during, and after a reading event (Grimmett, 1988). This reflection helps teachers know why they teach as they do and facilitates their explanations to others (Jaggar, 1989). The diagnostic teacher shifts between immersion in the reading event and distancing herself from it in order to critically analyze the experience. This distancing helps the diagnostic teacher reconsider reasons for her instruction and refocus on the theoretical framework that underpins these decisions (Walker, 1990a). Thus, in this reflection the diagnostic teacher continually evaluates her guiding theory of reading (see Chapter 1) and expands her awareness of individual differences among students.

Before the lesson, the diagnostic teacher plans her instruction based on her guiding theory of reading. She thinks about students' strengths and needs in relation to stages of reading development, students' strategies, and attributions. She reflects

Figure 3–2
Roles of Diagnos-
tic Teaching

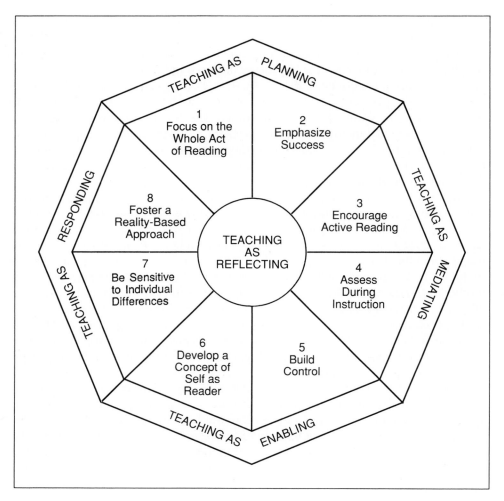

upon the instructional sequence as she plans each lesson. Diagnostic lessons are much more than a set of activities selected because they are fun. Diagnostic teaching involves the systematic orchestration of reading instruction. At this stage in the teacher's thinking (reflections before teaching), the students' attributes are matched with an instructional framework (see Chapter 4) and cross-checked with her guiding theory. These rationales continue to impact instruction as the diagnostic teacher implements her plans.

As the lesson is taught, the diagnostic teacher observes how the student is responding to the lesson (reflections during instruction). Using these observations, the diagnostic teacher changes original plans to modify instruction and thus to mediate student learning. Every day teachers make decisions that are often intuitive and unconscious; they are "knowledge in action" (Schon, 1988). These changes enable problem readers to employ independent strategies. For example, Jordan

(1989) reported: "During the lesson, I discarded the story map, modeled self-talk, self-questioning, and especially prediction. Used the story map as a summary . . . She elaborated and answered with background knowledge the comprehension questions, today." In this example the teacher makes adjustments during the lesson to improve the student's reading. The teacher is constantly sensitive to how the student-teacher interactions affected the goals of the lesson.

After the lesson, the diagnostic teacher evaluates what specific part of the lesson produced the desired reading behavior and she considers how the on-the-spot adjustments fit into the overall diagnostic lesson. She considers the amount of energy expended in order to encourage student understanding. Likewise, she reflects on the prompts and scaffolding she used to improve reading performance. Then she makes adjustments in subsequent lesson plans as she reflects on what occurred and how the interactions were consistent with her plans as well as her beliefs about reading.

The reflective teacher analyzes her own preferences for learning and how these preferences affect her teaching. She focuses on how she learns and how she teaches, not only on what she is teaching. She watches herself to cross-check strategies for teaching with personal beliefs about reading. Andrews (1977) found that teachers who believe that word recognition and accuracy are important in reading introduce isolated vocabulary words and practice them through flashcard drill, pointing to each word as they read it and using such phrases as "perfect," "that's exactly right," and "go back and read that again."

Finally, the diagnostic teacher thinks about how this instructional event brought a new understanding to her theory of reading instruction. For example, one diagnostic teacher was uncertain how to measure passive reading. After teaching, she decided to review several articles on passive behavior in reading. She later commented: "I understand that there is no testing that particularly tests this element. It is determined by observation and analysis of the reader and the reading event." After analyzing the characteristics described in the research literature, she felt she knew enough to identify one of her students as a passive reader. These reflections had led the diagnostic teacher to become more confident in her own knowledge. By reflecting on the various aspects of an instructional event and thinking about how they fit together, the diagnostic teacher elaborates and changes her model of the reading process. Through reflection she actively constructs her theory of reading and reading instruction.

Thus the diagnostic teacher reflects on her plans (the diagnostic session), her observations during instruction, and her intuitive decisions (adjustments). She does this as she plans lessons, mediates learning, enables student independence, and responds personally during the reading event.

PLANNING

Prior to the reading event, the teacher thinks about how instruction will occur. She thinks about the variables of the reading event: task, text, reader, and context. Then she selects teaching techniques that focus on reading stories that ensure success. As teachers focus on the broad aspects of reading, they talk with students about why and how the strategies of reading will improve their reading performance. In doing this, they create activities that are both challenging and successful.

This planning creates an expectation that the reading event will produce independent readers. Effective teachers expect the students in their classrooms to read and interpret stories. Furthermore, this prior planning allows the effective teacher to think about the strategies needed to complete the assigned reading task; therefore, she can attribute students' success to both their abilities and efforts. Teaching as planning means that the teacher preplans her lessons to focus on the whole act of reading and to ensure success. These two planning guidelines are delineated in the following section.

Guideline #1: Focus on the Whole Act of Reading

As the diagnostic teacher plans her instruction, she creates a literate environment by focusing on the whole act rather than the parts of reading. Furthermore, she realizes that children learn what teachers teach (Berliner, 1981). If teachers instruct children to recognize vowel sounds, they will learn vowel sounds. If teachers emphasize literal comprehension, they will, in fact, become excellent fact finders and comprehend the literal information of a story. However, if teachers instruct students to react to whole stories using important textual information and their own prior knowledge, they will actually become comprehenders who flexibly shift between reader-based and text-based knowledge. As a result, focusing instruction on the whole act of reading is extremely important.

Effective teachers focus on reading whole stories and relating them to relevant personal experiences. They encourage sustained silent reading of stories as well as mastering specific skills. However, studies have shown not all students receive the same amount of contextual reading instruction. A longitudinal study that investigated children's reading progress in first through third grade (Juel, 1988) found that poor readers read less than half as many words each year as good readers. In another study, good readers were observed to be engaged in contextual reading 57% of the time; poor readers, only 33% of the time. Poor readers, in fact, had an extended amount of time practicing the skills of reading in short, isolated drills (Gambrell, Wilson, & Gantt, 1981). The results are even more astounding in remedial programs. In these programs the average number of words read a day was 43 (Allington, 1977). Even though research supports the premise that skill knowledge is best mastered during contextual reading (Anderson, Hiebert, Scott, & Wilkinson, 1985), it appears that remedial instruction in both classrooms and clinics continues to focus on the parts rather than the whole act of reading. However, classrooms with high reading achievement are characterized by silent reading of selections followed by small group discussions where students exchange ideas about the meaning of the story (Rupley & Blair, 1978). Through the small group discussions, students justify their interpretations by relating the text to what they already know. This focuses instruction on meaning rather than decoding.

As teachers focus on the whole act of reading, they engage students in a discussion about both the content of the story and the strategies they use to construct meaning.

This social interaction is critical to the process of constructing knowledge. As students explain and defend their ideas to their peers, they refine and reorganize their knowledge. Likewise, students who hold misconceptions about the content need to be challenged by others to redefine their understanding and create new knowledge. By communicating ideas in discussion groups, children share their interpretations, focus their purposes, and think about the functions of reading and writing. The diagnostic teacher plans time for discussing stories in small and large group settings so students can explore their own interpretation of text with this valuable interaction with classmates.

In addition to discussing whole stories, the diagnostic teacher selects appropriate skills and strategies to teach. But, she teaches more than just the skill; she explains when and why the skill is used. The diagnostic teacher gives students reasons for learning the parts of reading and shows students how the parts affect the total reading process. As skills or strategies are presented, therefore, the teacher explains when it is most appropriate to use them. For example, when reading different types of text, the teacher explains the utility of using or not using the particular reading strategy she is teaching. If the teacher is instructing the use of formulating predictions based on prior knowledge, she explains that if the student does not know anything about the topic, he must read two or three paragraphs, summarize the information, and then create a prediction based on the new information and what he knows about it.

In summary, the effective diagnostic teacher encourages students to discuss ideas within the reading event. She explains the process of shifting between reader-based knowledge and the text and how the strategies of reading will influence reading efficiency when problems in text interpretation arise. This focus means that students are given rationales for the various reading activities and are shown how these activities relate to the whole act of reading.

GUIDELINE #1: FOCUS ON THE WHOLE ACT OF READING

- □ *Focus on reading entire stories.*
- □ *Plan time for discussing content and strategies.*
- □ *Provide rationales for how the parts (skills and strategies) of reading relate to the whole act of reading.*

Guideline #2: Emphasize Success

As the diagnostic teacher focuses on the whole act of reading, she must at the same time ensure successful reading for students. Berliner (1981) stresses that reading achievement is directly related to the amount of time spent reading material where students have a high success rate. It is not only the amount of time engaged in reading that matters, but readers must experience a high level of success. Thus, in order to develop a notion of efficient reading, students must first experience numerous successful reading experiences. When students have success, they repeat the successful activity. Obviously, success is a powerful motivating factor.

On the other hand, if students experience numerous failures in an activity, they often give up and avoid subsequent opportunities to engage in this activity. Poor readers are often placed in material that is very difficult for them (Allington, 1984b; Clay, 1979; Juel, 1988). They have either a low rate of recognizing words or understanding the content, which discourages them from further reading. These unsuccessful reading experiences contribute to an unsystematic evaluation of reading performance. These students have a serendipitous notion about success. Success is attributed to external factors such as "baby reading material," "it was my lucky day," or "the teacher gave it away when she helped me."

To encourage a healthy attitude toward success, the diagnostic teacher creates a series of consistently successful reading events. She keeps a close match between the students' abilities and the texts that she chooses for reading instruction. When choosing texts, the diagnostic teacher not only considers the level of reading performance but also the extent of prior experiences. She chooses material that contains familiar concepts so students can readily use their prior knowledge to predict, monitor, and elaborate their understanding. She, then, plans for the students to read more material and to express ideas based on what they have read.

Not only does the diagnostic teacher plan successful reading experiences by placing the students at the appropriate reading level, but she also carefully selects authentic texts that are familiar and interesting to her students. In good children's literature readers and characters share similar experiences, thus promoting reading for meaning (Routman, 1988). When children's literature is matched with students' experiences, the problem reader readily identifies with the main character's conflict and can successfully predict solutions out of his own experiences. Therefore, the diagnostic teacher selects high caliber children's literature and reads with students to establish a successful reading experience. The students continue to read on their own and feel the success of reading an entire book. This success can spill over into other literacy activities by giving them confidence in writing or in taking on other reading tasks.

However, many problem readers have a hazy notion of success and do not recognize when they are successful. Therefore, besides creating successful experiences, the diagnostic teacher designs activities that concretely show students how they are progressing. This self-assessment helps readers evaluate and recognize their success. Portfolios, where students choose what is included in their assessment folder, can help students evaluate their success on various activities and show them their progress over time. Periodically, the teacher uses these portfolios to show students their growth in strategic reading and knowledge acquisition. Students can also evaluate their success on individual reading activities as they complete them by using teacher-developed check-sheets related to the task. For example, a check-sheet was designed with story grammar questions (see Story Mapping, Chapter 9). The students marked whether or not their retelling included main characters, setting, problem, major events, and problem resolution (Glazer & Searfoss, 1988). Using the check-sheet, the students and teacher assess literacy and discuss student success. Self-assessment helps problem readers develop a more systematic evaluation of reading performance and attribute their success to internal factors such as knowledge and strategies rather than to luck or easy materials.

GUIDELINE #2: EMPHASIZE SUCCESS

□ *Create a series of successful reading events.*
□ *Use authentic texts that are familiar and interesting.*
□ *Encourage self-assessment.*

MEDIATING

The diagnostic teacher mediates learning by phasing in and out of the reading event as she guides student learning. She asks questions that promote an active interpretation of text. She listens to the students and uses what they understand about the story to elicit more elaborate interpretations and applications of the text. She gives them time to develop predictions and formulate answers. When students are unsure of a response, she asks them what they know so far about the story. Then she asks them to explain how they came to that conclusion. From this information the teacher develops leading questions or examples that will guide the students' interpretation. Using students' responses, the diagnostic teacher assesses their learning as a result of her instruction. Teaching as mediating means that the teacher phases in and out of the reading event in order to encourage active reading and assess learning as a result of her instruction. These two mediating guidelines are detailed in the following section.

Guideline #3: Encourage Active Reading

Reading is an active, problem-solving process that involves predicting (or guessing) what the author is going to say, based on expectations about story events. After making a guess, children select clues from the story to confirm their guesses and then check this knowledge with what they already know. The diagnostic teacher engages students in this active problem-solving process so they construct meaning as they read. This engagement fosters an exploration of their own concepts and strategies. From a very young age, children strive to make sense of their world and the diagnostic teacher builds on this natural aptitude by supporting students in making sense of reading and writing events. The diagnostic teacher, then, encourages students to evaluate their guesses from a "making sense" perspective. She assists students to extend ideas, revise misconceptions, develop opinions, and prove beliefs. In their search for meaning, students invent their own explanations for print, examine and justify these reasons, and finally refute or rework their explanations. Thus, "What a reader reads may mean more to the reader than it did to the author" (Harste et al., 1984, p. 122). To mediate learning, the diagnostic teacher constantly engages students in an active meaning search.

To do so the diagnostic teacher checks her behavior with both proficient and problem readers to see if her prompts focus on meaning. Research shows that teachers treat their students in low reading groups differently from those in their high reading groups. This indicates that they view the reading needs of poor readers as different from the reading needs of good readers (Cazden, 1981).

Teachers allow more interruptions in low groups and are more engaged as teachers when instructing high groups. They interrupt poor readers at the point of error, while they let good readers continue reading to see if they are going to recover meaning. They use more word-level prompting with poor readers, while they use meaning-level prompting with readers in their high groups (Allington, 1980). These teaching behaviors affect reading performance. Often this causes poor readers to miscall words or ideas and continue reading without checking these words or ideas against an overall meaning to see if they fit. For these readers, the diagnostic teacher needs to frame her prompts from a making-sense perspective. As students miscall a word or miscomprehend an idea, she indicates her inability to make sense of their response and encourages them to rethink their explanation. This focuses the problem reader on making sense of text.

The diagnostic teacher can encourage active reading by asking questions that require students to construct ideas rather than give right or wrong answers. In these lessons, the diagnostic teacher creates an expectation about the story before a story is read. She asks the children what they already know about the topic and to think about what the text might say. As the children read, the teacher asks questions that focus on comparing what they thought the text might say with what was written. This process encourages an active reading of text based on reader knowledge and textual information.

The line of questioning also influences active comprehension of text. If questions focus on the important organizational parts of the story (setting, problem, goal, events, and resolution), comprehension is enhanced (Beck et al., 1982; Singer & Donlan, 1982). When developing her questions, the diagnostic teacher reads the text, selects the most important points of the passage, and constructs questions that will lead students to think about these important points (Pearson, 1985a). She also encourages active comprehension by directing students to formulate their own questions. Students who generate their own questions during reading perform better on interpretive comprehension tasks than students who answer only teacher-posed questions (Helfeldt & Lalik, 1979; Walker & Mohr, 1985).

Although teacher-originated questions are prevalent in the classroom, asking appropriate questions is a complex skill. Learning what to ask and how to ask questions is extremely demanding. The diagnostic teacher learns to monitor not only the kinds of questions she asks but also the way she asks them. She thinks about how to orchestrate her support. The effective diagnostic teacher phases in to support the students' sense making and phases out to allow students to think independently (Singer, 1989). Initially, she allows three to five seconds between the original question and her probes. Increasing the wait time from one second to three seconds positively affects the number of student responses as well as the organization of the response (Rowe, 1973). Furthermore, the amount of time between the students' responses and the teacher's response affects the elaboration of the answer. Thinking takes time. Silence may mean that students are constructing thoughtful answers to higher level questions.

Not only should the diagnostic teacher increase her wait time, but she must also deal effectively with inappropriate responses. Initially, the teacher uses part of the students' answers to probe reasoning. Sometimes she rephrases or reduces her question so that a response is more manageable. At other times she asks students to justify their answers by supplying information from the text. During the lesson, she remains flexible, interacting with students to show them how to justify their answers using the text and what they already know. Finally, if the line of reasoning is justifiable, the diagnostic teacher accepts the response as a valid point of view. As the diagnostic teacher increases her wait time and deals creatively with inappropriate responses, she develops an atmosphere that promotes active interpretation of text.

In summary, the diagnostic teacher encourages active reading by focusing on making sense of text and asking logical questions that promote active reflection. She phases in and out of the lesson to create an atmosphere that promotes thinking rather than interrogation.

GUIDELINE #3: ENCOURAGE ACTIVE READING

☐ *Focus on "Making Sense" with text.*
☐ *Ask questions that focus on key ideas.*
☐ *Phase in and out to support active thinking.*

Guideline #4: Assess During Instruction

As the diagnostic teacher implements the lessons that she planned, she keeps a mental log of the students' responses. Her instruction, therefore, not only creates active readers but also provides a means for assessment. As the diagnostic teacher mediates learning, she observes how she modifies the initial reading task to create learning. This record of students' responses to instructional modifications is called dynamic assessment. Dynamic assessment evaluates students' performances as they are guided to use more effective reading strategies. This type of assessment reveals the students' acquisition of strategies during instruction rather than unaided levels of competence (Brown & Campione, 1986).

During dynamic assessment the teacher probes responses when questions are missed or answers are not clear. For example, when a child read a story about two mountain climbers in Chile, South America, he miscalled the word *Chile* (actually he pronounced the *ch* sound and then mumbled). In the oral retelling, he referred to Chile as the location. When the diagnostic teacher probed how he got the answer, the student said, "Well, the author talked about the Andes Mountains, and I know the Andes Mountains are on the west coast of South America . . . so I decided that the country must have been Chile."

From this information, the teacher assessed that this student had a wide range of prior experiences and used them to interpret text. He was also able to mentally self-correct word recognition errors. This was a sign that he was an active rather than a passive reader. His reading problem stemmed from overrelying on his background knowledge when he encountered several words that he could not recognize. Probing the student about how he arrived at an answer during the instructional situation gave the diagnostic teacher a more accurate picture of the student's potential for learning new information.

Finally, as the diagnostic teacher assesses learning while she teaches, she evaluates whether or not her instruction is appropriate for her learners. She evaluates the reading event and asks if there is another way to teach students the task. She asks herself:

1. Am I leading students through the task according to their present strategy use? If not, should I try another way?
2. Is this an appropriate text for these students? If not, should I try another text?
3. Am I using the students' strengths as I am teaching? If not, should I try another way?
4. Is this an appropriate technique for these students? If not, should I try another way?
5. Is this an appropriate learning context for these students? If not, should I try another situation?

As key variables of instruction are changed, assessment is based on the resulting changes in reading performance. The diagnostic teacher evaluates students' improvement due to her instruction. If students do not improve, the diagnostic teacher looks for another way to modify her instruction to produce improved reading performance.

GUIDELINE #4: ASSESS DURING INSTRUCTION

☐ *Assess reading change due to mediated learning.*
☐ *Probe students' answers to evaluate how they arrive at answers.*
☐ *If reading performance does not change, try another adjustment.*

ENABLING

During the reading event, the diagnostic teacher enables students to control their own learning and, therefore, think of themselves as readers. To enable students, the diagnostic teacher helps them develop control by sharing how she thinks while she is reading. The students and teacher work together to figure out a story and then discuss how they reached their conclusions. As the teacher shares her thinking and works with the students to gain understanding, she enables them to control their own learning and talk with themselves about their own understanding of a story. As the diagnostic teacher builds control, she finds ways to show students that they can read and think. She acknowledges the effective strategies they use when they read efficiently. At times, she allows students to read for their own purposes without teacher questions and discussion. These guidelines for enabling students are elaborated in the following section.

Guideline #5: Build Control

The fifth guideline requires that the teacher not only instruct the strategies of reading but systematically plan how students will assume responsibility for their own learning. The diagnostic teacher not only directs the learning process by explaining the steps and guiding the practice; she also gives students ownership of their learning by encouraging them to think about their thinking. Efficient readers monitor their understanding. As they are reading, they monitor their comprehension by actively choosing alternate strategies when reading does not make sense. Remedial readers, on the other hand, are characterized by disorganized strategies and failing to spontaneously self-monitor (Bristow, 1985). Consequently, they continue to rely on the teacher to monitor reading performance.

To change this dependence, remedial readers need explicit instruction in effective monitoring behaviors so that they can progress from teacher-directed to self-directed learning. The initial step is to redirect assessment from the teacher to the child by thinking out loud about reading. To do so, the teacher purposely makes mistakes while reading so that she can model how she monitors an active meaning search. Too often remedial readers perceive proficient reading as error-free reading. By making mistakes, the teacher can model her own coping behaviors.

The teacher begins the modeling by saying, "Oops, did that make sense?" When the answer is negative, various alternative corrective strategies are modeled. She shows readers that they can ignore the mistake and read on to see if they can figure out the meaning. Or that they can reread the sentence to check the overall meaning to see what might fit.

As she continues to model this active meaning search, the teacher illustrates the self-questioning process that goes through the mind of an active reader:

> If I don't understand, I ask myself a series of questions, the first one being "What would make sense?" If I can't regain the meaning, I ask more questions. Most of the time I need to figure out either a word I don't know or what the author was trying to say. I can use two different sequences.
>
> First, to figure out a word, I ask myself, "Can I say it that way?" (syntactic fit) or "What word does it look like?" (graphic fit) or "What does it sound like?" (phonic fit).
>
> Second, to figure out meaning, I ask myself, "What does the text say? What do I already know about what the text says? How does this information fit together?"

After modeling the self-questioning process, the teacher and students work through a couple of examples. The students follow the teacher's model and think aloud, asking themselves questions about their reading. The students actually talk about how they solve the reading task. The teacher, in turn, provides encouragement for their thinking about thinking. Pearson (1985a, p. 736) states that "teachers assume new and different roles: they become sharers of secrets, coconspirators, coaches and cheerleaders."

Guided practice involves an interaction between students and teacher that begins with talking about how to solve the reading problem. This thinking aloud allows the teacher to provide feedback about the appropriateness of strategies used. She comments, "Did you notice how you reread that sentence to see if it made sense? That was very effective." When necessary, she models appropriate trouble-shooting strategies. This is an intermediate step between teacher direction and student control of the reading process.

As the teacher builds control by modeling active reading and the flexible use of trouble-shooting strategies, she encourages internalization of these strategies. She assumes an active role by asking students to explain what they are going to do the next time they read a passage they cannot understand. This type of questioning focuses instruction on the inner speech that accompanies logical thought, heightening students' awareness of the problem-solving process.

The diagnostic teacher builds student control of the reading process by modeling the process of active reading and the corresponding trouble-shooting strategies that efficient readers use. In addition, the teacher thinks out loud, showing students how she knows what she knows. In turn, students think out loud using the steps of active reading, and the teacher reinforces the thinking process rather than focuses on right or wrong answers. Finally, control of the process is gradually released by the teacher, who encourages students to actively think about the strategies they are using.

GUIDELINE #5: BUILD CONTROL

☐ *Model your own thinking while reading to students.*
☐ *Collaborate in thinking about how reading is occurring.*
☐ *Release teacher control by encouraging self-talk about how students solve their reading problems.*

Guideline #6: Develop a Concept of Self as Reader

Children come to school with well-developed problem-solving abilities; they have learned to walk, to talk, and so on. Through their everyday living, they have learned many of the principles of communicating their ideas through language. However, because disabled readers repeatedly fail when learning to read, they develop a concept of themselves as nonreaders. This self-assessment is very difficult to change. As inefficient readers learn to read, word identification is difficult, and the sympathetic teacher assists these students more readily, allowing them to depend on teacher assistance rather than using textual meaning to correct errors. This type of interaction inhibits an active search for meaning and encourages a passive view of reading, emphasizing word calling rather than meaning as the goal of reading.

While listening to such readers, one notices that they "read as if they do not expect what they read to make sense, as if getting every individual word right were the key" (Smith, 1978, p. 34). This passive attitude is also exhibited when comprehending text. Disabled readers seem to monitor their reading less frequently and accept whatever argument is presented in the text without applying their prior knowledge. They seldom reread text to check initial interpretations and try to maintain interpretations even in light of contradictory information (Palincsar & Brown, 1984). These ineffective strategies can be altered by the teacher who is sensitive to her influence on the students' concept of themselves as readers. This concept can be developed using three teaching strategies: immersing students in reading, attributing success to effective strategy use, and allowing time for personal reading.

To be engaged in the actual reading of text is the first important requisite for developing a concept of self as reader. Immersing students in relevant reading activities will increase their concept of themselves as readers. As they read material that is repetitive, relevant, and rythmic, they can feel themselves reading. Poor readers, however, have few opportunities to read connected text. In first-grade classrooms, Allington (1984a) found that children in high reading groups read 10 times as many words as children in low reading groups. In this study, children in low reading groups read silently a total of only 60 words during the five-day sample period. It is difficult to consider oneself a reader when one only reads 12 words a day. Therefore, increasing the amount of fluent contextual reading each day is the first step toward developing a concept of self as reader. Difficult reading material causes students to focus on the word level of reading, precluding an active search for meaning. Reading text fluently at an independent level allows students to read enough words correctly so that they can engage in an active search for meaning.

Inefficient readers, however, need more than easy reading material to change their concept of themselves as readers (Johnston & Winograd, 1985). Because of the repeated failures of problem readers, they do not recognize the effective strategies that they do use. When asked how they got an answer, students often respond with "I don't know." Because of their continual failure, these students do not have enough experience with successful reading to recognize when and how their effective strategies work. They have developed a view that reading is simply calling words correctly and waiting for teacher assistance when reading breaks down. They attribute their reading performance to forces outside their control rather than to effective use of strategies. To change this attitude, teachers show students how their strategies influence reading performance. Then changing reading behavior is a mutual responsibility demanding effort from both teacher and students. The teacher acknowledges students' strategy use by charting their reading progress (see Chapter 4). In this way the students' attention is refocused on those behaviors that they can control.

When effective strategies are reinforced, students can attribute their comprehension not only to the product but also to the process of active reading. They begin to see themselves as active readers who can construct meaning from text. As the children build their self-concepts as readers, a second major task of the teacher is to talk about the strategies used to derive meaning from text and attribute active reading to effective strategy use and effort.

The purpose for reading can also influence children's concepts of themselves as readers. When children read for their own purposes and enjoyment, their interactions with text are perceived as real and relevant reading; consequently, they perceive themselves as readers. Teachers need to set aside time in the classroom for children to read for their own enjoyment and then share their reading. In building the students' concept of themselves as readers, the teacher allows time for them to share the knowledge they have gained from reading in a creative way with their peers. She creates a "read and tell" time that reinforces individual variation in text interpretation. This allows students to have ownership of their own responses to text and builds the concept of themselves as readers.

When students think of themselves as readers, they identify questions to be answered, read to answer those questions, and actively engage in text interpretation. They view themselves as in control of their reading. Teaching strategies can build children's concepts of themselves as readers. The sensitive teacher creates independent readers by having them read a lot of text, stressing the strategies of active reading, and having them read relevant materials for their own enjoyment.

GUIDELINE #6: DEVELOP THE CONCEPT OF SELF AS READER

☐ *Immerse students in reading.*
☐ *Attribute active reading to effective strategy use.*
☐ *Allow students to read for their own individual purposes.*

RESPONDING

In all her interactions, the teacher responds as a person rather than a controller of activities. She responds to the different children she has in her classroom and challenges them according to their individual needs. She uses what they already know to present concepts in the way they learn best. Using the unique strengths of the individual learners in her classroom, she reduces stress for each learner. Furthermore, she acknowledges the realities of the educational situation. Using personal statements about her own reading process and laughing about her own mistakes increases students' awareness that reading is constructing a response rather than getting the answer right. The guidelines for responding to students are explained in the following section.

Guideline #7: Be Sensitive to Individual Differences

Students bring to the reading task their own sets of experiences and knowledge that affect their reading behavior. At the same time, they bring their own strategies for dealing with the world. Some children are impulsive, some are simultaneous, and some are quiet, while others are highly distractible. Even though each of them is different, seldom do these differences affect instruction in public schools. This is partly due to a limited exploration of how learners are alike and different. Understanding human similarities increase one's sensitivity to human differences. When learning something new, people are alike because new learning creates disequilibrium, or stress. As people solve the problem or learn the information, they reduce this stress (Elkind, 1983).

People learn this new information in two ways. First, they all use what they already know to formulate hypotheses about new information (Pearson & Johnson, 1978). Second, they use their strengths to reduce this stress (learn the information). Therefore, in this state of disequilibrium (new learning), people use what they already know to make sense of the new information. However, people differ not only on *what* they already know (knowledge-based differences) but also on *how* they integrate new information with what they already know (strategy-based differences).

Knowledge-based differences are evident in the scope of vocabulary knowledge and the variety of experiences that students have. Some children come to school with a rich variety of experiences and a well-developed oral language. Some children have had repeated experiences with books and have developed concepts about print. Other children come to school with limited experiences with reading events and require more exposure to a variety of experiences with both print and concepts.

These knowledge-based differences are accentuated by differences in problem-solving strategies. All remedial students do not learn the same way (Bond & Dykstra, 1967; Juel, 1984). Some students select meaning cues, while others select graphic cues. For example, Clay (1979) found that many young readers did not integrate cueing systems. Some of these students used a visual cueing system; they matched the missed word with the initial letters of other words they knew. Other students used the phonic cueing system; they matched the missed word to the sounds they knew.

Some students rely heavily on their background knowledge to form hypotheses while they are reading. These students check what they already know without thinking about the text. Other students rely heavily on the text to form their hypotheses while reading (Strange, 1980). Some students summarize stories, giving the overall gist of the text, while other students give explicitly stated information (Moore & Cunningham, 1984). Some students revise and monitor their model of meaning readily, while others need concrete facts before they revise their model of meaning (Collins, Brown, & Larkin, 1980). Some students organize information within broad, simultaneous categories, while others organize information in discrete, hierarchical categories (Kaufman & Kaufman, 1983).

Because the reading event is more stressful for remedial readers (Gentile, 1983; Gentile & McMillan, 1987), the demand for instruction using background knowledge and processing strengths is greater for them. By using appropriate instructional methods that utilize learning strengths, the diagnostic teacher can reduce the stress associated with the reading task and increase learning (Kogan, 1971). For example, teachers have differentiated prompting by using language that emphasizes the preferred cueing system and then encouraging the integration of word identification cueing systems (Clay, 1979). For instance, the child using the visual cueing system can be prompted with "what makes sense?" and "begins with. . . ." Teacher prompting can effectively differentiate instruction by using children's processing strengths and then encouraging them to incorporate more flexible strategies.

Individual sense making is encouraged through the use of *I* statements. The teacher models "I think . . .," talking about her own reading and thinking aloud about how she figured out a particular answer. Showing the *how* and modeling "I think . . ." release students from the necessity of having to do the process in the same way. "I do it this way" implies that others can do it a different way but that the question needs to be resolved. Furthermore, this attitude eases the need to conform and acknowledges that even though a particular process or strategy for solving problems is not a very effective strategy for reading, it may be effective in other situations. For the impulsive child, the teacher often remarks, "Someday your rapid-fire decision making may help you become a great artist, but when you are reading text, you need to think about what the author is trying to say."

Being sensitive to individual differences requires that the diagnostic teacher evaluates two broad categories of learner differences. First, she evaluates what the students already know, because using what they already know will increase what is learned. Secondly, she assesses the way the students learned what they already know so that new information can be presented using the children's strengths. These two categories, knowledge-based differences and strategy-based differences, help the diagnostic teacher adjust instruction for individual students. As the teacher learns to make sense in her classroom, she uses students' strengths and models *I* statements (which release everyone from doing things in the same way). Thus she encourages individual variation in problem solving.

GUIDELINE #7: BE SENSITIVE TO INDIVIDUAL DIFFERENCES

☐ *Adjust instruction to what children already know and do.*
☐ *Reduce stress by using students' strengths.*
☐ *Use* I *statements to acknowledge individual variation in problem solving.*

Guideline #8: Foster a Reality-Based Approach to Instruction

Even though each child is different and some are harder to teach than others, the diagnostic teacher interacts with her students as a person. She is a participant in the learning process, sharing with them her reactions to reading events and student learning. Honest communication and sharing of the knowledge of the students' strategies for reading set the stage.

The diagnostic teacher helps students develop a realistic assessment of their own reading behavior, as opposed to a tense, perfectionist view of their learning. She becomes human as she talks about her own mistakes and coping behaviors, focusing on the process rather than the products of reading. As the teacher finds humor in her mistakes and proceeds to correct them, so too will remedial readers learn to reflect on their mistakes in a lighthearted manner, realizing that they can correct incongruencies as they read. Mistakes become a tool for learning rather than an indication of failure. Modeling self-correcting strategies in a relaxed atmosphere helps students develop a risk-taking attitude toward reading (Gentile, 1983) and increases their active reading behavior.

Likewise, effective teachers expect students to think, cope with their mistakes, and resolve problems as they read. They expect students to read lots of words and to express ideas based on what they have read. A major characteristic contributing to the success of all readers is the teacher's expectation that all students will read and learn (Berliner, 1981). Maintaining appropriate expectations is extremely demanding for the diagnostic teacher. It is important, however, not only to maintain high expectations but also to share with students how those expectations are to be met. Once the diagnostic teacher has made adjustments during instruction, she tells students she expects them to complete the necessary reading. She emphasizes that real life involves coping with limitations and using one's strengths to solve difficult problems.

Finally, the diagnostic teacher engages students by personally responding to literature discussing her own personal change as a result of reading and writing experiences. This personal response draws students into discussing their own individual reactions to literature. Consequently, both the students and the teacher talk about how their world view is changing as a result of being literate. In this way, she fosters reality-based instruction that gives the student more than a reading experience; it provides a model for how literacy stimulates people to outgrow their own knowledge.

In her classroom, the effective teacher creates a relaxed environment where students can take risks and correct mistakes as they try out new ideas. She expects that all students will grow and learn from their mistakes. She interacts with her students personally sharing with them her own interpretations and growth. Thus, a reality approach to instruction is just that: it makes reading a real, personal event.

GUIDELINE #8: FOSTER REALITY-BASED INSTRUCTION

- □ *Teach that real life requires coping with errors.*
- □ *Maintain high expectations.*
- □ *Discuss personal change as a result of reading.*

SUMMARY

Effective diagnostic teaching is coordinated by the reflective teacher, who bases her decision making on individual assessment of the readers' responses during instruction. Thus, at the core of diagnostic teaching is reflective teaching. The effective diagnostic teacher plans instruction, mediates learning, enables thinking, and responds honestly so that children experience success when reading interesting stories that require personal interpretation. Consequently, diagnostic teaching requires planning a whole reading event, the emphasis of which is success. Furthermore, the diagnostic teacher's goal is to create active, engaged readers who use what they already know to interpret text.

With this goal in mind, she encourages active reading by assessing reader response while she instructs. She is sensitive to the individual differences among her students and accepts the uniqueness of each reader in her classroom. She enables students to read with confidence, creating the expectation in students that they can read. Doing this, she reacts to the instructional event not only as the planner, mediator, and enabler, but also as a participant in the reading event. She acknowledges her own personal response to literature, modeling her control of the reading process and then fostering in her classroom real responses to reading, learning, and thinking.

The Diagnostic Teaching Session: An Overview

The diagnostic teaching session places a premium on tailoring programs that specifically fit problem readers. It provides a structure for lesson planning that uses both assessment and instruction to identify instructional alternatives and monitor their effectiveness. The session is composed of the following four elements: (a) continuous diagnostic assessment, (b) guided contextual reading, (c) strategy and skill instruction, and (d) personalized reading and writing. Each element performs a distinct function and combines with the others to form a complete diagnostic teaching session that can be completed in an hour. However, the session may be spread out over several days or a week, depending on the amount of individual contact the teacher has with the student.

During the session, these four elements find expression in the various steps of the decision-making cycle (see Figure 4–1). *Continuous diagnostic assessment* uses the principles of dynamic assessment to monitor the effect of mediated instruction on students' learning. It is a way to assess growth by gathering data about students' unaided performance in the text that is used for guided contextual reading. Within the diagnostic decision-making cycle (see Figure 4–1), the element of assessment incorporates the aspects of formulating diagnostic hypotheses and assessing growth while *guided contextual reading* includes teaching the diagnostic lesson within the reading event. *Guided contextual reading* focuses on meaningful interpretation of whole stories, while allowing students to demonstrate their strengths. This involves the planning and mediating roles of the diagnostic teacher. The diagnostic teaching session also includes the other two elements that are embedded in the reading event. *Skill and strategy instruction* explicitly remediates those skills and strategies that are inhibiting performance. During *personalized reading and writing,* both the students and the teacher engage in reading and writing for their own purposes and self-fulfillment. These two elements extend the roles of the diagnostic teacher to enable the problem reader by building control and developing a self-concept as a reader. Throughout the diagnostic teaching session, the teacher responds to each student's differences and fosters a reality approach to learning. This chapter explains the instructional premises of the diagnostic teaching session as well as discusses its features, which are further elaborated in the chapters on instruction and assessment that follow.

The diagnostic teaching session is based on a teaching procedure developed by Darrel D. Ray and used in the Oklahoma State University Reading Clinic. The author is grateful for the perceptive insights gleaned from her work in that clinic.

Figure 4–1
The Decision-
Making Cycle of
Diagnostic
Teaching

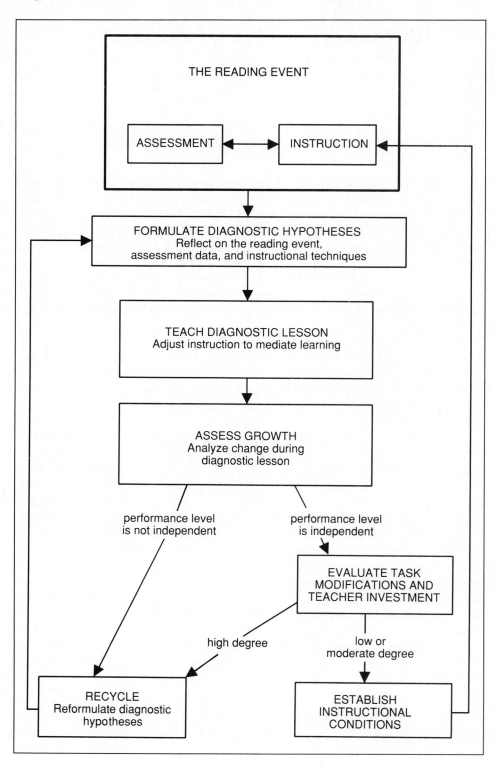

PREMISES

In addition to the components of the reading event and the roles of the diagnostic teacher, the diagnostic teaching session is based on several premises:

1. Effective diagnostic teaching results from monitoring the effect instructional adjustments have on reading performance. Continuous diagnostic assessment provides baseline data about students' reading performance prior to instruction. During guided contextual reading, the reading lesson is adjusted to meet the students' needs. The difference between performance without aid and performance with aid is recorded using the data from these two elements.
2. Effective diagnostic teaching allows students to demonstrate their strengths (what they already know and do) by overlapping what is known and done with new information and new strategies. In other words, the diagnostic teacher uses the students' strengths to understand problem areas when reading a particular story. This enables problem readers to read with success.
3. Effective diagnostic teaching results in an interplay of contextual reading with skills and strategy instruction. Guided contextual reading uses whole stories to teach reading as interpreting and discussing text. Skill and strategy instruction provides minilessons in specific skills or strategies that are inhibiting reading performance.
4. Effective diagnostic teaching results from an interplay of implicit and explicit instruction. Guided contextual reading is characterized by implicit (guided) instruction during which the teacher acts as guide and participant in the learning process. The focus is on the meaningful interpretation of the text while practicing the whole skill of reading. Skill and strategy instruction, on the other hand, is characterized by explicit (direct) instruction in skills and strategies.
5. Effective diagnostic teaching results from an interplay of challenging and easy reading tasks (Beck, 1981). Schneider (1979) has found that a balance of high-success and medium-success reading tasks results in higher student achievement. Thus, reading materials are validated by the diagnostic teacher, and texts are chosen to maximize success on both independent and mediated reading levels. Guided contextual reading provides instruction in material that is moderately difficult, while personalized reading and writing are characterized by easy reading material. During skill and strategy instruction, the diagnostic teacher uses a combination of moderately difficult texts and easy texts, depending on the instructional needs of the learners.

These premises underlie the elements of the diagnostic teaching sessions. Taken together, the elements provide a vehicle for monitoring the effect of instructional adjustments and the interplay between instruction using strengths and instruction in areas of need, between contextual reading and skill lessons, between implicit and explicit instruction, and between challenging and easy reading tasks.

CONTINUOUS DIAGNOSTIC ASSESSMENT (CDA)

Continuous diagnostic assessment (CDA) contains an unaided, "at sight" assessment taken from the selected text used during guided contextual reading. This is the vehicle used to monitor reading performance. During the other elements, the diagnostic teacher adjusts instruction as the students read; therefore, the students' performance without instruction is not evaluated. Continuous diagnostic assessment allows the diagnostic teacher to collect a sample of reading behavior prior to instruction. Then the diagnostic teacher compares performance data without guided instruction (CDA) and reading performance during guided contextual reading (GCR). This sample of reading behavior allows the diagnostic teacher to develop hypotheses about the changing reading needs of the students.

The assessment provides two kinds of information. First it provides information about the appropriateness of the text that is being used during the guided contextual reading element. If the material proves too difficult (at frustration level) or too easy (at independent level), an alternate text is selected and checked for an appropriate match (see Chapter 5 for procedures to determine performance level). Basically the teacher asks himself, "Am I using an appropriate text (moderately difficult) in GCR?" Second, this assessment provides baseline data so that the teacher can analyze the difference between unaided reading performance and the students' reading perfor- mance with instruction. He asks himself, "Is the student profiting from my instruction? Is there a difference between the reading performance in GCR and CDA?"

To monitor progress, the teacher follows the procedures found in Chapter 5, "Gathering Diagnostic Data." First, a segment from the text used in guided contextual reading is read without prior instruction (at sight). A passage about 50–125 words long is selected and questions written that focus on the main idea or problem, key facts or events, key vocabulary words, and inferences. The selection is read orally or silently, depending on the reading concerns for the students (see Chapter 5). Error or miscue rates and percentage of comprehension are calculated. Decisions are made as to the appropriateness of the text. If the selection is at frustration reading level (oral accuracy below 1/10 running words and comprehension below 50%), the teacher immediately moves to easier reading material in the GCR segment. For example, Chris reads a selection from a trade book with an error rate of 1/7 and 60% comprehension on constructed questions. Since this indicates frustration-level reading, the clinician selects an easier text to use during guided contextual reading.

If the selection reflects the mediated reading level, the diagnostic teacher continues using the material and records errors to establish a pattern of reading performance. For example, Sally reads a selection from a novel with an error rate of 1/15 and 80% comprehension. After three samplings in this text, the error pattern indicates that the substitution errors most prevalent are key vocabulary words that are limiting comprehension. The diagnostic teacher develops a program of word identification based on word meanings related to both the text to be read and the background knowledge. He adapts instruction during GCR by using a vocabulary map of key words to increase both word identification and word meanings of those words (see "Vocabulary Maps" in Chapter 9). After the story is read, he returns to the map and adds new understandings to reinforce word meaning with word identification.

If the selection is at an independent level, a more difficult text needs to be evaluated in the continuous diagnostic assessment phase. The diagnostic teacher selects a more difficult text and prepares a segment for evaluation. For example, Toni can read silently a segment from a third-grade text with 100% comprehension. There is no previous instruction before this segment is read. Therefore, a text at the fourth-grade level is selected. An on-level assessment is conducted and scored. This on-level evaluation is read silently with 70% comprehension on the constructed questions. As a result, the text used in GCR is changed to the fourth-grade text, which reflects a level that is challenging and has a moderate success rate.

In all the elements, the diagnostic teacher is assessing the response of the children to instruction. To monitor progress, however, a segment of a text is read without prior instruction (at sight). Continuous diagnostic assessment is an integral part of the diagnostic teaching session because it provides the framework for dynamic assessment by providing baseline data about the students' performance in the selected text without instruction.

FOCUS OF CONTINUOUS DIAGNOSTIC ASSESSMENT

□ *Monitor reading behavior.*
□ *Maintain baseline data.*
□ *Analyze reading growth.*

GUIDED CONTEXTUAL READING (GCR)

Each teaching session includes a guided contextual reading lesson (GCR) that focuses instruction on the communication of the ideas gleaned from reading whole stories. Guided contextual reading involves 60% of instruction in the diagnostic teaching session; therefore, students read contextual material for the majority of the time. The reading selection is of sufficient length to allow for comprehension of story line and character development; however, it is short enough to provide a sense of closure for the reader. During GCR, the diagnostic teacher differentiates instruction according to the strengths and reading levels of the students. Texts that maximize student performance are chosen.

The guided contextual reading element can incorporate specialized methods, but the generic format of readiness, active reading, and reacting needs to be followed consistently in a text that is moderately difficult. The diagnostic teacher thinks about the kind of instruction needed before, during, and after the student reads the selected story or chapter. He considers the support needed before the story to enable the student to read fluently with comprehension. The teacher asks himself, "Can I provide support before reading to help the student anticipate the meaning?" If support is needed, he reviews the charts (Tables 8–1 and 8–2) that suggest techniques to use before reading a story. This means that the students' attention is focused on the key concepts of the story prior to reading. These concepts are then related to the students' own experiences. Predictions related to the story theme are developed by the teacher and students together, thus increasing students' active reading of the story. Open-ended questions need to focus on predictions that will engage the students in active reading through the entire length of the story (Pearson, 1982). Therefore, purposes or predictions that can be answered on the first page of the story hardly represent the main story theme.

During this brief discussion, the teacher anticipates problem vocabulary words and, if needed, provides instruction in either word identification or word meaning. This instruction needs to be directly related to the story to be read, predictions that have been made, and the key concepts or story theme. Time is of the essence in diagnostic teaching. Consequently, only the important words, meanings, and concepts need to be stressed.

The second step of the guided contextual reading is silent reading to confirm the predictions. This is called *active reading*. The diagnostic teacher thinks about what kind of support is needed as the students read the story or chapter. If support is needed, he reviews the charts (Tables 8–1 and 8–2) that suggest techniques to use during instruction. Questioning is the key tool for the teacher as a dialogue about the story is maintained and he helps students construct their interpretations. Realizing the importance of questions, Beck and McKeown (1981) suggest that teachers develop story maps (see "Story Maps" in Chapter 9) to serve as a guide to logical questioning of story events. Rather than questions that are text-based, literal, and often unrelated to the story theme, questions developed from the story map should lead the students in developing an understanding of the purposeful actions of the characters to resolve the problems in the story. In other words, logical questions help summarize the main actions and events that occur in the story to resolve the problem.

The third step of guided contextual reading is *reacting* to the story as a whole. This requires an analysis of the story in terms of the characters' motivations, the author's purpose for writing the story, and other stories and experiences with similar themes. A key component of this phase is relating the story to similar personal experiences and analyzing the effect these experiences have on the comprehension of the story. Experiences may include other stories, movies, songs, and personal situations the students have encountered with similar plots and characters. Analysis should focus on the similarities and differences of these cases, using textual and nontextual information to support statements.

These steps form the framework for guided contextual reading, the major component of the diagnostic teaching session. Basic to the development of guided contextual reading is an instructional sequence that uses the students' strengths; therefore, specialized techniques are selected that compensate for reading deficiencies so that the reading selection can be read fluently with comprehension. In other words, the diagnostic teacher asks, "What can I do to make these stories more understandable for my students? Do I need specialized reading techniques to ensure fluent reading of these stories? At what point in the instructional sequence do I need to adjust my instruction?"

Students who have a limited ability to deal with oral language receive an extended vocabulary development program and direct experiences with the prerequisite concepts that are necessary to read a particular selection with understanding. For these students, GCR requires an extended amount of instruction before they read the story. Vocabulary maps (see "Vocabulary Maps" in Chapter 9), which require students and teacher to construct a visual diagram relating the vocabulary words to background knowledge, are used to introduce the story. Therefore, the instructional adjustment occurs prior to reading the story. This facilitates the students' understanding of the concepts in the story and increases their ability to read the story fluently with comprehension.

When students experience little difficulty with understanding what the words mean, however, the instructional adjustments are different. For students who show extreme difficulty with oral accuracy, the diagnostic teacher spends more time on word identification and fluency and less time on developing word meanings. Before a story is read, for example, a language experience story (see "Language Experience" in Chapter 9) might be written using the targeted vocabulary words. The teacher encourages rereading of this story to create an expectation for the vocabulary in the text. After the selected story is read, readers theatre scripts (see "Readers Theatre" in Chapter 9) could be constructed from the story so that increasing oral reading fluency becomes purposeful. The diagnostic teacher incorporates specialized techniques both before and after reading the story. For these students, the adjustments facilitate reading the story fluently with comprehension. During GCR, the diagnostic teacher differentiates instruction according to learner strengths in order to provide fluent reading with comprehension. The ultimate goal is to focus on the whole act of reading in connected text that will allow the students to integrate their prior knowledge with the text to develop personal interpretations.

FOCUS OF GUIDED CONTEXTUAL READING

- ☐ *Read whole stories.*
- ☐ *Focus on meaningful interpretation of text.*
- ☐ *Support active reading before, during and after the lesson.*
- ☐ *Differentiate instruction so that the text can be read fluently with comprehension.*
- ☐ *Encourage personal interpretations.*

STRATEGY AND SKILL INSTRUCTION (SAS)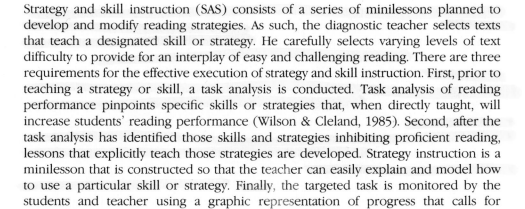

Strategy and skill instruction (SAS) consists of a series of minilessons planned to develop and modify reading strategies. As such, the diagnostic teacher selects texts that teach a designated skill or strategy. He carefully selects varying levels of text difficulty to provide for an interplay of easy and challenging reading. There are three requirements for the effective execution of strategy and skill instruction. First, prior to teaching a strategy or skill, a task analysis is conducted. Task analysis of reading performance pinpoints specific skills or strategies that, when directly taught, will increase students' reading performance (Wilson & Cleland, 1985). Second, after the task analysis has identified those skills and strategies inhibiting proficient reading, lessons that explicitly teach those strategies are developed. Strategy instruction is a minilesson that is constructed so that the teacher can easily explain and model how to use a particular skill or strategy. Finally, the targeted task is monitored by the students and teacher using a graphic representation of progress that calls for self-assessment.

Task Analysis

Task analysis identifies inhibiting behaviors and isolates the specific strategy or skill to be taught. Using the constructs of informal assessment, miscue analysis, and think aloud procedures (see Chapter 5), the diagnostic teacher identifies particular reading skills and strategies that if learned would *easily* increase student performance.

An initial informal assessment of Mary, for example, identifies fluency of word identification as inhibiting reading performance. Further analysis indicates that she can decode words in isolation. During the diagnostic lesson, however, it is evident that when miscues are made, Mary does not use what the word looks like or means in the story to correct the miscue. In other words, she does not ask herself, "What makes sense and starts with a . . .?" This analysis indicates that she would benefit from instruction in applying a making-sense framework, or using the overall context to self-correct errors. Therefore, the task analysis results in recommending strategy instruction in self-correction.

Strategy Instruction

After the task analysis has identified those strategies and skills inhibiting proficient reading, lessons that explicitly teach those strategies are selected. For most skills or strategies, the diagnostic teacher selects an easy text to introduce the targeted strategy or skill. This limits other possible problems in text interpretation. As the task is learned, the diagnostic teacher increases the difficulty level of the text so as to lead students to use the targeted strategy or skill in reading situations that are moderately difficult. The activities need to be carefully chosen so that the teacher can model active reading. For Mary, therefore, an effective diagnostic technique would be an adapted repeated reading (see "Repeated Readings" in Chapter 9) that incorporates strategy instruction of the self-talk "What would make sense and starts with a . . ." as an intervention between the first and second readings.

Initially, students are informed of their inefficient strategies and shown the efficient counterpart, as modeled by the teacher (see "Strategy Instruction" in Chapter 9). After explicitly stating how the skill or strategy works, the teacher gives students a rationale for its inclusion in their program and tells them why doing these specific exercises will increase reading performance. Then students are led systematically through a series of short activities. In the first examples, the teacher models the desired reading behavior. Then students imitate the teacher's model.

In Mary's case, after the first reading of a selection, the teacher reviews miscues and suggests that reading would be more effective if she would check the miscue to see if it made sense. Then he explains how he would self-correct those errors using a making-sense framework and checking the initial letter. For example, before the second reading, the teacher explains that when reading breaks down, Mary should ask what would make sense and starts with a ". . . ." "If I had made this mistake," says the teacher, "I would have asked, 'What would Dad use that starts with a *sh?*' Then I would have corrected the sentence to read 'Dad shoveled the garden' and said, 'That's good! I can make sense of my reading by fixing up my mistakes.' Then I would continue to read. Now *you* try the next sentence with a miscue."

Finally, the diagnostic teacher reinforces active reading with task-specific comments. His comments are directed to the targeted tasks and students' improvement in those tasks. Furthermore, he encourages self-evaluation. For Mary, the teacher says, "I like the way you reread that sentence to correct your mistake. What do you say to yourself when you correct your mistakes?"

Self-assessment

The third aspect of strategy and skill instruction is helping students evaluate their increasing use of strategic reading processes. Self-assessment, therefore, directs the students' attention to the use of various strategies and the effect their implementation has on their reading comprehension. It also helps students draw relationships among their strategy use, skill knowledge, and personal effort.

Constructing a graph of reading progress or strategy use provides an avenue for the students and teacher to discuss the strategies that the students are using and how this strategy or skill will improve reading performance. The students, therefore, assume increasing responsibility for changing their reading behaviors. Progress charts can vary in complexity; however, the focus of charting should be the evaluation of progress toward the goal and how this progress fits into the whole skill of reading. Charts can be skill oriented, as in the sight-word card chart in Table 4–1. Or they can be a self-evaluation chart like the chart of reading fluency in Table 4–2. As progress toward the goal is made, the teacher allows students to assume the role of monitoring

Word	M	T	W	Th	F
GO	●	●	●	●	●
RUN		●	●	●	
COME	●		●		●
CANDY	●		●	●	●

Table 4–1
Progress Chart for Word Card Review

How I Read Today	M	T	W	Th	F
FLUENTLY IN PHRASES					
MOSTLY IN PHRASES				●	●
SOMETIMES WORD BY WORD		●	●		
MOSTLY WORD BY WORD	●				

Table 4–2
Progress Chart for Self-Evaluation of Fluency

their own performances. He reinforces their trouble-shooting strategies and encourages self-assessment.

Strategy and skill instruction is like many regular classroom lessons; however, it is different because it is specific to the readers' weaknesses. In diagnostic teaching, it is important to identify those skills and strategies that are limiting reading improvement. The diagnostic teacher asks, "What skills and strategies are limiting reading improvement? Will instruction in these skills or strategies improve reading performance?" It is important to identify which skills and strategies will improve overall reading performance if they are taught directly. Therefore, SAS is different from regular classroom instruction's sequential introduction of reading skills because here the skill instruction is specific to students' reading development and identified through a task analysis.

In *Becoming a Nation of Readers,* Anderson et al. report that "though children of all levels require direct instruction from teachers, low-ability children usually do less well than high-ability children when working alone or in small groups without a teacher" (1985, p. 91). Therefore, the key characteristic of SAS is the identification of specific skills and strategies that problem readers lack and that, when directly taught, will improve reading performance.

FOCUS OF SKILL AND STRATEGY INSTRUCTION

☐ *Conduct a task analysis of inhibiting skills and strategies.*
☐ *Implement strategy instruction of those skills.*
☐ *Graph student progress.*

 ## PERSONALIZED READING AND WRITING (PRW)

In personalized reading and writing (PRW), students are engaged in 10 to 15 minutes of personal reading and writing. This element offers students a time of quiet reflection to respond personally to the language arts. Writing and reading "positively influence each other and both develop as a natural extension of children's desire to communicate" (Gambrell, 1985, p. 512). In this phase, time is set aside for the students and teacher to read and write for their own purposes. Easing the structure of the teaching session is crucial. If the students do not experience "choosing to read and write," they may not choose to read and write for their own purposes later on as adults.

For the silent reading time (see "Sustained Silent Reading" in Chapter 9), children select books, magazines, newspapers, or their own writing to read during the designated time period. This is a time for students to read for their own individual purposes. As Berglund and Johns (1983, p. 534) suggest, "It frees their minds to enjoy reading on their own terms in materials they have selected." Encouraging students to read books for their own enjoyment rather than instructional purposes develops the desire to read. They learn to ask themselves, "What do I want to read about? What kind of stories do I find more interesting?" This facilitates habits of book selection and defining interests (Trelease, 1985).

Students are taught to match the book to their reading levels by using the rule of thumb (Glazer, 1984; Glazer & Searfoss, 1988). This means that as they read a page from their selected book, they put a finger on each unknown word starting with the little finger. If they reach their thumb before the end of the page, the book is too difficult and another should be selected. Therefore, personalized reading and writing experience encourages children to select books they can successfully read and moves the control of the selection of reading material from the teacher to the students. In fact, during this element, the students are in control; there is no have-to reading. If the students want to skip pages, look at pictures, laugh or cry, they can read and think whatever they want. The students control what they learn from books.

For the sustained silent writing (see "Dialogue Journals" in Chapter 9), the students and teacher communicate through writing. During each session, students write to the teacher about anything of interest or importance to them. Following the journal entry, the teacher comments with a brief, personal, and honest reaction to what was written. For example, a student wrote: "Today my cat died." The teacher responded: "I bet you are sad. My cat died last year and I cried." According to Glazer (1984), "comments concerning content should be empathetic, noncritical, and encouraging." In other words, the teacher responds during each session to what the children have written.

The teacher comments can be an empathetic response or can ask for more information. Such comments (e.g., "That sounds like fun, I would like to know more about . . ." or "Can you describe what it looked like?") allow the diagnostic teacher to encourage the fluent writing of ideas without evaluations. The focus is communication between students and teacher; therefore, the teacher should not correct any spelling or grammatical errors.

The teacher encourages the writing of ideas as he models correct writing forms in his responses to the student. This stream-of-consciousness communication is based on the students' personal, real-life experiences. The topics, length, and format are self-selected. As children compose text, they think about ways to express ideas. This thinking about how ideas are expressed sensitizes students to the visual aspects of text (how words are spelled and the order of words in sentences); consequently, students become more aware of how words are used.

Personal reading and writing develop within students an interest in reading and writing for their own enjoyment. It releases students from the have-to assignments made during direct and guided instruction, thus placing them in control of their interests, ideas, and emotions. Besides being an avenue of control, personal reading

---

FOCUS OF PERSONALIZED READING AND WRITING

☐ *Encourage self-direction.*
☐ *Evoke a personal response.*
☐ *Allow time for quiet reflection.*

is a major source of knowledge about word meaning and sentence and text structure (Anderson et al., 1985). Personal writing is a major vehicle for self-reflection because the students have written their thoughts and can now reflect on them. Furthermore, during personal reading and writing, there are no wrong answers. In fact, there are *no* answers; thus students cannot fail.

SUMMARY

Reflecting on his roles as a diagnostic teacher and the variables of the reading event, the diagnostic teacher plans a teaching session which allows him to assess and instruct at the same time. During continuous diagnostic assessment, the diagnostic teacher monitors the effects of his instruction by comparing unaided reading performance and mediated reading behavior. During guided contextual reading, he guides students' learning; therefore, he is constantly asking what will make this a successful reading event for the students. As he teaches the planned lesson, he encourages active reading by focusing on deriving meaning from text. He probes with leading questions: "What did the author mean when she said? Does that (the answer) make sense in relation to the other ideas presented in the story?"

During *strategy and skill* instruction, the diagnostic teacher decides which strategies and skills would, if directly taught, result in higher reading achievement. Then he develops short demonstration activities to teach a skill and its strategic application. He uses progress charts to encourage self-assessment of reading performance. Therefore, he builds responsibility within the students by gradually giving them the control to monitor their own reading behavior.

During personalized reading and writing, the diagnostic teacher allows time for students to read and write for their own purposes. In these situations, the readers are in control of the meaning they derive from print.

The format of the diagnostic teaching session allows the diagnostic teacher to develop instructional alternatives that fit the strengths and needs of problem readers. By systematically planning instruction, the diagnostic teacher provides learning opportunities that enable problem readers to become independent learners.

Gathering Diagnostic Data

Teachers gather data to formulate diagnostic hypotheses about the strategies a reader uses to interpret text (see Figure 5–1). Diagnostic decisions are made based on data gathered without prior instruction and also after instructional adjustments have been made. This chapter focuses on data acquired when the student does not receive instruction. Such data provide needed information about the independent problem-solving strategies of the learner.

In the decision-making cycle of diagnostic teaching, data are gathered to make initial decisions and to monitor changes in reading performance. The initial decisions are made using informal reading inventories, including the selection of a text that is moderately difficult for the student. The diagnostic teacher then chooses a story and conducts an assessment using the first section of the story. This is referred to as an on-level assessment. The data gathered from it are used to monitor the student's changes. This assessment can be taken from the first phase of the diagnostic lesson, which establishes baseline data (see "Establishing Baseline Data" in Chapter 7), or it can be the information that is continuously gathered (see "Continuous Diagnostic Assessment" in Chapter 4). These procedures provide detailed information about the reader's strategies for regaining meaning when text interpretation becomes difficult. The diagnostic teacher uses these data to formulate hypotheses about a particular student's instructional needs. This chapter elaborates the sources of data: the level of text needed for instruction, the major presenting problem, and the reader's strategies.

ESTABLISHING THE LEVEL OF STUDENT PERFORMANCE

To begin gathering data, the diagnostic teacher samples reading behavior across levels of text difficulty to identify the student's performance without assistance. To make this assessment, the teacher uses, a series of graded passages that range in difficulty from first grade to junior high. This procedure is known as *informal reading assessment.* Reader responses in easy, moderate, and difficult texts establish a level where the student will experience success in classroom instruction. Three estimates of reading performance are derived.

☐ *The student's independent reading level* provides an estimate of the level where the student can read fluently with a high level of comprehension. The student reads and understands enough of the text to monitor his own reading performance. He applies appropriate correction strategies when reading breaks down, using both reader–based and text–based processing; therefore, teacher-directed instruction is not necessary.

Figure 5–1
The Decision-
Making Cycle of
Diagnostic
Teaching

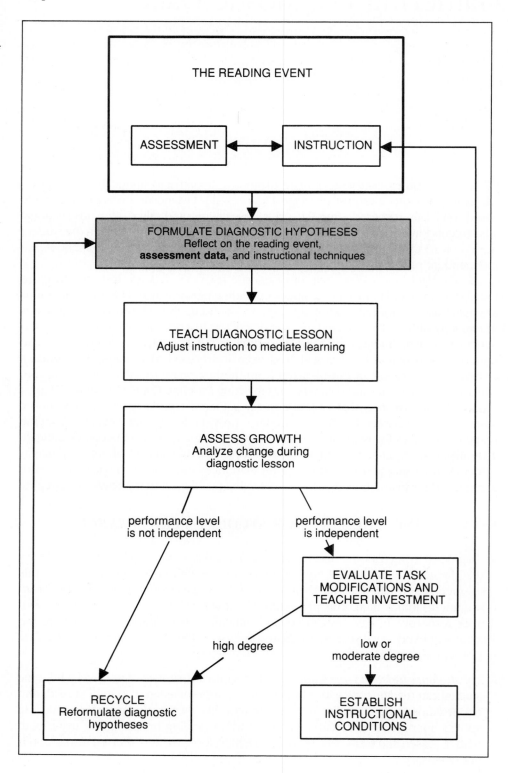

☐ *The student's instructional reading level* provides an estimate of the level where the student experiences a mild level of stress between the text and his present reading strategies. It is assumed that classroom instruction would increase the student's understanding of new textual information.

☐ *The student's frustration reading level* provides an estimate of the level where the reader is not fluent and has little recall of textual information. It is projected that at this level, guided instruction would be extremely demanding and time consuming because the reader does not know enough about what he is reading to make adequate connections between the new information and prior knowledge.

Informal reading assessment provides an estimate of reading performance in selected texts based on oral reading errors and percentage of comprehension. The instructional reading level is an estimate of the level where the student "might experience some difficulties when reading classroom materials at sight, but most of these difficulties should be overcome after the student has had an opportunity to read the same material silently" (Johns, 1981, p. 7). Therefore, the guidelines for regular classroom instruction are more in line with traditional scoring criteria in informal assessment (Betts, 1946). These criteria use 95% word identification and 75% comprehension as an estimate of instructional reading level.

The diagnostic teacher uses the inventory to assess a number of potential problem areas. In a standarized inventory, there are equivalent passages. Therefore, the diagnostic teacher administers one form for the oral reading analysis and another form for the silent reading analysis. After each passage has been read, comprehension is evaluated by computing the percentage of correct answers to various types of comprehension questions, such as main idea, supporting details, inferences, and vocabulary. As the student reads orally, errors (deviations from the text) are recorded. These errors are used to compute an error rate or percentage of word recognition. Although variation exists in what constitutes an error, substitutions, mispronunciations, omissions, insertions, and unknown words are usually used to compute the error rate (see Table 5–1). Other reading behaviors such as repetitions, punctuation errors, and self-corrections are analyzed when conducting a qualitative assessment of oral reading performance (see Table 5–2). (Further directions for conducting informal reading assessments can be found in the Appendix.)

From the information derived from the informal reading inventory, the diagnostic teacher identifies a level that would be moderately difficult for the student. She thinks again about the criteria for frustration and independent reading level and mentally pictures the ranges shown in Figure 5–2 (p. 66). Word recognition and comprehension criteria for *independent* reading are 1 error in 100 words (1/100 or 99% accuracy) and 90% comprehension accuracy. Word recognition and comprehension criteria for *frustration* reading are 1 error in 10 words (1/10 or 90% accuracy) and 50% comprehension accuracy. "If there is more than 10 percent of error in the record rate this is a 'hard' text for this child" (Clay, 1979, p. 14). Also, according to Barr and Sadow (1985),

When individual students are missing more than half the questions posed or having difficulty with more than 1 word in every 10, the materials are inappropriate, represent-

Table 5–1
Scoreable Errors
(to be used in
computing error
rate)

Substitutions or mispronunciations (the replacement of one word for another): Mark the mispronounced word by drawing a line through it and writing the substitution above the word.

want
"The man ~~went~~ to the store," said Ann.

Omissions (leaving out words): Circle the word omitted.

"The man went to (the) store," said Ann.

Insertions (adding extra words): Draw a caret and write the inserted word above it.

away
"The man went ∧ to the store," said Ann.

Transpositions (changing the word order): Mark with a ‾‾‾‾⌐ .

"The man went to the store," said⌐Ann.

Prompted words (words that have to be prompted or supplied by the teacher): Write the letter *P* above these words.

P
"The man went to the store," said Ann.

---

ing frustration-level work. . . . By contrast, students who perform in the borderline region between frustration level and acceptable instructional level may be helped by instruction that has been developed with their particular problem in mind. This border-line region is characterized by an accuracy of 90–94% on oral reading and 50–74% on comprehension questions. (p. 177)

This borderline region represents a text level that is moderately difficult. The diagnostic teacher uses this information to select appropriate materials for instruction (see Chapter 4).

While analyzing the student's performance using the traditional criteria on the informal reading inventory, the diagnostic teacher also evaluates the student's fluency as she listens to him read orally. To do so, she asks herself three questions:

Is the student's reading fairly smooth?
Does the student read words in meaningful phrases?
Does the student's pitch, stress, and intonation convey the meaning of the text?

Using these questions the diagnostic teacher determines the level of the student's fluent reading with comprehension and adds this information to that obtained from the traditional informal reading assessment. Sometimes the informal reading

Repetitions (words or phrases that are repeated more than once): Draw a line over the word and write the letter *R* over the line.

"The man <u>went</u> to the store," said Ann.

Repeated repetitions (words or phrases that are repeated several times): Draw a line over the word or phrase and mark it with a *2R* over the line.

"The man <u>went</u> to the store," said Ann.

Self-correction: If the child corrects an error, a line is drawn through the previously marked error and the letter *C* is written at the end of the line.

"The man ~~went~~ C went to the store," said Ann.

Pauses: Long pauses that are used to gain meaning are marked with slashes.

"The man//went to the store," said Ann.

Punctuation errors (ignoring punctuation symbols): Draw a circle around the omitted punctuation mark.

"The man went to the store," said Ann. "Then he went home."

inventory does not reveal a problem with oral reading (few substitutions, omissions, or prompts), but the phrasing seems atypical. "Reading occurs word-by-word . . . as if print knowledge has not become sufficiently automatic to permit attention to phrasing . . ." (Barr, Sadow, & Blachowicz, 1990, p. 70). Thus, print processing must also be evaluated by rating fluency. The diagnostic teacher notes how the student's oral reading misuses and comprehension interface with his reading fluency on the informal reading assessment (Hoffman, 1988). Teachers have used a four-point fluency scale to evaluate upper elementary schoolchildren's reading fluency (Zutell, 1988). This scale is a valid and reliable measure of the student's fluent reading and correlates with overall reading ability (Rasinski, 1985; Zutell, 1988). The modified scale has the following descriptions of oral reading behavior.

1. Clearly labored and disfluent reading, marked by very slow pace (less than 60 wpm), word-by-word reading, numerous pauses, sound-outs, repetitions, and/or lack of intonation and expression.
2. Slow and choppy reading, marked by slow pace (roughly 60–80 wpm), reading in two- and three-word phrases, many pauses, sound-outs, and/or repetitions, some difficulty with phrase, cause and sentence boundaries and/or intonation problems at the ends of sentences.

Figure 5–2
Performance
Ranges

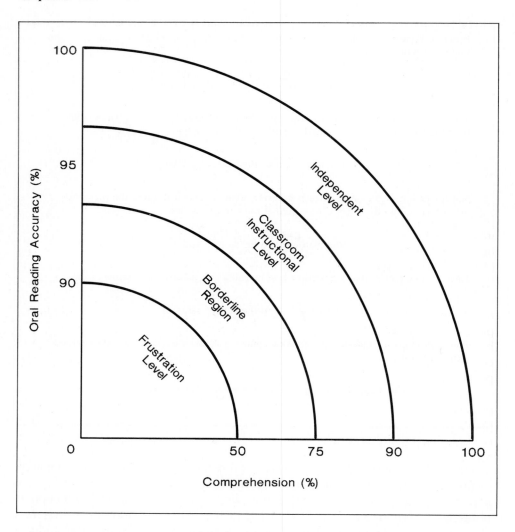

3. Poor phrasing and intonation, marked by reasonable pace (roughly 80–105 wpm), but with some choppiness and possibly several repetitions, sound-outs, and/or run-ons.

4. Fairly fluent reading, marked by good pace (more than 110 wpm), longer phrases, and a good sense of expression and intonation. While there may be some difficulties with aspects of fluent reading behavior, this reader is aware of the need for appropriate phrasing and intonation; repetitions may be used to correct phrasing/expression errors.*

Using this scale, a student's rating of 1 would indicate that the student is experiencing a great deal of stress when reading and is at frustration level. A rating of 2 or 3 would

*Reprinted with permission from Zutell, J. (May 1988). *Developing a procedure for assessing oral reading fluency: Establishing validity and reliability.* Paper presented at 33rd Annual Convention, International Reading Association, Toronto, Canada.

indicate a mild amount of stress and reading at instructional levels. A score of 4 would indicate fluent, independent reading. After listening to the students read, the diagnostic teacher uses the fluency rating in conjunction with the information obtained from the informal reading assessment to identify performance levels and major presenting problems.

IDENTIFYING THE MAJOR PRESENTING PROBLEM

The ultimate goal of reading is to read fluently with comprehension. Two major processes contribute to fluent reading with comprehension. Both print and meaning processing occur simultaneously as one reads. Students combine sources of information and shift between the text, print knowledge, and personal knowledge to figure out what the text says. Meaning processing involves predicting, monitoring, and elaborating the author's intended meaning. This is usually the predominant focus while reading. In other words, when reading, students are constantly striving to derive meaning from text. On the other hand, print processing involves predicting, monitoring, and elaborating what the words on the page look like. This is the predominant focus when the meaning becomes unclear to the reader, and he shifts his attention to a close examination of single words. When students read fluently with comprehension, they strategically combine all their resources to smoothly process print and meaning to construct the author's message.

Based on an informal reading inventory, the diagnostic teacher decides whether print processing or meaning processing is the major inhibiting factor in fluent reading performance. As the diagnostic teacher works with a student, she asks herself, "What is inhibiting fluent reading with comprehension? Is the student having difficulty recognizing the words (print processing), or understanding the content (meaning processing), or both?" She knows that fluent reading requires that the student use both printed words and background knowledge to interpret the text. She also realizes that oral reading is a different task from silent reading.

When reading orally, the reader must attend not only to meaning but also to the oral production of the text. According to Allington (1984b, p. 853), "the instructional setting for oral reading imposes different demands from that of silent reading (e.g., public vs. private performance, personal vs. external monitor of performance, emphasis on accuracy of production vs. accuracy of meaning construction)." Therefore, if the diagnostic teacher needs information on print-processing ability, she uses an oral reading assessment. She observes how the student attends to print when reading breaks down. If fluent reading with comprehension is impaired by print processing, the diagnostic teacher listens to the child read orally and asks him questions to check comprehension. This is known as *oral reading analysis*. Some students call words fluently but need assistance in how to derive meaning from the words that they recognize (meaning processing). If the diagnostic teacher needs further information on meaning processing, she uses silent reading analysis and asks the student to think aloud at critical points in the story. She breaks a story into segments and discusses the story after each segment. These procedures are known as *silent reading analysis*. For the diagnostic teacher, this initial decision merely begins her analysis of how the student is approaching the reading task. Figure 5–3 illustrates the types of extended assessment.

> *The diagnostic teacher establishes the major presenting problem. She thinks about how print processing and meaning processing affect the student's reading.*

To formulate hypotheses, the diagnostic teacher selects a text that is suspected to be in the borderline area, or moderately difficult (90% oral accuracy or 60% comprehension), for the student. She also decides if the major inhibiting factor is print processing or meaning processing. Then she prepares an extended passage that is read either orally or silently. In either case, she constructs questions that require the student to understand the main idea or theme, identify supporting details or events,

Figure 5–3
Types of Extended Assessment

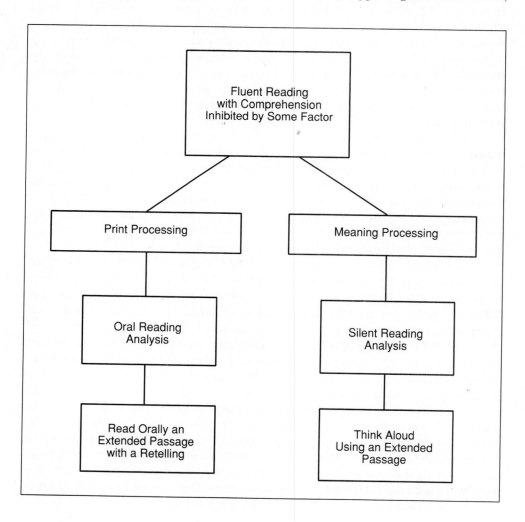

infer relationships within the information, and explain how the key words are used in the text.

If print processing is inhibiting fluent reading comprehension, the diagnostic teacher interprets oral reading behavior. She asks the student to read the selected text aloud while she records the errors or miscues (see "Scoring Criteria" in the Appendix). To cross-check oral reading behavior with comprehension, the oral reading is followed by an oral retelling. Then she asks the constructed comprehension questions that have not been answered. Finally, the student's reading errors or miscues are analyzed to identify the cueing system used to repair the reading error (see Goodman & Burke, 1980, for detailed procedures) and the pattern of reading behavior employed.

If meaning processing is the major concern, however, the teacher conducts a *think-aloud* assessment. She divides the selected passage at strategic points. First, she asks the student to predict what the story is about and to read silently to strategic points in the story. Next she asks the student to summarize the information read. Using teacher-constructed questions, she then probes for a higher-level analysis of the text and key information omitted from the summary. When the student cannot answer the question, she knows that either reading understanding has broken down or that the question needs to be rephrased. When rephrasing the question does result in a response, the diagnostic teacher asks the student to find support for the answer in the text and read it out loud, which permits her to assess if word identification is interfering with comprehension (Cioffi & Carney, 1983). Then she asks the student to predict what will happen in the next segment of the story and why he thinks it will happen. She asks him to evaluate his previous prediction in light of the new information read and to decide if he wants to change the prediction, keep it, or discard it. When the student finishes reading the selected text, she asks any prepared questions that have not yet been answered. Each exchange during the think-aloud period is analyzed to identify patterns of reading behavior.

To assess the pattern of reading performance, the diagnostic teacher looks at the data collected when the student reads without assistance. When the student reads an extended passage that is moderately difficult, a pattern of trouble spots and correction strategies emerges. The diagnostic teacher analyzes the miscues and/or miscomprehensions to evaluate both the student's patterns when reading breaks down and the strategies he uses to fix mistakes while reading. Both oral reading analysis (of print processing) and silent reading analysis (of meaning processing) result in a more comprehensive understanding of the strategies that students use to interpret the text as they are reading. In the discussion that follows, the premises for each analytic process are laid out, together with the kinds of diagnostic data collected.

ANALYZING ORAL READING

Premises

To interpret oral reading behavior, the diagnostic teacher evaluates how the reader miscalls words as he is reading. An error (or miscue) is an oral response that deviates from the printed text. The reader is viewed as an active interpreter of text. He creates an expectation, using his background knowledge. Then he confirms and/or revises this expectation as he reads and checks the text to see if his interpretation is making sense. A reader's miscues, therefore, are systematic attempts to derive meaning from text (Goodman, 1967).

Miscue analysis is a tool for evaluating the relative significance of miscues in the context of both the entire passage and the reader's experiences. Several frameworks for evaluating miscues have been developed; in this text, however, an adaptation of the procedures suggested by Goodman and Burke (1980) is used. This analysis is based on several theoretical assumptions:

1. Readers read to gain meaning.
2. Reading is not an exact process.
3. Some miscues or errors are more significant than others.
4. Miscues should be evaluated based on the degree to which they change meaning.
5. Readers use a consistent pattern of correction strategies that indicate their preferences for text processing.

In other words, miscues indicate the cue selected or the source of information the reader tends to use to gain meaning from the text. Miscues that change meaning and remain uncorrected are viewed as diagnostically significant. They indicate what happens when a reader cannot regain meaning as he is reading. Miscues that change meaning but are subsequently corrected reveal self-monitoring strategies and are viewed as efficient strategies. They offer information about how the reader regains meaning. Miscues that do not alter the meaning of the text are viewed as nonsignificant. Evaluating the nature of the information used to regain meaning reveals the student's approach to text interpretation.

The student may use various sources of information when he encounters an unknown word in his reading: (a) the context and his experience, (b) the way words sound in conversational speech, (c) graphic information, and (d) phonic information. Using the context and his own experience, he might try various words to see if they make sense in the context of the sentence and the story.

Sentence: The girl hit the baseball.
Reader: The girl bit the baseball. *(Oops that doesn't make sense. I'll try again.)* The girl hit the baseball.

Sometimes, he might check to see if how he is reading the sentence sounds like a real sentence.

Sentence: The girl hit the baseball.
Reader: The girl hitted the baseball. *(Oops that's not the way we talk. I'll try again.)* The girl hit the baseball.

At other times, he might check the graphic information by asking himself how the word begins and how long it is.

Sentence: The girl hit the baseball.
Reader: The boy hit the baseball. *(Oops the word is not* boy *because it starts with a* g *not a* b, *but it is the same length. It must be* girl *instead of* boy. *Yes, that looks right.)* The girl hit the baseball.

At still other times, he might check the phonic information to decipher unknown words by asking himself what sounds these letters make.

> Sentence: The girl hit the baseball.
> Reader: The girl hit the brassball. *(Oops, that doesn't sound right. Let's see* bbb-aaa--ss--bbb-all . . . baseball. *Yes, that sounds right.)* The girl hit the baseball.

Diagnostic Questions

Using these premises, diagnostic hypotheses can be developed. The diagnostic questions that follow are used to analyze oral reading behavior.

1. How close is the reader's interpretation (i.e., how much meaning change results from the miscue)?
2. Does the reader monitor oral reading (i.e., does he self–correct miscues that do not fit the context)?
3. Does the reader use top-down or bottom–up strategies to regain meaning?
4. How has previous instruction influenced the child's miscue pattern?
5. Do the words in the text influence the miscue pattern?

The pattern of strategies revealed by these questions indicates the student's application of reading skills in text. Each of the questions elicits data that contribute to a comprehensive analysis of the student's reading behavior.

1. How Close Is the Reader's Interpretation? Proficient readers' text interpretations maintain the basic intent of the author. Although they miscue and continue reading, their miscues are insignificant in terms of the context of the entire selection. However, problem readers make miscues that change the meaning. Instead of correcting themselves, they continue reading "as if they do not expect the text to make sense" (Smith, 1978, p. 34).

The diagnostic teacher evaluates each miscue as to the degree it changed the author's intended meaning. She uses this information to designate the significance of the miscue. As she continues her evaluation, she thinks about what the student did when the miscue changed the meaning. Those miscues that did not change meaning are not evaluated.

2. Does the Reader Monitor Oral Reading? Proficient readers typically correct those errors that change meaning but pay little attention to those oral reading errors that do not change the meaning (Clay, 1969). Inefficient readers, however, do not distinguish between the miscues that affect meaning and those that do not. There is little difference in the frequencies with which they correct either type of miscue. Therefore, inefficient readers do not *consistently* read for meaning and do not monitor their oral reading behavior. As a result, inefficient readers make more errors and correct them less often.

The diagnostic teacher summarizes the number of miscues that are corrected and those that are not corrected. She uses this information to decide which miscues to evaluate further. Miscues that change meaning and are corrected are closely evaluated to predict how the student combines sources of information when reading is efficient.

The miscues that are left uncorrected and change meaning are evaluated to look for the student's attempts to trouble shoot when reading problems occur.

3. What Source of Information Does the Reader Use to Regain Meaning? Proficient readers flexibly shift between sources of information when what they are reading does not make sense. They use what they already know (top-down approach) as well as what the text says (bottom-up approach) to check and revise their miscues. However, inefficient readers use only one source of information to correct problems when reading orally (Allington, 1984b). Whether they rely too much on what they already know or how the text looks, they invariably limit their remedial strategies to one source of information. This leads to one of three diagnostic hypotheses.

The first hypothesis is that when reading breaks down, the student makes his miscues fit *his* interpretation and background information rather than uses information from the text. For example, a student who consistently substitutes a word that does not resemble the text but retains the meaning reflects a processing preference for a top-down meaning search. He does not revise a miscue on the basis of the words in the text but relies solely on his background knowledge. If this is the pattern, the diagnostic teacher works with the student to encourage him to use how the words look as well as what he already knows. She chooses techniques that teach word identification as well as emphasize monitoring print processing.

The second hypothesis considered is that when reading breaks down, the student's miscues are similar to the graphic form of the text. For example, a student who depends on the graphic form for figuring out unknown words often produces a miscue that has the same initial letter and is approximately the same length as the word in the text and is a word that he has been taught. This reader is using what the text looks like but does not ask what the word would mean in this sentence. He needs to check not only the words he has been taught but also what word would fit in the meaning of the story. In this case, the diagnostic teacher chooses techniques that teach word identification using text cues as well as meaning cues.

The third hypothesis evaluated is that when reading breaks down, the student's miscues reflect an attempt to employ sound-symbol (phonic) associations. For example, a student who depends on graphophonic information produces miscues by sounding out a word one letter at a time, blending those sounds to form a nonword, and continuing to read. He sacrifices meaning for inaccurate decoding. This reader is said to be bound by the text and uses a bottom-up processing strategy. In this case, the diagnostic teacher decides if decoding is a proficient strategy. If it is, she uses techniques for word attack and incorporates strategy instruction in word identification into the remedial program. If decoding is an inefficient strategy for this reader, however, the diagnostic teacher looks for strategies that use overall meaning of the text rather than sounds of letters to decode unknown words.

The diagnostic teacher summarizes the data about the sources of information to look for a consistent pattern of print processing.

4. How Has Previous Instruction Influenced the Child's Miscue Pattern? Young readers use the strategies that they have been taught. Therefore, readers differ in their strategies to regain meaning because of the instructional emphasis in their initial reading programs (Barr, 1974–1975). This emphasis affects a child's correction strategies through the third-grade reading level. Some reading programs emphasize using meaning and the initial letter of the word to remember words (meaning-emphasis programs). Other programs emphasize blending sounds together to remember words (phonics programs). Miscue patterns often reflect the type of initial reading instruction received.

Sometimes the child is using a system that he has been taught effectively. In a meaning-emphasis program, the student's attention is focused on the initial letter and word length along with context to figure out unknown words. As he reads for meaning, he develops fluent and appropriate phrasing while checking his guesses with the initial letter and word length. However, in a structured phonics program, the reader's attention is focused on the letter-sound relationships to identify words. Therefore, he sacrifices meaning for phonic decoding, reflecting less use of context and a higher tendency to focus on individual words to remedy reading errors (Dank, 1977).

The diagnostic teacher evaluates whether the student is using effectively the system he has been taught. If so, she plans a program to help him refine this system and integrate it with other cueing systems. In other words, if the student was taught phonics and is using it well, the diagnostic teacher continues to emphasize this cueing system while simultaneously asking the student to double-check his responses to see if they make sense.

At other times, however, the child may try to use a system that he has been taught but reverts to using sources of information more in line with his cognitive abilities. When there is a mismatch between the way a student has been taught to read and his cognitive abilities, often the student tries to use the cueing system that he has been taught but usually abandons this technique to rely on a source of information that seems more natural to him (Juel, 1984; Stanovich, 1981). For example, if a student has been taught to sound out words letter by letter but has no ability to synthesize sounds, he will *try* to sound out the word but abandon this strategy in favor of using meaning cues and the initial letter. Because he has been taught a system that he cannot use, he reverts to a strategy more in line with his cognitive abilities.

If the diagnostic teacher observes these phenomena, she can change her instruction to match the reader's strengths in word identification. She reinforces these strengths and plans for a more integrative use of cueing systems. For example, a reader who was taught phonics continually miscues by substituting a word that makes sense in the context without regard for the letters in the word. The teacher notes that he is overriding his instruction and using his preference. Therefore, she chooses techniques that develop word recognition using the overall meaning of the text. As the student becomes more accurate with this system, she calls attention to initial letter and word length.

5. Do the Words in the Text Influence the Miscue Pattern?   The type of words in the text can affect the miscue pattern. A text that contains many decodable words is easier to read for the child who has had phonics instruction. However, if the text contains high-frequency words with a mixture of regular and irregular decodable words, the student who uses intial-letter and word-length cues has more success in reading the text (Juel, 1984). Consequently, before making final decisions about the student's correction strategies, the diagnostic teacher checks the text to see if it has caused an atypical error pattern.

In conclusion, oral reading patterns give insight into how the student is monitoring his reading behavior. The student's reading errors or miscues are analyzed to find the source of information used to remedy the reading error. The strategies that the student uses are affected by previous instruction, his cognitive abilities, and the text that is being read. The sensitive teacher considers all these influences when interpreting the student's oral reading behavior.

ANALYZING SILENT READING

Premises

To analyze comprehension, the diagnostic teacher evaluates how the reader thinks through the comprehension of a passage. Using a *think-aloud* format of interrupted reading, the teacher observes how the student uses the text and what he knows to interpret the passage. A think-aloud analysis, therefore, is a tool for evaluating the reader's comprehension strategies in the context of the entire passage. Although several researchers have outlined think-aloud procedures, the approach discussed here has been drawn from the work of Olson, Duffy, and Mack (1984).

A think-aloud analysis is based on the three theoretical assumptions that follow.

1. Reading is an active process (i.e., a reader constructs a model of meaning as he reads).
2. To construct this model, the reader uses what he already knows (reader-based inferencing) and the information in the text (text-based inferencing).
3. Reading is a strategic process (i.e., the reader checks his model of meaning to see if it makes sense).

In other words, the reader is viewed as an active interpreter of text. He predicts what is going to happen. Then he confirms or revises this expectation using both what he already knows (reader-based inferencing) and the important information from the text (text-based inferencing). Finally, he checks his interpretations to see if they are making sense.

Asking the student to think aloud gives an indication of how the student is processing text. The think-aloud process shows the diagnostic teacher the strategies that the student uses to make sense of what he is reading (Brown & Lytle, 1988). As with the oral reading analysis, interpretations that change the author's intended meaning and the reader does not revise are seen as diagnostically significant. They indicate what the reader does when he cannot interpret the text. Interpetations changing the author's intended meaning that the reader later revises are viewed as efficient strategies. They offer information about how the reader regains meaning. Interpretations that do not alter the author's intended meaning are viewed as nonsignificant. Evaluating the nature of the information used to regain meaning reveals the active comprehension strategies. Basically, the student uses various sources of information for text interpretation: (a) what he already knows, (b) facts stated in the text, and (c) a combination of both the text and what he already knows.

Diagnostic Questions

Based upon these premises, diagnostic hypotheses can be developed using the following questions.

1. How close is the reader's interpretation (i.e., how elaborate is the summary and are the important points covered)?
2. Does the reader monitor comprehension (i.e., how does he use new information to predict and revise his model of meaning)?
3. What sources of information (reader-based, text-based, or both) does the reader use?
4. How has previous instruction influenced the think-aloud process?
5. Does the text influence the think-aloud process?

The diagnostic teacher uses these questions to analyze silent reading behavior during the think-aloud experience. The pattern of strategies indicates the student's application of reading skills in text. When the student's interpretation changes the meaning, a careful analysis is needed to assess the strategies he uses to regain meaning. Each of these questions is designed to elicit the particular kinds of data necessary for a complete assessment of his silent reading behavior.

1. How Close Is the Reader's Interpretation?   During the think-aloud assessment, the student summarizes out loud what he read silently. Summarizing, or retelling, forces the student to select information important in illustrating the message as he perceived it (Harste et al., 1984). It reveals the student's ability to recall textual information and make inferences using his own experiences. For narrative text, a good summary includes the important elements of story grammar: setting (characters and place), problem, key events, and resolution (see Morrow, 1988, for detailed procedures). For expository text, a good summary contains the main idea and key details (Taylor, 1985). During the discussion, the diagnostic teacher evaluates how inclusive or narrow the summary is, the completeness of verbal responses, and the cohesiveness of the summary. After the student has finished his summary, the teacher uses questions to probe higher-level thinking, to focus on key ideas in the text, and to assess the student's knowledge of the meaning of the key words (Barr & Sadow, 1985).

The diagnostic teacher uses this information to designate the significance of the miscomprehension. As she continues her evaluation, she thinks about how the interpretation affects how the student constructs meaning. Summaries that do not change the overall interpretation of the story are considered the result of effective strategies. However, summaries where the student changes the meaning of the text are evaluated to form hypotheses about the reader's strategies. Often poor readers do not organize textual information as they read (Paris & Oka, 1989). The details or events they include in their summaries become increasingly random and show a decreasing relationship to the text (Winograd, 1984). Thus, summaries can alert the diagnostic teacher to problems in text processing that will be uncovered as she continues her analysis.

2. Does the Reader Monitor Comprehension?   The diagnostic teacher uses this question to evaluate how the student uses new information to predict and revise his model of meaning. At each interruption, the teacher asks him to predict what will happen next in the story and why he thinks so. She asks him to evaluate his previous prediction in light of the new information read, and then she gives him the option of changing the prediction, keeping it, or discarding it. As the student makes predictions and evaluates them, the teacher observes his strategies for monitoring comprehension. She observes the inclusiveness of the prediction and the amount of textual information used up to the point of interruption.

Basically, inefficient readers have been found to be less active than more efficient readers. They change their predictions less often than more proficient readers. Some students rely too heavily on their initial prediction and make the entire story fit it (Maria & MacGinitie, 1982). When they do revise their predictions, passive readers change only one part of their predictions. These readers do not use new textual information to revise predictions; rather they keep a prediction when it is no longer supported by the text (Baker & Brown, 1984). Less active readers hold onto previous predictions rather than become more tentative.

Active readers seem more comfortable keeping their models of meaning tentative. If there is no new information in the text, they delay making a prediction (Dybdahl, 1983). However, during a think-aloud experience, they change their predictions, adding and revising new information provided in the text and relating information throughout the procedure.

This phase provides diagnostic information about how the student is monitoring his reading comprehension. The teacher notes the point at which the reader realizes that his model of meaning does not fit the stated information in the text. Since the story has been presented in segments, the diagnostic teacher can easily observe strategies such as rereading previous segments to check the text, modifying predictions, or remaining tentative until more information has been read. She uses this information to decide which summaries and predictions to evaluate further. Those interpretations that changed meaning but were subsequently revised are closely evaluated to predict how the student combines sources of information when he encounters trouble spots in reading. The interpretations that were not revised and changed meaning are further analyzed to evaluate how the student attempts to make sense of what he is reading.

3. What Sources of Information (Reader-Based, Text-Based, or Both) Does the Reader Use? Beginning the think-aloud procedure by using the title of the text, the diagnostic teacher can assess the student's prior knowledge about the topic. Questioning the student about how he arrives at a prediction from just the title allows the diagnostic teacher to probe further background knowledge and begin to assess how the student uses this background knowledge as he reads the text (Watson, 1985). The teacher can observe the student as he constructs a rationale to support his prediction, and evaluate whether the support is text-based or reader-based. This process leads to one of three diagnostic hypotheses.

The first hypothesis is that when reading breaks down, the student's interpretation fits something he can understand instead of what the whole text says. Some readers ignore information that they do not understand. (They actually do not *know* that they do not understand.) When this happens, their responses are marked with an elaborate interpretation of the one or two events that they were able to comprehend. There is no line of reasoning that connects these students' responses to the story because they lack sufficient knowledge to interpret the text. If this pattern occurs, the diagnostic teacher needs to develop the necessary background knowledge for this particular student before he reads a story.

The second hypothesis suggests that when reading breaks down, the student's interpretations fit what he already knows and not what the text says. Some problem readers rely too heavily on their own knowledge and actually make their interpretations fit what they already know. For example, some students consistently answer questions with information that they know, using it to explain a line of reasoning for their answers rather than using information provided by the author. In these cases, the student understands what he reads but relies too heavily on his own experiences to develop reasons that are close to, but not exactly like what the author intended. When this pattern occurs, the diagnostic teacher uses techniques that show the student how to use what he knows in combination with what the text says.

The third hypothesis proposes that when reading breaks down, the student's interpretations fit what the text says without tying together information. Some problem readers rely too heavily on the text and fail to use their own knowledge to interpret the text (Spiro, 1979). They have too narrow an interpretation because they do not draw relationships between information in different parts of the text. If this pattern occurs, the diagnostic teacher uses techniques that first allow the student to discuss what the text says and then show him how to use what he knows to elaborate on it.

During the think-aloud process, the diagnostic teacher evaluates the source of information used to construct responses as well as the accuracy of the interpretation.

4. How Has Previous Instruction Influenced the Think-Aloud Procedure? The number and types of questions teachers ask students when discussing text affect children's comprehension. Guszak (1967) found that teachers ask predominately literal questions (70%) in classroom instruction and have an increasing tendency to ask more nonliteral questions at higher grade levels. Additionally, teachers discriminate between high-ability students and low-ability students. By sixth grade, half the questions asked the high-ability students are nonliteral, while only *30%* of the questions asked the low-ability students are nonliteral (Pearson, 1983). Furthermore, studies indicate that when teacher-generated questions are posed prior to reading, comprehension narrows because students read to answer those specific questions rather than to construct meaning (Singer & Donlan, 1982). Some students have learned to rely on the teacher's direction rather than to think independently. The diagnostic teacher analyzes the focus of previous instruction to find out how that focus has affected comprehension.

5. Does the Text Influence the Think-Aloud Process? Poor story construction affects the student's think-aloud process and the choice of interruption points. When story plots are engaging enough to motivate readers to find out what happens, then the teacher-reader interactions during the analysis period are elaborate; however, bland and boring texts give the students no reason to read (Olson, Duffy, & Mack, 1984). The diagnostic teacher needs to construct a story map of the selected story to determine if the story actually lends itself to a think-aloud process and is engaging enough to elicit an elaborate interaction. Some initial ambiguity of the story plot allows the diagnostic teacher to observe the child's approach to problem solving when reading. The type of text also affects the think-aloud analysis. Narrative text lends itself to prediction, revision, and monitoring, while expository text lends itself to summarizing, clarifying, and discussing the line of argument used by the author (Olson et al., 1984).

In conclusion, having the student think aloud as he reads allows the teacher to assess the strategies that he uses to construct meaning. This procedure provides diagnostic data to formulate instructional hypotheses and subsequently to select appropriate techniques for improving reading comprehension.

SUMMARY

The diagnostic teacher gathers data by asking questions that focus her evaluation of the strategies of the problem reader. First, she evaluates the student's performance across levels of text difficulty using the informal reading inventory. From this information, she designates a level that is moderately difficult for the student. She evaluates both oral and silent reading performance and determines the major presenting problem. After she decides whether print processing or meaning processing is inhibiting fluent reading with comprehension, she selects a story to continue her assessment. From the story, she constructs an on-level assessment that is either an oral reading or a think-aloud experience. This assessment gives her more data about the student's strategies when reading is difficult. The data about the reader's strategies consider influencing factors from the reading event, especially the text and past learning experiences. Then she conducts the assessment and analyzes the data to formulate her diagnostic hypotheses.

Formulating Diagnostic Hypotheses

To formulate the diagnostic hypotheses, the diagnostic teacher analyzes the information that he has gathered through the assessments in Chapter 7 and within the reading event (see Figure 6–1). He uses data from the informal reading inventory to assess the student's reading pattern in texts across a range of difficulty levels for both oral and silent reading. He performs an on-level reading analysis to assess the student's reading pattern when she reads a text that is moderately difficult either orally or silently. As he evaluates this information, he increases his specificity by reflecting on the diagnostic questions in Chapter 5. He reflects on the reading event and how it has influenced the data he has gathered. Then he reflects on instruction and predicts which technique(s) will produce the desired reader change based on these data.

REFLECTING ON DIAGNOSTIC QUESTIONS

After collecting the data from the extended analysis, the diagnostic teacher reflects on the diagnostic questions. This analysis provides detailed information about the strategies the reader uses to recover from difficulties in processing print or meaning in a text. The diagnostic teacher uses these data to formulate hypotheses about the most advantageous instructional design for the student. How a diagnostic teacher uses this data is described in this section within the framework of a case study of a hypothetical third grader named Jenny who is experiencing difficulty in fluent oral reading.

Print Processing Questions

After analyzing the diagnostic questions in Chapter 5, the diagnostic teacher uses this information to identify patterns and suggest instructional frames. The following discussion delineates patterns representative of ineffective reading. The instructional techniques and major categories referred to in this section are explained in Chapter 8, "Selecting Instructional Techniques."

Meaning Change. The diagnostic teacher analyzes the amount of meaning change that results from the student's miscues or errors. If the errors do not significantly change the meaning of the passage, then the student is reading for meaning; however, if the meaning of the text is substantially changed due to the miscues, then the diagnostic teacher designs lessons that encourage sense making while reading.

Figure 6–1
The Decision-
Making Cycle of
Diagnostic
Teaching

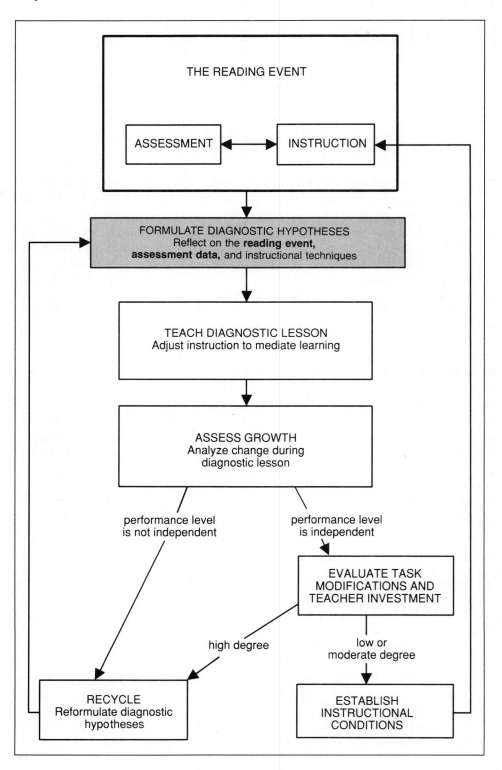

1. First, the diagnostic teacher investigates whether the student is familiar with the concepts in the text. This requisite knowledge helps the student decode the words by asking what would make sense. If the student is not familiar with the concepts, the teacher carefully selects texts that include familiar topics that are easy to read. This enables the student to make sense of the story and use her understanding to correct miscues.
2. If the text is familiar, then as the student reads, the diagnostic teacher prompts the student using "making sense" comments such as "Did that make sense?" or "Try that again, I didn't understand." or "Oops, what did you say?" These questions and non-verbal prompts can help students monitor their reading.
3. The diagnostic teacher selects techniques that naturally encourage students to predict and monitor their print processing (see Table 8–4). These teaching techniques are coupled with "sense-making prompts."

☐ *How Close Is Jenny's Print Processing?* When reading orally, Jenny reads to make sense of text as long as the topic is familiar. When Jenny makes a string of miscues, she misconstrues meaning and makes up the text. She ceases checking to see if what she is reading fits with the words in the text (monitoring print processing).

☐ *Diagnostic Hypothesis:* Jenny reads for meaning. However if she reads a string of miscues, she reverts to word calling rather than sense making. Jenny needs to read in interesting, familiar material so she can check her print processing by asking what makes sense.

Strategic Print Processing. The diagnostic teacher analyzes how students predict, monitor, and elaborate their model of meaning using the printed words in the text. She evaluates how actively students attend to what they read. Effective readers actively monitor their print processing, correcting miscues that significantly change meaning. In fact, effective readers have twice as many self-corrections as ineffective readers. Ineffective readers often exhibit one of the following patterns:

1. Some students simply call words and fail to correct miscues. They believe that reading is orally reading words without constructing meaning. They are unaware of the mistakes they make since they are not reading to make sense of text. When students exhibit this behavior, the diagnostic teacher constructs reading experiences in which the student will naturally make sense of text. Language experience is an excellent technique to help the student use prediction and to elaborate print processing strategies. Other techniques in Table 8–4 can also improve self-correction strategies.
2. Other students guess at words, but fail to check if the words they say match the words on the page. They continue to read, changing the story to fit the miscue rather than actively monitoring their print processing. When students exhibit this behavior, the diagnostic teacher constructs reading experiences that encourage the student to monitor and elaborate print processing. The use of repeated readings is an excellent technique for this purpose. Other techniques in Table 8–4 can also improve these strategies.

☐ *Does Jenny Use Strategic Print Processing?* Jenny predicts what words are by using overall textual meaning and her background knowledge. However, if she miscues, she does not check the print in the text to confirm her guesses. If her miscues don't make sense, she begins to decode every word and ceases to predict or recover meaning. Since this process has continued over a period of time, Jenny has not elaborated flexible strategies for print processing.

☐ *Diagnostic Hypothesis:* Jenny would profit from instruction that helps her monitor and elaborate strategies for processing print. Reading predictable books and then writing a new story using the same pattern would focus Jenny's attention on elaborating how print works.

Sources of Information.   Through print processing analysis, the sources of information a student uses can be identified. This leads the diagnostic teacher to describe a consistent pattern of using information sources as well as how the student is processing that information. From this pattern, the diagnostic teacher can make hypotheses about instruction. Although students vary in their use of the sources of information, three of the predominant patterns used by ineffective readers and appropriate instructional responses follow:

1. If the student uses his background knowledge at the expense of text-based information, the diagnostic teacher uses prompts that focus on "sense making" (a strength) and the letters in the text (a weakness) at the same time. Additionally, the diagnostic teacher selects techniques that emphasize monitoring print processing from a top-down perspective. Predictable language techniques used in combination with repeated readings encourage combining sources of information. Other techniques can be found in Tables 8–4 and 8–6.
2. If the student uses graphic clues from the text but fails to supply a word that makes sense, the diagnostic teacher prompts using "What word do you know that would make sense in this text?" Additionally, the diagnostic teacher selects techniques that emphasize predicting what would come next in the sentence. Predictable books coupled with cloze techniques would be useful for this type of reader. Other techniques can be found in Tables 8–4 and 8–6.
3. If the student overrelies on phonic information (a strength) without integrating this strength with sense-making strategies, the diagnostic teacher prompts using "What word has those same sounds (a strength) and would make sense in this story (a weakness)?" At the same time, the diagnostic teacher selects techniques that emphasize monitoring print processing (see Tables 8–4 and 8–6).

☐ *What Source of Information Does Jenny Use When Solving Print Problems?* Jenny predicts what the text will say using her own ideas about the story. When she is on the right track, reading progresses. However, when Jenny has misconceptions about the story content, she adds words to fit her understanding.

☐ *Diagnostic Hypothesis:* Jenny would profit from instruction that shows her how to monitor her predictions using the words in the story. Repeated readings in interesting and predictable texts can encourage Jenny to monitor her print processing.

Previous Instruction.   As stated in Chapter 3, the instruction a student receives affects his reading pattern. However, the most significant effect occurs when the student overrides his previous instruction, reverting to his natural cognitive abilities.

In these cases, reading problems often grow out of confusion about how to approach print processing and result in a disorganized set of strategies. The following patterns are most prevalent:

1. The student has been taught to sound out words, but often abandons this strategy in favor of using meaning cues (a strength). If the student is somewhat successful in using phonics, the diagnostic teacher focuses her prompting and instruction on first using meaning cues and then phonics when the student encounters difficulty in a text. The predictable language approach allows the student to easily combine these two sources of information. Predictable books like *The Hungry Giant,* where many of the words are decodable, facilitate the integration of these cue systems.
2. The student has been taught to think about the meaning and how a word begins but guesses wildly using only the meaning. These students need to be encouraged to look at more of the letters in the word to regain meaning. The diagnostic teacher prompts using "What would make sense?" (a strength) and "Look closely at the letters" (a weakness). The language experience approach and others that encourage monitoring and elaborating print processing are excellent techniques for this type of reader.

□ *How Has Previous Instruction Influenced Jenny's Print Processing?* Because of a deficit in visual processing, Jenny has had three years of a structured synthetic phonics program. Thus, Jenny often tries to sound out words at the expense of using her natural cue system of meaning processing. Since this is a laborious process for Jenny, she gives up using her strength and simply calls words only half-heartedly searching for meaning.

□ *Diagnostic Hypothesis.* Jenny needs experiences where she can first use meaning cues and then use her learned strategy of sounding out words. Techniques that encourage the student to use top-down processing while focusing on printed words are the most appropriate.

Textual Influence.   Since the type of text can influence the miscue pattern, the diagnostic teacher thinks about the reading strategies that the problem reader uses and selects texts that will extend those strategies so they become more integrated and automatic (see Table 8–2 for a more complete analysis).

□ *How Does the Text Influence Jenny's Print Processing?* Jenny has had numerous experiences reading decodable words in isolated word practice, however, she does not efficiently use phonic analysis when reading authentic texts.

□ *Diagnostic Hypothesis.* Jenny would profit from reading many meaningful stories where she can use both reader-based inferencing and phonic knowledge at the same time. The diagnostic teacher needs to look for predictable stories that contain an abundance of decodable words.

Meaning Processing Questions

After analyzing the diagnostic questions for strategies for gaining meaning from text in Chapter 5, the diagnostic teacher uses this information to identify patterns and suggest instructional procedures. The following discussion portrays typical patterns of ineffective readers. The instructional techniques recommended are found in Chapter 8, "Selecting Instructional Techniques."

Meaning Change.   The diagnostic teacher analyzes the degree to which the students' summaries differ significantly from the author's intended meaning. Effective readers use the critical information when summarizing text while ineffective readers fail to recount important information. If the student changes the meaning substantially, the diagnostic teacher designs lessons that encourage sense making while reading.

1. First, the diagnostic teacher makes sure that the student is familiar enough with the topic to construct summaries. If the student is not familiar with key vocabulary words or larger concepts, then the teacher carefully selects texts that include familiar topics and less challenging vocabulary.
2. If the text is familiar, then as the student reads, the diagnostic teacher prompts using leading questions that encourage students to integrate the major concepts within the framework of the story. Techniques such as story mapping, herringbone diagraming, retelling, and summarizing help students develop a textual framework for elaborating comprehension (see Table 8–4).

☐ *How Close Is Jenny's Meaning Processing?* When Jenny was asked to retell the story section by section, her interpretation was extremely close, indicating that she strives to make sense of text. However, she omitted some information in her summaries. This information was later evaluated as containing words that were difficult for her to decipher.
☐ *Diagnostic Hypothesis:* Jenny's desire to make sense of text is a processing strength and should be included in all instructional activities.

Strategic Meaning Processing.   The diagnostic teacher analyzes how the student constructs a model of meaning by analyzing how students predict, monitor, and elaborate their model of meaning during the think-aloud procedure. Effective readers actively predict and revise their understanding, clarifying difficult areas by rereading and reading ahead. Ineffective readers passively read without revising or elaborating their understanding. These passive readers may demonstrate one of the following patterns:

1. Some students hang on to an initial incorrect prediction, or change it infrequently, by ignoring information that does not fit their interpretation. When this occurs, the diagnostic teacher models her own predictions and how they change as the story progresses. Techniques such as self-questioning and prediction mapping show students how to monitor their comprehension (see Table 8–4). Ambiguous scary stories and mysteries where the plot changes near the middle and end of the story are excellent materials for these activities.
2. Some students refuse to predict because they don't want to be wrong. Often their instruction has focused on getting answers correct. These students need to learn how to guess, realizing they can change their predictions when they get new information. To help these students, the diagnostic teacher encourages them to predict more frequently and to make several guesses at a time. Techniques such as request and question-generation aid them in predicting a model of meaning (see Table 8–4).

☐ *Does Jenny Use Strategic Meaning Processing?* During a think-aloud, Jenny was able to predict and revise her understanding, elaborating ideas using her personal knowledge. Sometimes, however, her elaborations included tangential information that had little to do with the theme or main idea.

☐ *Diagnostic Hypothesis:* Using Jenny's active processing strength, the diagnostic teacher needs to help Jenny focus her attention on key ideas and concepts. Although elaboration is a strength, Jenny should be encouraged to use her knowledge selectively.

Sources of Information.   Through the think-aloud analysis, the sources of information a student uses can be identified. Effective readers combine information sources (text and background knowledge) while ineffective readers overrely on a single source of information. From the think-aloud, the diagnostic teacher can make hypotheses about instruction to help readers to strategically combine information sources. Two predominant patterns and suggestions for appropriate instruction follow:

1. If the student uses his background knowledge at the expense of text-based information, the diagnostic teacher uses prompts that focus on "sense making" (a strength) and uses the information in the text to verify guesses. She selects techniques that emphasize monitoring meaning (see Table 8–4).
2. If students rely heavily on the text without thinking about what they know, the diagnostic teacher asks them to restate the text and then think about what they know that relates to the text. He selects techniques that emphasize predicting what the text might say and elaborating textual meaning (see Table 8–4).

☐ *What Sources of Information Does Jenny Use for Meaning Processing?* When constructing meaning, Jenny relies heavily on her own knowledge about the topic. She does use the text to verify her response. Occasionally, however, she overrides the text by supplying information she already knew to support her interpretation. Most of the time this is effective for Jenny.

☐ *Diagnostic Hypothesis:* Because meaning processing is a strength, Jenny is asked to explain her reasoning and then orally read sections of the text that support the explanation. This uses a strength to improve a weakness (print processing).

Previous Instruction.   The instruction students receive affects how they strategically read text. Some students rely on the teacher's direction rather than constructing their own meaning. The diagnostic teacher decides if previous instruction has affected the strategic application of meaning processes. The following may be found:

1. The student has been taught to answer questions literally using the text and, therefore, fails to infer or elaborate meaning. In these cases, the diagnostic teacher uses text-based techniques like story mapping and then asks the student to retell the story using what they know.
2. The student's use of extensive background knowledge when retelling or answering comprehension questions has been reinforced. Therefore, she tends to disregard the text. In these cases, the diagnostic teacher uses reader-based techniques like the DRTA, but focuses on using the text to verify answers or completing a story map after discussion.

☐ *How Has Previous Instruction Influenced Jenny's Meaning Construction?* Previously, Jenny has been rewarded for embellishing the text with her own topic knowledge. This instruction, however, has caused Jenny to rely too heavily on topic knowledge when reading. She needs to learn to verify her answers using the text.

☐ *Diagnostic Hypothesis:* Again Jenny is asked to verify her explanations using the text. However, she is also asked to generate in writing new questions for other students to answer. This uses her strength of meaning processing to develop attention to print through writing.

Textual Influence. Since the type of text can influence meaning processing, the diagnostic teacher thinks about the reading strategies that problem readers use and their preference for narrative or expository texts. She selects texts that build on preferences, and then extends strategies so they become more integrated and automatic (see Table 8–1 for a more complete analysis).

☐ *How Does the Text Influence Jenny's Meaning Processing?* Jenny enjoys reading information about science concepts. Her reading is more fluent, and her retellings are more elaborate in science text. Jenny also has a high need to read authentic text.

☐ *Diagnostic Hypothesis:* Jenny would profit from reading science texts about familiar topics that are well constructed so the information makes sense.

After the diagnostic teacher has reflected on print and meaning processing, she thinks about how the student has responded during an instructional event. She reflects on the reading event and how these factors have influenced the data.

REFLECTING ON THE READING EVENT

After collecting the data, the diagnostic teacher reflects on the reading event. He returns to the model of the reading event discussed in Chapter 2 and uses it to evaluate the influence of the variables on the student's reading behavior. He remembers that the information he has collected is a result of the interactions that occurred in the reading event. He systematically evaluates the influence of the task, the text, the reader, and the context of the reading event on the data. He looks for key factors by asking, for example, "What task did the child do? Is this task an important consideration in establishing this student's instructional program?" He considers the relative strengths of the student's oral and silent reading in promoting fluent reading with comprehension. From this analysis, he formulates diagnostic hypotheses and selects teaching techniques to enhance reading growth.

How the diagnostic teacher uses the data from the initial assessments and relates them to the elements of the reading event is described in the pages that follow. The case study of a hypothetical third grader named Jenny, who is experiencing difficulty in fluent oral reading is continued in this section. As the teacher reflects on the reading event, he makes observations about the student's performance using the data he has collected. The *asterisk* (*) indicates key factors he has to consider when establishing Jenny's instructional program.

The Task

The diagnostic teacher analyzes the reading tasks that the student completes during the reading event. He carefully considers the range of possibilities related to the task and looks for key factors that might affect the student's reading behavior. During the informal reading assessment, he has already decided on the major presenting problem; now he uses this information to evaluate the effect that the question type is having on the reader's responses and to evaluate reasoning requirements. He compares the reader's performance on the informal reading inventory and the extended passage. From this comparison, he ascertains whether the task segment is affecting reading performance and whether production requirements are affecting reader response.

☐ *How Does Jenny Approach Reading Tasks?* Task analysis for Jenny is given in Table 6–1.

Table 6–1
Task Analysis for Jenny

*Oral or silent reading: Both oral and silent reading behavior were evaluated, with the student comprehending all passages where she could decode the words. Oral reading was the more difficult task. At the instructional level, silent reading comprehension was not a concern.

Task segment (words, sentences, paragraphs, stories, etc.): Short paragraphs were used for the evaluation.

Availability of text: The text was not available for referral when answering questions; however, student comprehension was elaborate.

Production requirements: Retelling was used to assess comprehension, followed by inferential questions. Comprehension was high on each task.

Question type: Literal and nonliteral responses were evaluated. She performed equally well in both cases.

*Purpose for the task: Teacher-directed reading was used for evaluation. Informal conversation revealed that she liked to control her own learning.

Reasoning requirements of task: Factual recall and applicative reasoning was required. The student did well in both types of tasks.

☐ *Diagnostic Hypothesis:* Jenny reads with moderate difficulty at the second-grade level (1/11 oral accuracy and 75% comprehension) on an informal reading inventory. Oral reading presents the most difficulty for the student. Although she prefers silent reading, Jenny needs to read orally to improve fluency. Her informal comments ("I hate these stories") indicate that she prefers to choose her own stories.

The Text

The type of text read during a reading evaluation can influence significantly the data to be analyzed. The diagnostic teacher routinely assesses the text and its influence on reading behavior to identify which characteristics are affecting the student's reading. Again he seeks the key factors about the text that affect this student's reading behavior. To do so, he looks at the information from the informal reading inventory, the extended passage, and the final question of the oral/silent reading analysis (does the text influence the results of this procedure).

☐ *How Does the Type of Text Affect Jenny's Reading?* The text analysis for Jenny would contain the material covered in Table 6–2.

Table 6–2
Text Analysis for
Jenny

Passage length: Short passages produced more oral reading miscues. The extended passage gave the student more opportunities to use overall context to self-correct errors.

***Passage type:** Both expository and narrative passages were read. The student made fewer miscues on expository text.

Type of content: The student read various subject content. It did not seem to affect her performance.

Background knowledge required of reader: Various levels of background knowledge were needed in the text, but the student knew about most topics.

***Grammatical complexity:** The more complex the sentence structure, the better the student read.

Word choices: Short words that fit the text were used. Elaborate word meanings were not required for comprehension. Decodable words were easier to read.

Density of information: The high density of information did not affect comprehension, but this did affect the reader's miscue pattern. When too much information was presented, the student could not self-correct.

Elaboration or use of examples: Not enough examples of elaboration to establish a pattern.

Organizational structure: Not enough examples of organization to establish a pattern.

Coherence or unity of text: When the story structure did not reflect the title of the passage, the reader's miscues were affected because she tried to make the title fit the text.

☐ *Diagnostic Hypothesis:* Jenny needs a text that is coherently organized, and she appears to prefer expository text. Increasing the complexity of the sentence structure seems to have a positive effect on miscues (i.e., the longer the sentence, the more she is able to correct her miscues). Another possible influencing factor may be the word choices in the text. Since the student was taught with a synthetic phonic approach (see "Synthetic Phonics" in Chapter 9), words that are more decodable might improve performance.

The Reader

The reader is the major focus of traditional assessment. In diagnostic teaching, however, the reader is assessed in relation to herself as well as to the variables of the reading event. The teacher looks at the knowledge-based requirements of the tasks and how the student responds to them. From the informal reading inventory, the diagnostic teacher evaluates general skill proficiencies and deficiencies. Returning to the extended passages, the diagnostic teacher uses the answer to the first question ("how close is the reader's interpretation?") to assess general knowledge. He must judge whether the reader changes the meaning of the selection because she has no similar experience to use to evaluate the sense of the text. In addition, he uses data from the extended passage to evaluate the strategies the student employs as she reads. He specifically analyzes the data on self-corrections and revisions during oral and/or silent reading. Finally, he evaluates data on the sources of information used.

☐ *How Does Jenny's Reading Performance Relate to Her Knowledges, Strategies, and Attributions?* Jenny's reader analysis is shown in Table 6–3.

Table 6–3
Reader Analysis
for Jenny

Knowledge-Based Differences

*Level of performance: On the informal reading inventory, the student read at the border-line level (moderate difficulty) on the second-grade paragraph.

Skill proficiencies: Answering comprehension questions and retelling a story.

*Skill deficiencies: Nonfluent oral reading; phonic knowledge is inappropriately applied.

Language proficiencies: The student used language well and often engaged in elaborate descriptions related to the story.

Language deficiencies: None observed.

Strategy-Based Differences

*Strategies used: Context of the story was used to help identify unknown words. Many miscues were semantically based (i.e., she used reader-based inferencing more often than text-based knowledge).

*Strategies needed: Self-correction during oral readings using *both* the semantic and graphic cueing systems.

*Source of information used (text or background knowledge): During comprehension, the student used an integration of both textual knowledge and reader knowledge; however, during oral reading, she used either textual knowledge or reader knowledge but not both when she encountered difficulty.

Elaboration of response (one word or embellished): All responses were elaborate except when the student encountered frustration-level reading.

Level of response (literal or nonliteral): The student used both literal and nonliteral responses when answering questions.

Attribution Patterns

Attribution Patterns and Cultural Attributes: The student's cultural expectations are similar to those of the classroom.

Need for structure: The student preferred to answer questions without help. She seems to have little need for structure.

*Type and need for feedback: During comprehension, the student had little need for feedback, often supplying her own analysis of her answers. However, when reading orally, one miscue can trigger a series of errors due to the student's creating a new text that makes sense in light of the initial miscue; therefore, feedback is needed for monitoring print processing.

*Need for human sense: The student exhibited disdain for the mundane stories at the first- and second-grade levels.

*Attribution for success or failure: For print processing, the student attributed her failure to baby reading material, dumb stories, and bad luck rather than to the lack of appropriate strategies.

☐ *Diagnostic Hypothesis:* Jenny needs instruction in word identification and fluency. She needs to be shown the effective strategies that she uses (e.g., self-correction from background knowledge). She tries to use phonic knowledge but is consistently unsuccessful in her attempts. Jenny, therefore, relies too much on her background knowledge and general story meaning. When she does this, she reads a string of miscues that make sense. Her unsuccessful attempts at self-correction reflect the use of either meaning cues or phonic cues without the integration of both cueing systems. She appears to like to direct her own learning rather than have the teacher tell her what to do. Because of her continual failure, Jenny needs to identify her strategy strengths and attribute her success to the combination of strategy use and effort.

The Context

The diagnostic teacher evaluates the instructional context in which the assessment occurs and how much influence he is having on the reader's response. At the same time, he evaluates how previous instructional experiences might have affected the student's responses. He reevaluates the patterns of performance, thinking about how the student's previous instructional experiences have influenced her reading patterns. He double-checks his data, focusing on the context of the reading event.

☐ *How Does the Instructional Context Affect Jenny's Reading?* An analysis for the context of Jenny's reading behavior is shown in Table 6–4.

Table 6–4
Context Analysis for Jenny

Learning situations (Present and past):
*Focus on constructing meaning. Previous learning situations have focused on skill weakness: two-year program of intensive synthetic phonics.
*Focus on collaboration in thinking. Previous learning situations have included an extensive pull out program with one-on-one instruction. The present classroom placement encourages collaboration in thinking.
Teacher expectation: High.
Composition of instructional group: The student prefers group instruction where she can participate in the discussion using her background knowledge.
*Feedback or prompting: Instruction needs to have minimal feedback from the teacher and maximal from the student. The teacher needs to prompt with this question: "What would make sense and start with a _____?"
Wait time: Appropriate for the learner. She always had a response.
Time allowed on task: Not evaluated.
Point of intervention during the lesson: Before the student reads, she needs to review new words to facilitate print processing.

☐ *Diagnostic Hypotheses:* Jenny's previous learning experiences affect both her perception of reading and her miscue pattern. When she miscues, she tries to sound out unknown words because that is the way she has been taught (two years of instruction in synthetic phonics). This strategy usually fails, however, and Jenny becomes discouraged. Having forgotten the meaning of the story, Jenny creates a string of miscues that make sense for the sentence but not for the entire story.

SUMMARY

Formulating Hypotheses for Jenny

When cross-checking the elements of the reading event, the diagnostic teacher remembers that some of the factors may not be important in examining the particular reading event under scrutiny. Only the key factors affecting the student's reading performance are analyzed. For Jenny, the analysis resulted in the following key factors:

1. The type of text (expository) facilitates reading behavior and heightens interest.
2. The student has a negative attribution to reading (she states that she hates reading).
3. The student uses only one cueing system at a time when reading breaks down. (She tries to use phonics, but when this fails she uses sentence sense. She does not combine the sources.)
4. The more grammatically complex the sentence structure, the more the student can self-correct her errors.
5. The student would rather direct her own learning than have the teacher tell her what to do. (This may be a function of the extremely structured program that was used during her initial reading instruction.)
6. The student uses top-down sources to regain meaning when reading breaks down.
7. The student has a well-developed background of information that she uses when answering questions.

Having identified these key factors, the teacher is then able to select an appropriate diagnostic teaching technique.

Reviewing the Steps

To formulate the diagnostic hypotheses, the diagnostic teacher reflects on the reading event, considering each variable and its relationship to the reader's performance. He looks at the interactions among the task, the text, the reader, and the context to establish patterns of reading performance.

After he has formulated hypotheses, he selects instructional techniques to advance the students reading (see Chapter 8). To verify the hypotheses that have led to this selection, the teacher conducts a diagnostic lesson. The guidelines for conducting this lesson are found in Chapter 7, "Assessment Using Diagnostic Lessons."

Assessment Using
Diagnostic Lessons

Although the diagnostic teacher uses the constructs of informal assessment and extended assessment discussed in Chapter 5, she interprets the information in a different fashion. She uses the informal reading inventory as a measure of what the student can do when he independently (without instruction) solves the reading problem. However, she also establishes how the student solves the reading problem as she is teaching. Therefore, she continues her assessment and establishes a level where the student profits from her instruction. From this knowledge, she derives her hypotheses for the student's instruction.

After the diagnostic teacher formulates her hypotheses, she teaches a lesson using techniques based on the hypotheses (see Figure 7–1). Diagnostic lessons provide a tool to assess the amount of growth that actually occurs as a result of the instructional adjustments. Through the *diagnostic lesson,* the teacher *assesses* the student's *growth* and establishes the student's optimal *learning conditions* (see Figure 7–1) including the student's mediated reading level.

ESTABLISHING MEDIATED READING LEVEL

The student's mediated reading level determines the level where the student can efficiently be taught. This level is determined by evaluating the "distance between the actual developmental level as determined by independent problem solving and the level of potential development as determined through problem solving under adult guidance or in collaboration with more capable peers" (Vygotsky, 1978, p. 86). First, the diagnostic teacher identifies at what level the student can incorporate the targeted reading strategies as a result of specified instruction. This is determined by calculating the "difference between the level of unaided performance a child can achieve, and the level he could achieve with aid" (Powell, 1984, p. 248). Therefore, the diagnostic teacher establishes the highest difficulty level where the student profits from instruction.

Since the goal is to determine how instruction improves reading performance, a text that is moderately difficult (90% oral accuracy and 60% comprehension) provides a more appropriate measuring tool. Using a moderately difficult text (within the borderline range in Figure 5–2) allows the teacher to assess the student's growth in reading performance as a result of instruction. She wants to observe how the student learns from her instruction. After instruction, the selected text should be read at the independent level (98% accuracy and 90% comprehension). If this happens, the

Figure 7–1
The Decision-
Making Cycle of
Diagnostic
Teaching

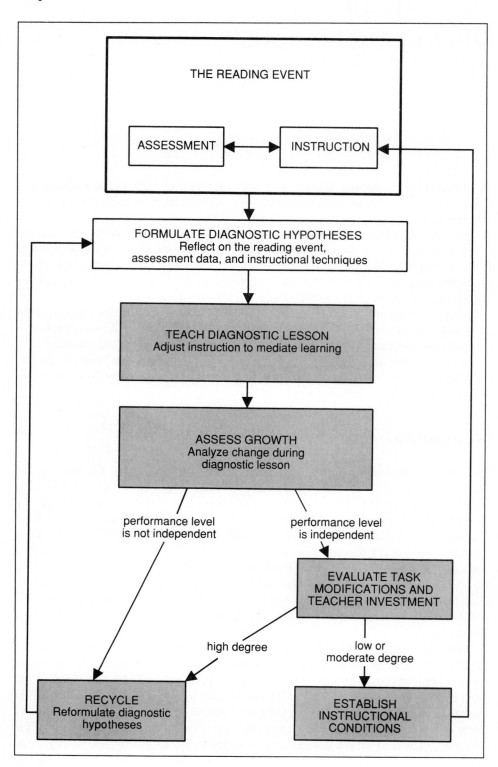

diagnostic teacher selects a more difficult text and teaches another lesson. She continues until the student does not achieve an independent reading level after instruction. Placement is thus determined by identifying the highest difficulty level where the student profits from instruction.

For example, a teacher took two short segments from a story in a text that was designated as moderately difficult for a student. Using the passages, she developed two assessments according to the constructs of informal reading assessment. Without teacher instruction, the student read the first segment with an error rate of 1/11 words and 60% comprehension. After the targeted vocabulary words were introduced and a discussion about how these words related to the selection was conducted, the second segment was read with an error rate of 1/50 and 90% comprehension. For this student, a text that was read near frustration without teacher direction could be read at independent reading level with instruction by the teacher.

The diagnostic teacher continued this procedure with a more difficult text. The highest level of text that the student read fluently after instruction was designated as the text to use during instruction. The level was then called the *mediated reading level*—the highest level of text that can be read fluently after instruction (Powell, 1986).

The diagnostic teacher establishes the mediated reading level, the highest level of text that can be read fluently after instruction.

For the diagnostician, decisions about placement involve more than just establishing at what level the student will profit from instruction. Since she is actually teaching during her assessment, she also evaluates the amount of task modification necessary to create the desired reading change (Feuerstein, 1979). Prior to instruction, the diagnostic teacher decides on certain task conditions that will enhance learning for a particular student. Some of these decisions include these questions: Will she segment the selection? If so, how will she do it—sentence by sentence, or paragraph by paragraph? Will the instruction be entirely silent reading? Or will oral rereading be necessary? How many new vocabulary words will be introduced before reading the selection and how will instruction occur? Should part of the discussion be written down so it can be referred to later? These decisions involve how she will modify the task so that learning will occur.

If there is a high degree of task modification, the diagnostic teacher needs to select either a less difficult text or a different teaching technique. If there is a low degree of task modification during the lesson, a more difficult text can be selected. Therefore, placement can be determined by the amount of task modification needed to ensure fluent reading comprehension.

The diagnostic teacher evaluates the amount of task modification (changes in the reading task) that she makes during instruction—like changing from oral to silent reading, or from one technique to another.

A third consideration is the amount of teacher investment necessary to engage the student in an active interpretation of text (Feuerstein, 1979). As she teaches, the diagnostic teacher adjusts her instruction to the needs of the student. She asks herself, "How can I phrase these questions so that the student will understand the main idea? What does he already know that will help him understand the story? How much time do I need to wait before I assist? What kind of assistance, questioning, or modeling will be most helpful?" These questions focus her involvement during instruction.

During instruction, the diagnostic teacher evaluates the amount of her investment. If the time investment is extremely high, changes in placement are needed that decrease the complexity of the task (an easier text or different teaching technique). If the investment is low, changes in placement are needed that increase the complexity of the task (a more difficult text or higher level questioning).

The diagnostic teacher evaluates the amount of teacher investment or the changes she makes regarding her interaction with the student, which includes prompting, rephrasing, and feedback.

The diagnostic teacher uses three criteria to determine the mediated reading level, the highest level where the student can profit from her instruction. She finds a reading level that is moderately difficult and teaches a lesson at this level. Then she evaluates the amount of reading growth due to instruction as well as the amount of teacher investment and task modification needed to ensure successful text interpretation.

After establishing a student's mediated reading level, the teacher continues her diagnostic lessons at this level. To begin, she chooses a reading passage that is at the student's mediated reading level and divides it into three sections. The diagnostic teacher uses the first section to assess reading performance without assistance. It is read *at sight* (without any period of familiarization) and without assistance to establish baseline data. The middle section of the passage is taught using the selected technique (see Chapters 8 and 9). This is the actual implementation of the hypotheses and requires keen observation of the changes that improve text interpretation. To assess the degree of change in reading due to instruction, the third section is also read at sight and without assistance. As a result of the mediated instruction, changes in reading performance should be apparent. If the instruction has been appropriate, the student should now be able to read the third section of the text at the independent reading level and exhibit patterns of performance that reflect a more integrated use of reader-based and text-based processing. Using the information from the diagnostic teaching lesson, the diagnostic teacher establishes the conditions that result in the optimal learning for the student. The following discussion delineates the purpose for each of the three sections of the diagnostic lesson.

PROCEDURES FOR DIAGNOSTIC LESSONS

Establishing Baseline Data

Having the student read the first section at sight and without assistance serves two functions: (a) to add information to the diagnostic hypotheses (see Chapter 6) and (b) to establish baseline behaviors so that the effectiveness of instruction can be evaluated. This section is about 100 to 200 words long and may be read either orally to evaluate print processing or silently to evaluate meaning processing (see Chapter 5). The data are analyzed by computing the percentage of comprehension and/or error rate as well as evaluating the patterns of the reading performance.

The diagnostic teacher reviews the data to expand her diagnostic hypotheses. However, her primary purpose for collecting baseline data is to measure growth due to instruction. Baseline data reflects the student's reading performance without aid and before adjusted instruction. During the instructional lesson, the teacher establishes the instructional conditions that mediate learning. To assess growth, the diagnostic teacher compares the student's performance without aid and his performance after specified instruction. This baseline data is used to evaluate reading growth due to instruction during the third section of the diagnostic lesson.

Establishing the Conditions of Learning

After the baseline data has been established, the teacher designs a diagnostic lesson based on her hypotheses about the student's reading performance. She selects a technique (see Chapter 8) that matches the reader's profile. However, the purpose of the second section is to establish the optimal conditions for learning new reading strategies. As she teaches the lesson, her modifications are summarized and become part of the diagnostic data collection. Unlike the first section, where the teacher constructs diagnostic hypotheses based on a relatively static assessment of reading performance, during the instructional lesson, the teacher's assessments are dynamic. Modifications of these hypotheses occur often as the teacher responds to the student's needs during instruction (Cioffi & Carney, 1983).

When using repeated readings with Ted, a second grader, for instance, the diagnostic teacher found that simply discussing the miscues did not result in decreased errors, so she modeled her own self-correction process by saying, "Oops, that doesn't make sense; let's see what would make sense and start with a *g*. Oh, *girl* starts with a *g*. *The girl hit the homerun*. Yes, that makes sense and sounds like it looks." Then Ted read the passage again, and the teacher recorded the errors and evaluated the amount and kind of change evidenced in the reading performance. Since there was a decrease in the number of errors and an increase in fluent reading, the teacher recommended the procedure with the modifications tried during the diagnostic lesson.

On another occasion, a fourth-grade student named John needed assistance in active comprehension. The diagnostic teacher formulated her hypotheses while she conducted a think-aloud assessment during the first section. During the second section, the teacher used a directed-reading-thinking activity. During the lesson, John could not answer an inferential question, so the diagnostic teacher rephrased the question to include some factual information to facilitate his answering the question. John still had no clue about how to arrive at an answer, so she asked him to find the part of the story that told about the factual information and to read it aloud. The ability of the student to perform this action indicates whether or not he understands the sequence of the story, as well as his ability to read the words without difficulty. He easily found the part of the text that contained the answer and read it without difficulty.

Again, the teacher began the line of questioning; however, this time she began with a factual question. Then she asked John to relate relevant personal experiences to the facts. After this discussion, the original inferential question was rephrased to see if instruction did result in an inferential understanding of the story based on factual information. Since this instructional sequence facilitated comprehension, the teacher hypothesized that John comprehends better if the instructional sequence begins with the facts and then develops an inferential understanding of the story.

During the diagnostic lesson, records of the instructional modifications are kept so that the amount and kinds of teacher intervention can be assessed. When conducting a diagnostic lesson, however, the teacher's primary goal is to teach the student. Her second goal is to assess those instructional modifications that are producing increased reading performance. In effect, the diagnostic teacher establishes the instructional conditions necessary to increase the reading performance.

Evaluating Growth

To evaluate the effect the instructional adjustments have on the student's reading performance, the diagnostic teacher conducts a final assessment using the third section of the passage. She uses the same format as for the first section, either recording oral reading responses or a think-aloud experience. The final assessment, conducted at sight and without assistance, provides a systematic method for assessing the effects of instructional intervention on the student's reading. The teacher assesses reading growth during the lesson as well as the amount of task modification and teacher investment needed to produce that growth. These measures not only determine placement but also establish optimal instructional conditions.

Reading Growth Due to Instruction.   First, the diagnostic teacher must establish the amount of change that has occurred as a result of instruction. If the instruction was appropriate, the resulting scores should indicate an independent reading level (98% word identification and 90% comprehension). Since the student received instruction in precisely those strategies that were inhibiting performance, there should be an increase in the number of questions answered correctly and a decrease in word identification errors. Reading growth should be evident.

Reading growth indicates a decrease in word recognition errors and an increase in the number of questions answered correctly.

Next, the diagnostic teacher compares the patterns of reading behavior assessed on the first section with those assessed on the third section. Oral reading should reflect more semantically and syntactically appropriate miscues and an increase in self-corrections. This pattern indicates that the student is using his knowledge of the story theme to figure out unknown words. The think-aloud experience should reflect a more integrated use of textual and nontextual information as well as more elaborate responses to questions. Spontaneous self-monitoring and the student's awareness of the sources of information he uses to construct responses should also be increasingly evident.

Reading growth is also indicated by an increasing use of both reader-based processing and text-based processing and by more self-monitoring for understanding.

Figure 7–1 highlights the final steps involved in assessing reading growth using diagnostic lessons. When the diagnostic teacher analyzes growth in this last phase of the decision-making cycle, two conclusions can result. There can be a positive change in reading behavior (independent level obtained) or there can be no change in reading behavior (independent level not obtained). These two outcomes necessitate different responses from the diagnostic teacher. If mediated instruction produces an independent reading level, the diagnostic teacher carefully evaluates the task modifications and teacher investment, or assistance, to establish the instructional modifications that produced the change. If mediated instruction does not produce reading growth, the diagnostic teacher eliminates those techniques and modifications that were used. She returns to her diagnostic hypotheses, adds any new information collected during the diagnostic lesson, and reformulates her hypotheses. Then she selects a new technique and conducts another diagnostic lesson.

Determining the Amount of Task Modification.   Prior to instruction, the diagnostic teacher selects a technique to implement during the diagnostic lesson. She determines how she is going to present the reading task. She decides if the reading task will be silent or oral and whether the story will be read as a whole or in segments. She decides if she will introduce new vocabulary words and how to do it. As she teaches the lesson, the teacher modifies these original tasks so that the student can read fluently with comprehension. It is these modifications that the teacher records and evaluates.

For example, the diagnostic teacher decided to use self-directed questioning (see "Self-Directed Questioning" in Chapter 9) with Luis, a third-grade student who was relatively passive when reading. He did not guess about the story or revise the few predictions he did make. The teacher began instruction by modeling the steps of self-directed questioning. As she silently read the text, she thought aloud when important information was presented. Next, she asked Luis to read silently and then to think aloud about the text. Luis readily began to talk about his interpretations. The teacher and student continued this process by alternately thinking aloud about the text. Luis began to make guesses and then to revise his thinking about the text.

In this example, the teacher needed to make relatively few task modifications. The student learned the new task and readily applied it. The teacher concluded that the passive reading behavior was due to a lack of experience with the task. It was evident that Luis had not transferred his active stance in other problem-solving situations to silent reading behavior before the instruction.

When evaluating Terry, another passive reader, the diagnostic teacher decided to use self-directed questioning again. As with the other student, the diagnostic teacher modeled the steps of self-directed questioning by thinking aloud about the text. Then she asked Terry to read silently and think aloud about the text when important information was presented. Terry read a long segment silently, then stopped and looked at the teacher for questions. However, he could not talk about the text. The teacher asked him to read the segment aloud and think out loud about the text. Again he read the words without stopping to think about their meaning. Therefore, the teacher modeled the same segment of the text, emphasizing how she thought about the text as she read out loud. Terry followed the teacher's model. However, he mainly recounted exactly what was stated in the text. He did not tie together events to make predictions or revise any previous thoughts.

The teacher modeled the next segment of the text. Terry was asked to follow the model, but he again read the words without thinking. The teacher, therefore, modified the task by segmenting the section into sentences. Reading sentence by sentence, she modeled her thinking about each sentence. Finally, Terry began to think aloud about the sentences and draw relationships among the sentences in the paragraph. During this segment, the teacher modified the procedures by asking questions like these: "What makes you say that? Was this character important? How do you know?"

To help this passive reader learn more active strategies for achieving reading comprehension, the diagnostic teacher needed to make modifications in a number of instructional areas. She changed the task from silent to oral reading when Terry could not talk about what he had read silently. She segmented the passage into sentences when he could not follow the modeled paragraphs. Moreover, she shifted from modeling only to modeling with inquiry questions to help him see relationships among the ideas in the text.

The diagnostic teacher evaluates the amount of modification necessary to create a change in the student's reading performance. Luis required little task modification for the original task and learned the task readily. Terry, however, required substantial modification. The degree of task modification becomes a key factor in determining future task assignments. If there is a high degree of task modification, a less difficult text or a different technique should be selected. If there is a low degree of task modification, however, a more difficult text or task can be employed.

The degree of task modification is considered in establishing the conditions necessary to produce reading growth.

Determining the Amount of Teacher Investment.   During assessment, the diagnostic teacher becomes a powerful determiner of reading performance. She thinks about how she set up instruction according to the procedures of the technique. Were these procedures sufficient for improving text interpretation? Or did she have to change the procedures, draw out of the student his own knowledge, and then show him how to relate this information to what he was reading? She evaluates how many times she had to rephrase questions and how many clues she needed to provide for the student.

Sometimes relatively little teacher investment, or assistance, is needed. For instance, Bobby could not recognize the word *skated* in this sentence: "The girl skated around the rink." The teacher told him to read to the end of the sentence. Bobby did so, thought for a minute about the word, and then read, "The girl skated around the rink." In this case, very little teacher investment was needed to encourage self-correction. With the simple prompt "read to the end of the sentence," the student was able to figure out the word.

Another student had the same difficulty with word recognition, but he needed more teacher investment. With the same prompt, Fred read to the end of the sentence but could not recognize the word *rink* either. In this case, the teacher had to probe further. She asked Fred to think about the story and what the girl might be doing. Still there was no response. The teacher then said, "In the picture there is an ice rink. Now, what do you think the girl is doing?" "Skating" was his reply. The teacher instructed him to read the sentence again. Fred now read: "The girl . . . skated around the . . . rink."

The diagnostic teacher assesses these modifications in terms of the amount of teacher investment necessary to create a change in the student's reading performance. Bobby required relatively little assistance, so there was minimal teacher investment. However, Fred required a great deal of assistance, so there was a higher degree of teacher investment.

The amount and kind of teacher investment are evaluated to identify the conditions that produce reading growth.

Conclusion

The diagnostic teacher assesses reading growth due to instruction by selecting a reading passage that is moderately difficult. She follows the procedures for the diagnostic lesson: establishing baseline data on the first section through the student's reading at sight, instruction during the second section, and establishing post-instruction data on the third section through more reading at sight. She evaluates whether or not the third section was read at an independent level. When the third section does not produce reader change, she reformulates her hypotheses and conducts another lesson. When the student reads the final section at an independent level, the diagnostic teacher assesses the amount of task modification and teacher investment that produced that growth. This assessment determines under what conditions subsequent instruction will be conducted.

1. If there was little task modification and teacher investment used to produce the desired change, the diagnostic teacher considers using a more difficult text for instruction.
2. If there was a moderate amount of task modification and teacher investment, the diagnostic teacher continues to use those adjustments in the same level of text.
3. If there was a great deal of task modification and teacher investment, the diagnostic teacher reformulates her hypotheses and selects either another technique or an easier text.

Special Considerations

The procedures outlined are used when considering only one technique or instructional modification for the student. In many instances, however, the diagnostic teacher needs to consider several options before establishing the optimal instructional conditions. Therefore, she compares growth under different techniques, uses several adapted lessons for the beginning reader, and combines techniques to increase her effectiveness.

Comparing Reading Growth Under Different Techniques. At times the diagnostic teacher will conduct a series of diagnostic lessons so that she can identify the most efficient instructional procedure. After the final assessment with each technique, the diagnostic teacher compares the performances under the different instructional conditions and evaluates the effectiveness of each technique. For example, Jason, a third-grade reader, was identified as having an oral reading fluency problem. In working with the child, the diagnostic teacher first formulated her hypotheses. From the data collected, the teacher designed a program of repeated readings (see "Repeated Readings" in Chapter 9), including a discussion of the errors after the first reading. She selected a text and conducted a reading-at-sight evaluation to establish baseline data. For the second section of the passage, she instructed Jason using a repeated readings format and discussed his errors with him. On the last section of the selected text, she conducted another reading at sight but without assistance. Jason decreased his error rate from 1/10 on the first section to 1/15 on the last section.

Since this technique resulted in only minimal change in reading performance, the diagnostic teacher designed another lesson. She decided to use the talking books technique (see "Talking Books" in Chapter 9) during the instructional phase of the diagnostic lesson. She followed the same procedure: first establishing baseline data through unaided reading at sight, next instruction, and finally establishing postinstructional data through more unaided reading at sight. This time Jason decreased his error rate from 1/10 on the first section to 1/50 on the last section.

The diagnostic teacher compared the resulting changes from the two sets of readings to decide which technique was most effective. The talking books technique produced the most change; moreover, it required less teacher investment since the tape recording provided the words that would have needed the teacher's prompting under the repeated readings approach. As a result, the teacher used taped stories in the diagnostic teaching program. Whenever the diagnostic teacher can conduct a series of diagnostic lessons to compare the effectiveness of several techniques, she increases her ability to confirm the diagnostic hypotheses and select the best possible instructional approach for the reader.

The Beginning Reader. The beginning reader requires a modification in the procedures of the diagnostic lesson since he cannot read enough text for a standard initial assessment. Consequently, the diagnostic teacher begins by teaching a lesson and *then* conducting an oral reading analysis of the student's reading. If the technique was effective, the passage should be read at the independent level even after a delayed period of time. These procedures are similar to the learning-methods tests developed by Mills (1956) and Ray (1970). After the lessons, the diagnostic teacher compares reading growth under several different techniques as recommended above.

A diagnostic teacher was working with Neil, a second grader who was a nonreader (he knew only five words by sight). The diagnostic teacher began her diagnostic assessment with a language experience lesson (see "Language Experience" in Chapter 9). She created an experience, Neil dictated a story, and they read the story together numerous times. The story was chunked onto cards and the cards flashed in story order. Then Neil read the story on his own and performed at the independent level (error rate 1/50). Later during the day, he read the story with an error rate of 1/10. This technique could be used for Neil in future instruction, but it required a high degree of teacher investment to achieve the recorded growth, and he seemed to memorize the story without looking at the words. Neil could, however, correct many of his mistakes when the teacher repeated the preceding part of the sentence (moderate teacher investment). Therefore, the teacher wanted to explore another approach.

For this diagnostic lesson, the teacher used the predictable language approach (see "Predictable Language Approach" in Chapter 9). Neil and the teacher were supposed to read the story simultaneously; however, he did not look at the text. Neil did, however, begin to read the text as the teacher omitted words in the language pattern. As she omitted more words, Neil paid more attention to the words on the page and reread the text with an error rate of 1/50. He also corrected many of his miscues by rereading sentences on his own. Later in the day, Neil still read the story with only 1 error every 50 words. The diagnostic teacher concluded that this technique was more effective than the language experience lesson because he was able to use the language pattern to self-correct his errors.

To see if there was a technique that required less teacher time but had similar results, the teacher conducted another diagnostic lesson. This time she used the talking books technique (see "Talking Books" in Chapter 9). Neil listened to a short story on a tape recorder until he had the story memorized. Then he read the story to the teacher, producing an error rate of 1/15 and losing his place many times. Listening to the book repeated, Neil had memorized the words but not associated them with the printed words. Later that day, he read the book with an error rate of 1/10. In this case, the diagnostic teacher continued using the predictable language technique and placed Neil in a small group where he was still able to maintain a high rate of success.

Using a series of modified diagnostic teaching lessons, the diagnostic teacher selects the most appropriate technique to teach the beginning reader. These lessons use two readings of the text—one immediately after instruction and another after several hours' delay—to establish a learning rate for that particular instructional technique. For the beginning reader, the diagnostic teacher pays special attention to the teacher investment and task modification needed to ensure fluent reading.

Using More Than One Technique at the Same Time. Sometimes the diagnostic teacher needs to combine several techniques to produce the desired change. In these cases, the combined techniques are more effective than using either one of them alone. The decision-making process that results in combining techniques is illustrated in the case of Charles, a fourth-grade reader with a comprehension problem. Initially, the diagnostic teacher designed a program using self-directed questioning (see "Self-Questioning" in Chapter 9). She selected a story, divided it into three sections, and conducted a think-aloud assessment that was unaided. She recorded her data. Next, she instructed the lesson using self-directed questioning. She modeled the process using the concepts missed during the first section. Charles had a great deal of difficulty remembering the steps in self-directed questioning, even after the diagnostic teacher had written them down (task modification). Charles was never able to do the task independently (high degree of teacher investment). The final section of the story was read like the first, as an unaided think-aloud assessment. There was only minimal change (from 55% to 65% improvement in comprehension).

The diagnostic teacher decided to try the reciprocal teaching technique (see "Reciprocal Teaching" in Chapter 9), which is similar to self-directed questioning but is more structured. She again conducted an unaided think-aloud assessment on the first section of the selected text. Next she instructed the lesson using reciprocal teaching, returning to concepts missed during the first section of the text to model the process and to clear up misconceptions about the story. Charles was to follow her model and summarize, ask a good question, clarify difficult parts, and predict what the next segment would say. However, he had a great deal of difficulty learning this task, so the teacher used a high degree of modeling on each segment. Charles was not able to do the task independently. The final section of the story was read like the first, as an unaided think-aloud assessment. When this technique resulted in only minimal change in reading performance (from 55% to 75% improvement in comprehension) despite a high degree of teacher modeling, the diagnostic teacher decided to add another technique to her procedure.

The teacher selected another story and followed the same procedure: having the student read at sight to establish baseline data, instruction, and having the student read at sight again to establish postinstructional data. During the instructional phase of the diagnostic lesson, the diagnostic teacher introduced a story map (see "Story Map" in Chapter 9) along with reciprocal teaching. First, she modeled the combined sequence: add new information to the story map, summarize using the story map, use the story map to ask a good question, clarify any difficult parts that do not fit on the map, and finally, use the components of the story map to predict what will happen next.

Following instruction in this combined approach, Charles began to take over the teaching. He began to teach the lesson independently. For him, using the story map was more concrete than either self-directed questioning or reciprocal teaching alone. During the final third of the lesson, the diagnostic teacher conducted a think-aloud assessment, which revealed a change in his monitoring of understanding. Charles had begun to revise his predictions as he encountered new information. This resulted in a growth from 55% to 90% in reading comprehension. As in this case, the diagnostic teacher may combine reading techniques to evaluate if the new combination results in greater reading growth. If it does, she uses the combined, or piggy-back, approach rather than either technique alone.

SUMMARY

The job of the diagnostic teacher is to identify appropriate techniques for instruction. By teaching a lesson using selected materials and techniques, the diagnostic teacher assesses the student's learning as she teaches and reading growth due to her instruction. She also measures the task modification and teacher investment needed to ensure this growth. Then she establishes the most appropriate instructional conditions for the student. Once these conditions are in place, the diagnostic teacher introduces more difficult tasks or texts and observes the student as he learns the task or reads the text. The diagnostic teacher becomes a teacher and an evaluator. Her purpose during the diagnostic lesson is to record changes in reading behaviors and the instructional adjustments that produced them. She focuses on teaching rather than testing to reveal those instructional adjustments that produce optimal reading growth for a particular student.

Selecting Techniques

Knowing *how* instruction occurs allows the teacher to modify his teaching effectively during the reading event. To mediate learning, he thinks about the techniques he uses and their influence on learning. A thorough analysis of each technique is necessary to provide the most efficient reading instruction. Therefore, this chapter classifies each teaching technique in the following ways:

1. the point at which the technique is implemented during the lesson
2. the type of text
3. the mode of response
4. the targeted reasoning strategy
5. the targeted reading skill
6. the information source
7. the type of structure embodied in implementing the technique
8. the cognitive process emphasized during implementation

This classification serves two functions: (a) to select techniques that fit the readers' patterns and (b) to focus instructional modifications during the reading event.

Initially, the diagnostic teacher selects a technique and analyzes its underlying characteristics. This analysis increases his effectiveness in implementing a particular technique as well as broadens his knowledge of instructional alternatives. According to Brophy, "most teachers seem to be reluctant to change their routines even if they are not working well, and when they do make changes, they tend to be minor adjustments rather than major revisions. This may occur mostly because teachers simply lack readily available alternatives, at least alternatives that they perceive to be preferable to the original plan" (1984, p. 83). Another reason teachers resist change is due to a lack of knowledge about why one technique may be more effective in certain situations. Chapters 8 and 9 provide reasons why one technique might be more effective under certain conditions than another. Knowledge about techniques allows teachers to make instructional changes that facilitate student learning and is a key factor in the decision-making cycle (see Figure 8–1) when formulating hypotheses or teaching a diagnostic lesson.

Knowledge of the techniques is important when considering an approach to instruction that mediates learning.

In this book, the instructional techniques can be used either as a part of the guided reading lesson to support authentic reading activities or as a specific strategy or skill lesson to improve weaknesses. The orchestration of the techniques depends on the strengths and needs of a particular reader. Thus, the classification of the

Figure 8–1
The Decision-
Making Cycle of
Diagnostic
Teaching

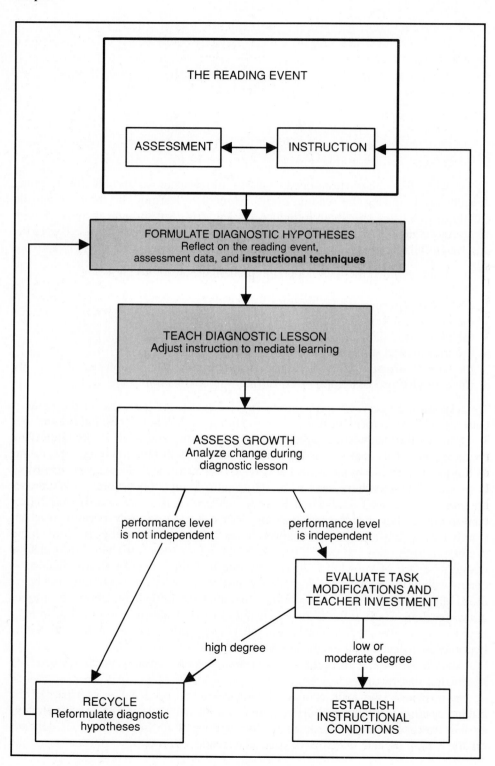

diagnostic teaching techniques is divided into three major categories. In the first, the techniques are classified according to their implementation within the instructional framework and fit appropriately during guided contextual reading (see Chapter 4). To select appropriate techniques for this part of the diagnostic teaching session, the teacher asks himself the following questions:

Do I want to focus on print or meaning processing to advance the understanding of the entire passage?

At what point during the guided reading lesson will the student need support in order to construct the entire message?

What techniques will best suit the type of text I am using?

Can using more writing or discussion during the lesson build on the strengths of the learner?

The second major category deals with the selection of techniques to encourage the students' use of weaker processing areas and fit appropriately during the element of strategy and skill instruction (see Chapter 4) of the diagnostic teaching session. Here the diagnostic teacher selects techniques that remediate weaknesses by showing the students how to use their strengths and weaknesses in combination. To select appropriate techniques for this part of the diagnostic teaching session, the teacher asks himself the following questions:

Is there a strategy that my students are not using? If so how should I approach instruction so that they can use the new strategy in combination with the strategies they already use?

Is there a skill that my students are not using when they read? If so, how should I mediate learning so that they incorporate this skill using their strengths?

The third major category deals with the specificity of selection. In either of the first two categories, the diagnostic teacher may need to identify specific strengths to utilize during instruction. For instance, a reader might need a great deal of teacher direction. In this case, the diagnostic teacher uses Table 8–7 on explicit instruction and narrows his previous options using this characteristic. To narrow his selection of techniques, the teacher asks himself the following questions:

If my students are overrelying on an information source, can I match this reliance with an instructional technique and show them how to integrate information sources?

How much explicit instruction do the students need?

If my students are compensating for deficits by using a strength in cognitive processing, can I match this strength in order to show them how to use their weaker processing style in combination with their strength?

Diagnostic teaching techniques from different views of reading have been classified according to these key questions so that the diagnostic teacher can match the students' strengths and needs to design lessons that mediate learning for each child. How a diagnostic teacher selects techniques according to the classifications is described in this chapter including the diagnostic hypotheses for Jenny (see Chapter 6), the third grader who is experiencing difficulty in fluent oral reading.

CLASSIFYING TECHNIQUES FOR GUIDED CONTEXTUAL READING

When considering the instructional framework, the diagnostic teacher selects techniques that support reading an entire story. The diagnostic teacher thinks about the element of guided contextual reading and considers how instruction will occur before, during, and after reading a particular selection so that the student constructs the meaning of the whole story. The teacher's instructional decisions involve deciding when to implement a technique within the reading event. The appropriate placement of instructional techniques facilitates students' learning by providing instruction at the precise point in the instructional framework at which the students can no longer learn independently. In other words, the instructional lesson is a planned exchange between independent student learning and teacher-guided learning. If the teacher intervenes at appropriate instructional points, he can move the students to more complex reading strategies. Therefore, the diagnostic teacher analyzes which phase of reading instruction is best to mediate these students' learning.

The diagnostic teacher first identifies the focus of instruction for the students. To read fluently with comprehension, some students need to focus on print processing because once they can read the words, they will comprehend. Other students call words fluently but need to focus on how to derive meaning from these words once they are recognized. Techniques can be classified, therefore, according to whether the instructional focus is on print processing or meaning processing. These techniques are then further classified by (a) instructional framework, (b) type of text, and (c) mode of response.

Classifying Techniques by Instructional Framework

The diagnostic teacher then analyzes the instructional framework. There are several critical points in the lesson framework for decision making during the instructional focus of guided contextual reading. To increase story understanding, techniques can supplement instruction either before, during, or after reading the text (McNeil, 1987). Sometimes it is most appropriate to provide instruction prior to reading so the students can read the text fluently. For example, students might need instruction in word meanings or word identification as related to the story. Before reading, some students will need assistance to think about how what they already know will help them interpret text.

Another critical point in the instructional framework is during the reading of the text. During this part of the lesson, the teacher needs to encourage inferencing, elaboration, and monitoring of text comprehension. In these instances, he intervenes during reading to build reading strategies such as self-questioning, summarization, visualizing difficult parts, and organizing the information.

The final critical point in the instructional framework is after the reading of the text. To mediate learning here, the diagnostic teacher provides instruction in integrating the text with personal experiences, and organizing the information. He may also need to reinforce word recognition strategies or develop fluency. In any case, using appropriate diagnostic teaching techniques at the critical points in the instructional framework increases student learning.

Classifying Techniques by Type of Text

The selection of appropriate techniques also depends on the type of text (narrative or expository) that is going to be read (McNeil, 1987). Techniques are often developed for a specific kind of text format. For example, story maps (see "Story Maps" in Chapter 9) are designed for narrative text and teach elements of story grammar, while reciprocal teaching (see "Reciprocal Teaching" in Chapter 9) is designed for expository text and teaches summarizing through the use of topic sentences. Techniques are most effective when used with the appropriate kind of text. The classification of techniques in Tables 8–1 and 8–2 is based on three instructional decisions: the type of text (expository or narrative), the presenting problem (meaning or print processing), and the phase of instruction where guided instruction is most appropriate (before, during, or after the lesson). The teacher thinks about the

Table 8–1
Classifying Techniques by Instructional Framework

Meaning Processing	
Narrative	*Expository*
Before	
Direct Experience	Contextual Processing
Experience-Text-Relationships	Direct Experience
Guided Imagery/Comprehension	Experience-Text-Relationships
Motor Imaging	Feature Analysis Grid
Vocabulary Maps	Graphic Organizers
	Guided Imagery/Comprehension
	K-W-L
	Motor Imaging
	Thematic Experience Approach
	Visualization
	Vocabulary Maps
During	
Directed Reading-Thinking Activity	Herringbone Technique
Prediction Maps	Reciprocal Teaching
Reading Logs	ReQuest
ReQuest	SQ3R
Say Something	Triple Read Outline
Self-Directed Questioning	
Story Drama	
Story Maps	
After	
Directed Reading-Thinking Activity	Cloze Instruction
Experience-Text-Relationships	Experience-Text-Relationships
Literature Circles	Feature Analysis Grid
Retelling	Question-Answer Relationships
Story Drama	K-W-L
Story Maps	Metaphors
	Opinion-Proof
	Question-Generation Strategy
	Summarization
	Thematic Experience Approach
	Vocabulary Maps

Note: Only the techniques that teach meaning processing are classified. The lesson frameworks of strategy instruction, explicit teaching, implicit teaching, dialogue journals, and sustained silent reading are not classified.

INST. EMPha.

Table 8–2
Classifying
Techniques by
Instructional
Framework

		Print Processing	
	Narrative		**Expository**
Before	Directed Reading Activity		Contextual Processing
	Language Experience		Language Experience
	Linguistic Method		Secondary Reading Sequence
	Secondary Reading Sequence		Vocabulary Maps
	Sight Word Approach		
	Synthetic Phonics		
	Talking Books		
During	Echo Reading		Secondary Reading Sequence
	Language Experience		
	Predictable Language		
	Talking Books		
After	Analytic Phonics		Cloze Instruction
	Chunking		Multisensory Approach
	Directed Reading Activity		Repeated Readings
	Message Writing		Word Cards
	Multisensory Approach		
	Readers Theatre		
	Repeated Readings		
	Word Cards		

Note: Only the techniques that teach print processing are classified. The lesson frameworks of strategy instruction, explicit teaching, implicit teaching, dialogue journals, and sustained silent reading are not classified.

framework of the diagnostic teaching session. He must decide how to orchestrate instruction during guided contextual reading. Therefore, he evaluates the underlying strengths and needs of the student and predicts at which points during the guided reading lesson she will profit most from mediated instruction. Augmenting instruction at critical points during the lesson enhances text interpretation. He returns to his analysis of the extended passage to look at monitoring and summarization strategies and to his evaluation of the data from the informal reading inventory. Using his interpretation, he refers to Tables 8–1 and 8–2 to select an appropriate technique for instructional intervention during the lesson.

Within the guided reading lesson, which process (print or meaning processing) do I need to highlight?
What type of text (narrative or expository) am I using?
At what point during the guided teaching lesson (before, during or after) will the student need support?

Diagnostic Hypothesis.   During guided contextual reading, Jenny needs assistance in recognizing new vocabulary words prior to the instruction of the story. However, she does not need instruction during the story because she monitors comprehension. After instruction, the diagnostic teacher needs only to reinforce word recognition. The student also shows a preference for reading expository text.

Classifying Techniques by Mode of Response

An additional decision about the instructional framework is the kind of response mode that will be used. Readers' responses can be either oral or written. The diagnostic teacher assesses students individually by asking himself, "Will discussing or writing help this student's reading performance? Which mode is this student's strength? Both a verbal discussion and writing a response change the task. Some students prefer to write about what they read while others prefer to discuss what they read. Both processes are constructive and facilitate reading growth.

Writing and Reading.   Much attention has recently been devoted to the writing process as an aid to improving reading. Writing about what they read facilitates reading by giving students a written record of their thoughts so that they can later reflect and elaborate on how they constructed meaning. The record offers the diagnostic teacher a tool for discussing how the students think. He can talk about the strategies they are using to construct meaning. As writing brings inner thoughts into the open for verification, it facilitates discussing the inner thoughts that happen as readers construct meaning.

Writing also facilitates reading because the instructional focus is on the process of constructing meaning. Reading and writing require similar processes: both readers and writers make plans about how they are going to construct meaning; both monitor their understandings to see if they are making sense; both revise their thinking by rereading, using what was written and comparing it to what they know; both elaborate what was written, making connections between what was written and what is known to create new ideas (Tierney & Pearson, 1983). In these ways, both reading and writing are constructive processes where one facilitates the other.

In addition, writing facilitates reading because both systems use the same writing conventions. Both use letters grouped together to form words, words grouped together to form sentences, and so on. The way the groups are formed follows certain patterns or conventions. Writing heightens students' awareness of how to use these conventions when they read (Duffy & Roehler, 1986). For instance, a young writer trying to spell *mother* thinks about how that word looked in the book *Are You My Mother?* Writing heightens an awareness of the visual features of words. It accomplishes the same task as flashing word cards. Writing facilitates reading through three avenues: reflective thinking, constructing meaning, and using writing conventions.

Discussion and Reading.   Much recent attention has also been focused on classroom interactions that facilitate learning. Discussing what students read does facilitate reading growth. When they verbalize their understanding of what they read, students reconstruct the text so that they can communicate their understanding to others. This is a constructive process, not simply a recall process. Readers think to themselves: "What is important and how do I communicate that to the others in the group? What did I learn that I want to communicate to this group? Did I think of something in a new light that would help others understand?"

Social interaction facilitates reading, therefore, because it provides a vehicle for interpersonal communication. The strategies, plans, and processes of meaning construction developed through social interaction later become individual mental processes (Vygotsky, 1978). In other words, thinking about what is read is facilitated by social activities that encourage students to elaborate and explain their thinking. In this social situation, the teacher also explains and elaborates his thinking. This allows the student to use tools for thinking (words, plans, strategies, ideas, etc.). The teacher responds, encouraging a refinement of thinking (use of tools) and showing students how he constructs his answer.

This interaction facilitates students' growth. As they discuss their thoughts and support their ideas by explaining how they construct their answers, the new ideas and strategies that they use become part of their internal thought processes. During discussion, the teacher facilitates reading by discussing interpretations, asking students to justify their interpretations, and sharing his own thought process. As a result, verbal discussion facilitates reading through three avenues: meaning construction, verbalizing plans and strategies for meaning construction, and making social thinking an internal process.

Conclusions About Mode of Response.   The diagnostic teacher thinks about the kind of responses that the student makes. He asks, "Will this student profit from discussing or writing about what she reads?" He realizes that both processes facilitate meaning construction. Writing provides a written record of thoughts so that the student can reflect on how she constructs meaning, while verbal discussion allows the reader to revise her ideas on the spot. The diagnostic teacher selects a technique that matches the learner's strengths and needs. He thinks about the mode of response that the techniques demand and refers to Table 8–3 to select one that will assist the reader.

Which mode of response (discussion or writing) will better assist this reader in analyzing her reading?

Diagnostic Hypothesis: For Jenny, whose language comprehension is elaborate and verbal abilities are strong, verbal discussion is most appropriate. During guided contextual reading, the diagnostic teacher allows ample time to discuss the stories that are read, thus using her strength. Furthermore, for skill and strategy instruction, the diagnostic teacher selects a technique that uses discussing fluency as well as practicing it.

CLASSIFYING TECHNIQUES FOR STRATEGY AND SKILL INSTRUCTION

The second major category is designed to help select techniques that remediate specific strategy and skill weaknesses. Although techniques can be used either during guided contextual reading or strategy and skill instruction, it is the purpose and focus of instruction that is different (see Chapter 4). During guided contextual reading, the focus is on reading entire stories and understanding the content. The techniques were

Response Mode (handwritten annotation)

Inst. Phase (handwritten annotation)

Table 8–3
Classifying Techniques by Mode of Response

Meaning Processing		
	Discussion	**Written Response**
Before	Contextual Processing	Feature Analysis Grid
	Direct Experience	Guided Imagery/Comprehension
	Experience-Text-Relationships	K-W-L
	Listening-Thinking Activity	Vocabulary Maps
	Metaphors	
	Visualization	
	Vocabulary Maps	
During	Directed Reading-Thinking Activity	Herringbone Technique
	Reciprocal Teaching	Prediction Maps
	ReQuest	Reading Logs
	Say Something	Story Maps
	Self-Directed Questioning	Triple Read Outline
	Story Drama	
After	Experience-Text-Relationships	K-W-L
	Literature Circles	Opinion Proof
	Question-Answer Relationships	Question-Generation Strategy
	Readers Theatre	Reading Logs
	Retelling	Story Maps
	Story Drama	Story Writing
		Summarization
		Thematic Experience Approach

selected to enhance story or passage understanding. However, during Strategy and Skill Instruction, the diagnostic teacher creates activities that remediate weaknesses. Because no one likes to focus on his weaknesses, these lessons are short and use engaging passages. The mini-lessons in this part of the diagnostic teaching session, focus on strategy deployment during reading. Rather than mastery of weaknesses, the diagnostic teacher encourages the use of unfamiliar strategies and skills showing the students how to use their strengths in combination with their weaknesses. With each lesson, he strives to promote student assessment of skill development or strategy use. The goal of the assessment is to discuss the student's development of effective reading behaviors.

During strategy and skill instruction, the diagnostic teacher identifies students' strategy and skill needs and provides mediated instruction showing students how a particular skill fits into their repertoire of reading strategies. When selecting skill activities, the teacher must also remember that students might not use a particular skill or strategy due to a deficit. Instruction that begins with students' strengths is often more effective (see Wilson & Cleland, 1985, for an elaboration of skill strengths and weaknesses).

For example, Student A uses background knowledge to identify unknown words; however, this is not always an effective strategy. She has a limited ability to manipulate the sounds of language (i.e., she cannot segment sounds and then synthesize them to form words). In this case the diagnostic teacher develops a large sight vocabulary using the impress method (see "Impress Method" in Chapter 9). This allows the student to bypass word analysis and use background knowledge and sentence comprehension to identify unknown words.

Although use of phonic knowledge would increase this student's reading performance, instruction in word analysis is futile without the ability to synthesize or segment sounds. As the student's reading fluency increases, the diagnostic teacher encourages decoding by analogy using this prompt: "What would make sense (strength) and sounds like another word you know (weakness)?" This latter instructional task is accomplished easily using repeated readings (see "Repeated Readings" in Chapter 9) with an intervention of strategy instruction.

In the preceding example, the diagnostic teacher used the strength of the problem reader to develop a successful reading program. Then he showed the student how to use her weaker skill area at times when using only her strength would not solve the reading problem. It is often necessary to try a variety of instructional techniques for these problem readers. For example, Student B is having difficulty with sight word identification. She is a bilingual student and has limited language development with no skill in sound synthesis. Typical techniques to develop sight word identification (word cards, language experience, etc.) prove futile until the new words are tied to a conceptual base. In this case, vocabulary maps (see "Vocabulary Maps" in Chapter 9) are used to tie background knowledge to the sight words so that the student can associate what the words mean with what the words look like.

The following sections elaborate the reasoning strategies and reading skills used during reading. The techniques in Tables 8–5 and 8–6 have been identified according to the targeted reading task developed when the technique is implemented in a diagnostic program.

Classifying Techniques by Reasoning Strategies

Readers strategically reason about what they are reading, applying skills when necessary. As students read, they select, sort, and evaluate the text against what they know. In essence, readers are involved in an active problem-solving process. They predict what is going to be communicated. Then they select and sort important information from the text and relate it to their prior knowledge. Next they confirm or revise their predictions based on new textual information. Finally, they elaborate their understanding. This reasoning process takes place automatically until readers cannot make sense of what they are reading.

Although children with reading problems exhibit individual variations in the strategies they employ, a body of research indicates that poor readers are not actively involved in constructing meaning (Paris & Myers, 1981; Paris & Oka, 1989). They view good reading as effortless; consequently, they do not make plans or vary their strategies as they read. Effective readers, however, are active. Before reading, "good readers use what they know about the topic, the type of text, the author's purposes and their own purposes to make predictions about the content of the text" (Duffy & Roehler, 1987, p. 416).

Predicting requires guessing about what the author is going to say. It occurs before and during reading.

As they read, effective readers remain tentative and revise their predictions frequently using a variety of reasons for their revisions. They intertwine the sources of information for revision (the text, background knowledge, or both) and the strategies for revisions (ignore the problem and read more, reread to check the facts, read ahead to clarify information, and consult an expert source if necessary) (Collins & Smith, 1980). Effective readers stop, reflect, and flexibly shift between reader-based processing ("Does that make sense?") and text-based processing ("What did the text say?"). This is called *monitoring reading.*

Monitoring requires checking the text or one's experience to see if what one is reading is making sense. Monitoring occurs during reading.

Finally, effective readers fit new information into what they know by elaborating relationships among information. They generate new thoughts by relating what they are reading to what they know, creating new connections among ideas (McNeil, 1987).

Elaborating requires relating new information to what is known in order to remember it. Thus the new information becomes part of what is known. Elaborating occurs during and after reading.

Problem readers, however, are less active. Their reading can break down in the predicting, monitoring, or elaborating phase of the reasoning process. Some readers do not use what they know to think about what the author might say. They read exactly what the text says without thinking about what it might mean. They need instruction that helps them make predictions about what the text would mean. Other readers venture a guess but hold on to the initial prediction even when the text does not support it. Other readers revise their predictions but change only one part of it, such as the *who, when, where,* or *how* information (Dybdahl, 1983). Some readers rely too heavily on the text or their background knowledge when monitoring their reading. They do not shift between knowledge sources to check their reading. These students need instruction in how to monitor their understanding of text. Other students fail to elaborate the relationship between what they know and the text; therefore, they cannot remember what they read. These readers need instruction in how to reason while they are reading.

Demonstrating reasoning strategies can improve the reading performance of poor readers (Duffy & Roehler, 1987; Palincsar & Brown, 1989). However, the diagnostic teacher needs to evaluate the various instructional techniques. Some techniques lend themselves readily to talking about the different strategies of effective reading; others do not. Therefore, diagnostic techniques have been classified here according to the reading strategy that they develop: predicting, monitoring, or elaborating. In addition, techniques can teach the reasoning process related to print processing or meaning processing. Table 8–4 classifies techniques for reasoning while processing print and meaning.

Table 8–4
Classifying Techniques by Reasoning Strategy

	Print Processing	Meaning Processing
Prediction	Echo Reading	Cloze Instruction
	Impress Method	Directed Reading-Thinking Activity
	Language Experience	Graphic Organizers
	Listening-Thinking Activity	Experience-Text-Relationship
	Message Writing	Guided Imagery/Comprehension
	Predictable Language	K-W-L
	Secondary Reading Sequence	Listening-Thinking Activity
	Talking Books	Motor Imaging
		ReQuest
		Self-Directed Questioning
		SQ3R
		Thematic Experience Approach
		Vocabulary Maps
Monitoring	Chunking	Directed Reading-Thinking Activity
	Guided Imagery/LEA	Herringbone
	Language Experience	Prediction Maps
	Predictable Language	Reading Logs
	Readers Theatre	Reciprocal Teaching
	Repeated Readings	Self-Directed Questioning
		Story Maps
		Triple Read Outline
		Visualization
Elaboration	Readers Theatre	Experience-Text-Relationship
	Repeated Readings	Herringbone Technique
	Secondary Reading Sequence	K-W-L
	Word Cards	Literature Circles
		Opinion-Proof
		Prediction Maps
		Question-Answer Relationships
		Question-Generation Strategy
		Reading Logs
		Reciprocal Teaching
		Retelling
		Story Drama
		Story Maps
		Summarization
		Thematic Experience Approach
		Triple Read Outline
		Vocabulary Maps

Note: The techniques listed are the most effective; however, other techniques can be used. See individual techniques in Chapter 9.

The diagnostic teacher then looks for a strategy that, if learned, will increase this student's reading. He reflects on the strategies that the effective reader uses and evaluates their influence on this reader's performance. He returns to the data he has collected and looks at the hypotheses he formed when he analyzed the reading event. He considers whether the context or the text is affecting the strategies employed by this reader. If a strategy needs to be taught, the diagnostic teacher uses Table 8–4, "Classifying Techniques by Reasoning Strategy," to identify techniques that facilitate learning the strategy. Again, he remains tentative in his selection until he completes all the diagnostic questions.

Is there a strategy (predict, monitor, or elaborate) that, if learned, will increase this student's reading?

Diagnostic Hypothesis: For Jenny, the diagnostic teacher decides that she needs instruction in monitoring print processing in order to check both what makes sense and what the word looks like. This strategy facilitates combining cueing systems when reading breaks down.

Classifying Techniques by Reading Skills

Although meaningful interpretation of the text is the ultimate goal of reading instruction, certain tasks consume a major portion of children's thinking capacity as they develop. The following explanation will provide a discussion first of the process of learning related to the targeted skills and then of the major skills involved at a given stage. Even though these skills have been associated with typical techniques, there are a variety of ways to develop each skill from various points of view. The diagnostic teacher selects the technique that mediates learning best for the particular child.

Stage One.   For beginning readers, the major task is the association of oral language with its written equivalent. Young children have learned to communicate using oral language within a social context. To read, however, they must infer the communicative intent of printed words. This new task places demands on learners. They must learn that printed words represent both a concept and spoken words. Therefore, the task of young readers is to develop this functional concept of printed language as well as the recognition of letters and sounds.

As these concepts of print develop, children begin to associate meaning with written words in stories. They automatically recognize a group of words at sight. They say, "I know a word that starts with *h* and is the same length, so this word must be *hat*." The development of a sight word vocabulary indicates that children are reasoning about the relationship between graphic symbols and meaning. Whether children use sounds, visual features, or background knowledge, their major task is to develop this automatic sight vocabulary, which generally consumes a major portion of their thinking through the middle of first-grade reading level.

TARGETED SKILLS FOR STAGE ONE

Word Identification

Based on
☐ *Association of prior knowledge with printed words*
☐ *Ability to remember the visual form (visual memory)*
☐ *Ability to use the initial letter and word length to remember words*

Typical techniques
☐ *Language experience method*
☐ *Sight word method*

Stage Two.   As children can read more words and longer stories, the major reading tasks change from oral reading to silent reading and from sight word recognition to decoding by analogy. Since they can read longer stories, they encounter new words that are not contained in their sight vocabularies. Therefore, emerging readers develop new skills and strategies to accommodate these new tasks. They begin to decode new words by sound analogies (i.e., "I know a sight word that looks similar to this new word; I will try substituting the sounds to see if this new word makes sense in the story"). This stage of reading development is marked by the ability to use the alphabetic principle; that words are made of sounds and letters that have a consistent pattern. Therefore, they match these patterns to known sight words.

This new strategy allows young children to read longer stories; silent reading, therefore, becomes more efficient than oral reading. Now in order to talk about what they read, they retell the story or answer questions. Since the simple stories in graded text place a high demand on literal comprehension, children's attention is focused on the logical development of a story line and proving answers using the text.

These skills occupy children's thinking capacity through the end of second grade, where techniques dealing with word attack and literal comprehension are most appropriately employed.

TARGETED SKILLS FOR STAGE TWO

Word Analysis

Based on
☐ *Ability to blend sounds (auditory synthesis)*
☐ *Ability to divide words into their sounds (sound segmentation)*
☐ *Use of sound-symbol word patterns*

Typical techniques
☐ *Analytic phonics*
☐ *Message Writing*

Literal Comprehension

Based on
☐ *Understanding of logical relationships in text (textual organization)*
☐ *How words go together in a sentence*
☐ *Background knowledge*

Typical techniques
☐ *Teacher questioning*
☐ *Retelling*

Stage Three. As reading development continues, the simple strategies of using known sight words, decoding by sound analogy, and thinking about the facts of a story are no longer sufficient to gain meaning from text. Because sentences are longer and more complex, children must use new strategies to interpret text. Developing readers respond with new strategies. At this stage, fluent word identification is necessary in order to allow more thinking capacity for word, sentence, and idea meaning. Because words with multiple meanings are used in the text, students must use more than decoding by analogy to figure out unknown words. Using sentence context to decode unknown words and to develop word meanings becomes a major task for these readers. Furthermore, this more difficult text has an abundance of new word meanings. Readers at this stage must think about what each new word means and how it is like other words and ideas that they already know. This stage occupies students' thinking capacity through the end of the fifth-grade reading level, where techniques developing fluency, sentence comprehension, and vocabulary knowledge are most appropriately employed.

TARGETED SKILLS FOR STAGE THREE

Fluency

Based on
☐ *Automatic association of what words look like with what words mean*
☐ *Breaking sentences into thought units*
☐ *Use of background knowledge to predict sentence meaning*

Typical techniques
☐ *Chunking method*
☐ *Repeated readings*

Sentence Comprehension

Based on
☐ *Use of sentence meaning to develop word meanings*
☐ *Use of context to organize information*
☐ *Familiarity with the content (background knowledge)*

Typical techniques
☐ *Cloze instruction*
☐ *Sentence combining*

Meaning Vocabulary

Based on
☐ *Requisite background knowledge*
☐ *Identification of likenesses and differences of word meanings*

Typical techniques
☐ *Vocabulary maps*
☐ *Contextual processing*

Stage Four.   As students read more difficult text, they find that the strategies that deal primarily with textual information are no longer sufficient. At this reading level, authors develop complex relationships that require an interpretation of text-based information within a reader's personal world view. Therefore, readers must be able to shift between text-based and reader-based processing to gain meaning from text. They read for a variety of purposes and monitor their own understanding of text. This stage of development continues through adult reading, where techniques emphasizing vocabulary knowledge and literal comprehension (described in Stage Three) are orchestrated with developing nonliteral comprehension and study skills.

TARGETED SKILLS FOR STAGE FOUR

Nonliteral Comprehension

Based on
☐ *Integration of background knowledge with textual information*
☐ *Self-monitoring (Does that make sense?)*
☐ *Self-questioning (I wonder what the author is going to say that is important to remember?)*

Typical techniques
☐ *Self-questioning*
☐ *Story drama*

Study Skills

Based on
☐ *Ability to organize information*
☐ *Knowledge of question-answer relationships*
☐ *Use of the structure of text*

Typical techniques
☐ *SQ3R (survey, question, read, recite, review)*
☐ *QAR's (question-answer relationships)*

Thus, the diagnostic teacher looks for a skill that, if learned, will increase this student's reading. He reflects on the major skills of reading and evaluates their influence on this reader's performance. He looks at the level of performance that is at the borderline range and matches it with the targeted skills for that reading level. Then he checks previous instructional experiences to evaluate their influence on the targeted skill. Basically, he asks, "Has this student received instruction in this skill and is still not proficient?" If a skill needs to be taught, the diagnostic teacher uses Table 8–5, "Classifying Techniques by Reading Skills," to identify techniques that facilitate learning that skill.

Are there skills that, if learned, would increase this student's reading?

Diagnostic Hypothesis.   For Jenny, whose borderline range is around the middle of second grade, the teacher decides that instruction in phonics is not appropriate because of her attempts and subsequent failures in using this cueing system. Literal comprehension is well developed and thus not the best choice for instruction now. Only when she read text with just 1/7 words correct did she ever miss a question. Therefore, the teacher decides to work on reading fluency, a skill that is at the third-grade level (i.e., the next higher level).

The instructional techniques in this book have been analyzed as to the major skill developed. Within each major area, the techniques differ in the focus of instruction (reader-based/text-based; implicit/explicit; or simultaneous/successive) but each technique can increase the specific skill mentioned. The diagnostic teacher checks the chart to identify how to remedy skill needs.

Conclusions About Reading Strategies and Skills.   After the diagnostic teacher evaluates the student's reading level and formulates hypotheses about how the student reads, he plans the strategy and skill lessons. Using the data collected, the diagnostic teacher identifies skills, strategies, or both that are inhibiting reading performance. He reviews the skill development and the strategies employed by the reader. Then he selects an appropriate technique that will focus instruction on the targeted concern in order to improve the student's reading performance.

CLASSIFYING TECHNIQUES FOR INCREASED SPECIFICITY

The tables in this section are used in conjunction with the other tables. They increase the specificity of the previous selections. Readers demonstrate strengths and preferences that can be used to enhance active reading. Techniques that focus on critical areas for readers' progress are classified in this section in three ways: (a) by sources of information, (b) by type of structure, and (c) by strengths in cognitive processing.

Basically, reading is an interactive process where readers use various sources of information (reader-based and text-based) at the same time to interpret text.

Table 8–5
Classifying Techniques by Reading Skills

	Word Identification	Word Analysis	Fluency	Meaning Vocabulary	Sentence Comprehension	Literal Comprehension	Nonliteral Comprehension	Study Skills
Alternate Writing					*	*	*	
Analytic Phonics		*						
Chunking			*		*	*		
Cloze Instruction				*	*	*		
Contextual Processing				*	*			
Direct Experience				*			*	
Directed Reading Activity	*			*		*	*	
Directed Reading-Thinking Activity						*	*	
Echo Reading	*		*		*			
Experience-Text-Relationship				*		*	*	
Feature Analysis Grid				*				
Graphic Organizer						*		*
Guided Imagery/Comprehension						*	*	*
Herringbone Technique						*		*
Impress Method	*		*					
K-W-L						*	*	
Language Experience	*		*					
Linguistic Method	*	*						
Listening-Thinking Activity						*	*	
Literature Circles							*	
Message Writing		*						
Metaphors				*			*	*
Motor Imaging				*				
Multisensory Approaches	*	*						
Opinion-Proof						*	*	
Phonogram Approach		*						
Predictable Language	*		*					

Table 8–5
continued

	Word Identification	Word Analysis	Fluency	Meaning Vocabulary	Sentence Comprehension	Literal Comprehension	Nonliteral Comprehension	Study Skills
Prediction Maps						*	*	
Question-Answer Relationships						*	*	*
Question-Generation Strategy						*	*	*
Readers Theatre			*			*	*	
Reading Logs						*	*	
Reciprocal Teaching						*	*	*
Repeated Readings	*	*	*					
ReQuest						*	*	
Retelling						*	*	
Say Something						*	*	
Secondary Reading Sequence	*		*			*		
Self-Directed Questioning						*	*	
Sentence Combining				*	*			
Sight Word Approach	*							
SQ3R						*		*
Story Drama						*	*	
Story Maps						*	*	
Story Writing					*	*	*	
Summarization						*	*	*
Synthetic Phonics		*						
Talking Books	*		*					
Thematic Experience Approach						*		*
Triple Read Outline						*		*
Visualization				*			*	
Vocabulary Maps				*		*	*	
Word Cards	*	*	*					

Note: 1) These classifications represent common uses for the techniques. Techniques can be adapted to accommodate the task demands of related skill areas; thus, word attack technique (synthetic phonics) might be used to establish a sight word vocabulary. 2) The lesson frameworks of strategy instruction, explicit teaching, implicit teaching, dialogue journals, and sustained silent reading are not classified.

However, techniques differ in which information sources are emphasized during instruction. Some techniques emphasize reader-based sources of information, while others stress text-based sources of information. Furthermore, problem readers often experience a deficit in either a skill or strategy that causes them to shift away from one information source. They compensate by using their strength and thus eliminate a need to use their deficient knowledge source (Stanovich, 1980). Therefore, a variety of techniques that remediate major reading problems have been classified, enabling the diagnostic teacher to select techniques that match the students' strengths as he is teaching a new task. As the task is learned, he can select techniques that have a more integrative instructional approach. The diagnostic teacher can thus use learner strengths to show students how to use their weaker information sources when text interpretation breaks down.

Also, the type of structure needed during the diagnostic lesson varies depending on the strengths and preferences of the problem reader. Some students profit from a structured, direct approach to the material while other students prefer to structure their own learning and discover rules.

Finally, readers exhibit strengths in cognitive processing and these strengths can be matched with appropriate techniques.

The following discussion and tables elaborate these areas.

Classifying Techniques by Sources of Information

Students vary the use of information sources as they read depending on the situation and their purposes for reading. Since active-constructive reading depends on combining all available sources of information, readers use reader-based sources (topic knowledge, rhetorical knowledge, phonological knowledge, etc.) and text-based sources (letters, pictures, words, etc.) as needed to meaningfully interpret the text.

Sometimes readers employ reader-based processes to predict what the text will say using their own knowledge. These predictions frame the text-based processing and are subsequently confirmed or revised. The degree to which the reader engages in reader-based processing depends on her purposes for the task of reading. For example, one Saturday a young teen was reading a romance novel during the afternoon. As she read, she embellished the story making inferences from her own life, rapidly predicting what the characters would do next. In this instance, the young teen used a great deal of reader-based information as she read. However, at other times, readers choose to engage in text-based processing where they defer evaluation until they have read enough textual information to form a conclusion (Garcia and Pearson, 1990). This kind of processing occurs when readers encounter unfamiliar information, when their previous predictions have been disproved, when they read new directions, or when text fails to make sense. For example, on the next Saturday afternoon, this same young teenager was taking a college entrance examination. As she read the test directions, she read and reread the printed page, focusing on the information as it was exactly stated in the text. In this case, she used the text predominantly as an information source.

Effective readers perpetually shift between information sources to select, combine, and restructure data from the text and their personal knowledge. However, ineffective readers circumvent using their weaker information sources and, as a result, often depend on a single source related to their strength.

Some readers have a wealth of general and topic knowledge which they use continually to add to their general knowledge. They employ reader-based processes to predict what the text will say using their topic knowledge and paying little attention to the text. This inhibits the development of knowledge sources dealing with the conventions of print. Because these readers overrely on top-down or reader-based processing of the content, they fail to develop knowledge sources dealing with the text (Walker, 1990b). For example, Mandy entered first grade with poor phonemic awareness, as many potentially poor readers do (Juel, 1988). This weakness in a knowledge source inhibited her understanding of the phonetic system which hindered her progress in the basal reader program that was used in the classroom. Therefore, Mandy used her strength of background knowledge to figure out words. When this did not work, she made up the text by looking at the pictures. Thus, Mandy began to overrely on her reader-based strength which inhibited her flexible meaning construction.

Some problem readers overrely on reader-based information making inferences from topic knowledge when a more careful reliance on the text is warranted.

Other problem readers, however, learn phonics easily and believe reading is accurately calling a string of words. When asked comprehension questions, they give answers using the exact words in the text when inferences to topic knowledge are more appropriate. They have come to believe that meaning is found in the text. But as stories become more complex, they find that simply repeating sentences from the text cannot indicate understanding (Walker, 1990b). For example, Gerry rapidly reads words seldom needing to monitor her understanding. This strategy seemed to work well when she read novels where the plot was similar to her own experiences. However, as she began reading more content area texts, she became lost. She could read the words, but she failed to check her understanding and elaborate new word meaning. Gerry continued to passively read words and repeat text-based definitions (her strength) without relating ideas. This inhibited the development of strategic reading.

Some problem readers overrely on text-based information, repeating text segments when inferences from background knowledge are more appropriate.

Instructional decision-making is facilitated by knowing which information sources the problem reader is using and then matching those with particular techniques so that readers demonstrate their strength. After several successful reading experiences, the diagnostic teacher chooses techniques that encourage strategically combining information sources. The techniques in this book have been classified by the source of information that is emphasized during instruction: (a) reader-based and (b) text-based. Some techniques initially ask children to use their prior knowledge while other techniques ask children to use the information in the text.

Reader-based Sources.   When selecting approaches that mediate learning using reader-based information sources, the diagnostic teacher identifies techniques that initially have the students use their background knowledge in relation to the content of the story. In using these techniques, the diagnostic teacher continually asks students to think about what they know in order to create an expectation about what the text may say. For example, when using the Directed Reading Thinking Approach, the teacher asks the students to predict what the story might be about. Then, after reading sections of the story, the teacher asks the students if their predictions were on the right track or if they would like to keep, add to, or change predictions. Thus, throughout the discussion, the teacher focuses on using reader-based inferencing to construct story understanding. Likewise, when using the Language Experience Approach (see Chapter 9), students are asked to tell a story which is recorded. This story constructed from their own words becomes the text and the students are continually asked to refer to what they said (reader-based source) when they cannot figure out a word.

Text-based Sources.   When selecting approaches that mediate learning using text-based information sources, the diagnostic teacher identifies techniques that initially ask students to use text-based information. In using these techniques, the diagnostic teacher focuses on how the information in the text explains and describes major characters, events, and ideas. For example, in the story mapping approach, the diagnostic teacher asks students to identify the setting (characters and place), the problems, the events that lead to the problem resolution, and the resolution, and then write this information on a visual framework (map) for the story. The focus is on putting the text-based information on the story map. Likewise, when using the synthetic phonics approach, students are asked to look closely at words and sound them out letter by letter. The students are continually asked to refer to the text when problems in print processing occur.

Conclusions About Sources of Information.   Effective readers do not operate using either reader-based information or text-based information sources, but rather strategically combine these sources of information. What is necessary for fluent reading is a flexible interplay between these sources. To develop more efficient use of both sources of information, the diagnostic teacher begins by using the reader's strength (reader-based inferencing or text-based inferencing) and gradually intro-duces a merging of both sources of information by using scaffolding statements that prompt the student to combine sources. To expedite the selection of teaching techniques, Table 8–6 analyzes teaching techniques in terms of the major tasks and information sources. The teacher appraises the students' use of information sources and analyzes the requisite task to be taught. He, then, selects a technique and constructs a diagnostic lesson to verify the appropriateness of the technique.

Source of Info.

Table 8–6
Classifying Techniques by Sources of Information

	Reader-based	*Text-based*
Word Identification	Language Experience Listening-Thinking Activity Predictable Language Secondary Reading Sequence	Linguistic Method Multisensory Approach Word Cards Echo Reading* Impress Method* Sight Words
Word Analysis	Language Experience Message Writing Secondary Reading Sequence	Analytic Phonics Linguistic Method Multisensory Approach Synthetic Phonics
Fluency	Chunking* Language Experience Readers Theatre	Cloze Instruction Echo Reading* Impress Method* Repeated Readings
Vocabulary	Direct Experience Metaphors Motor Imaging Visualization Vocabulary Maps Feature Analysis Grid	Contextual Processing Cloze Instruction
Sentence Comprehension	Readers Theatre Story Writing	Contextual Processing Cloze Instruction Sentence Combining
Literal Comprehension	Experience-Text Relationships K-W-L Retelling Say Something Story Writing Visualization Vocabulary Maps	Herringbone Technique Question-Answer Relationships Reciprocal Teaching ReQuest* Summarization Story Maps
Nonliteral Comprehension	Experience-Text Relationships Guided Imagery/Comprehension Literature Circles Opinion-Proof *Prediction Maps Reading Logs Story Drama *Self-Directed Questioning	Question-Answer Relationships Reciprocal Teaching
Study Skills	Guided Imagery/Comprehension *Question-Generation Strategy Thematic Experience Approach	Graphic Organizer Herringbone Technique Question-Answer Relationships Summarization *Triple Read Outline

*These techniques utilize both reader-based and text-based sources of information but focus slightly more on one or the other.

Note: The lesson frameworks of strategy instruction, explicit teaching, implicit teaching, directed reading activity, directed reading-thinking activity, dialogue journals, and sustained silent reading are not classified.

Classifying Techniques by Type of Structure

Instructional decision making also includes an analysis of how mediated instruction will occur. The diagnostic teacher asks how much explicit instruction will be necessary for students to regulate their own learning. Learners differ in how they approach the reading event. Some readers are active, while others are passive.

Active Readers.   Active readers automatically structure new learning situations by identifying key features, developing plausible solutions, and evaluating their effectiveness. These readers select key characteristics by sampling several alternatives and flexibly shifting among sources of information. As they solve these problems, they create their own rules for what they observe. This may be an inherent way to process information (Witkin, Moore, Goodenough, & Cox, 1977), or it may be developed through the social interactions that students experience daily. Often the more active, independent learners have had numerous experiences with school-book language when they communicate ideas. To communicate socially, these students use a wide variety of words to describe events and elaborate descriptions to justify their actions. Through previous social interactions, they become more active and explicit when they solve verbal problems (Finn, 1985).

Passive Readers.   Passive learners, however, learn by watching how other students and the teacher solve the problem. They have difficulty distinguishing between the context of learning (such as teacher praise and peer approval) and the task of learning. They approach problem solving as a spectator and remain passive toward their own process of learning, preferring to follow the teacher's model whenever possible. This passive stance may be an inherent way to process information (Witkin et al., 1977), or it may be a result of the daily social interactions that the students experience (Finn, 1985).

Often, the more passive students have relied on shared understandings during their social interactions. Communication is often limited to information that refers to events or ideas that are known to the listener; therefore, passive learners use less precise words and nonverbal language to communicate meaning. They rely on their listeners to infer meaning based on shared knowledge rather than speaker explanations. When learning demands a more active verbal stance, these students are unfamiliar with the elaborate language that can be used to justify their actions. They remain passive, therefore, preferring to follow the teacher's model to solve problems.

Previous Experiences.   For both active and passive students, previous experience with the task being taught affects the need for explicit instruction. If they have not had prior experiences related to the task, they might need some explicit instruction in the new task. If they have had prior experiences and *failed,* they might profit from explicit instruction that is very different from the initial instructional context (Paris & Oka, 1989).

The diagnostic teacher analyzes the students' need for explicit instruction by evaluating how active they are when solving the reading problem. If the students are active and have positive experiences with the task, the diagnostic teacher chooses a task that focuses on implicit instruction (students read texts rich in language and figure out the underlying consistency as the teacher guides inquiry). However, if students are passive and have few positive experiences with the task, the diagnostic teacher chooses a technique that focuses on explicit instruction (students are directly informed of what they are learning, provided a model, and given directed practice).

Explicit Instruction.   In explicit instruction (see "Explicit Teaching" in Chapter 9), the diagnostic teacher precisely states what is to be learned and models the thinking process that accompanies this new skill or strategy. Students are given reasons why this new skill will help them read better (Garcia & Pearson, 1990). Minilessons are constructed to show them how to use the reading skill or strategy, with the teacher modeling the steps of the task. Guided practice with a high level of teacher feedback is then provided. The feedback explicitly explains when and where students would use the skill or strategy. In the explicit teaching model, however, there is a gradual release of teacher-directed instruction to allow students to direct their own learning. The diagnostic teacher identifies students who initially lack control of their own learning; then he explicitly teaches the new strategy. Finally, he plans for the independent use of the strategy.

Explicit Instruction

Based on
□ *Reasons for learning*
□ *Teacher modeling how it works*
□ *Directed practice*
□ *Gradual release of control*

Typical techniques
□ *Synthetic phonics*
□ *Reciprocal teaching*
□ *Question-answer relationships*

Implicit Instruction.   Implicit instruction (see "Implicit Instruction" in Chapter 9) is characterized by an emphasis on the text, the reading event, and the child as informant. Large quantities of text are read that require students to use the targeted skill or strategy. Students apply the skill to make sense of what is read without consciously understanding the principle. Because the context has been carefully arranged, students can readily decide which mistakes make a difference in understanding. From these choices, they reason about text interpretation. The teacher plays the role of linguistic inquirer, asking students, "How did you know that . . . ?" (Haussler, 1985). This role allows students to generate their own rules for text interpretation.

Implicit Instruction

Based on
□ *Immersion in reading*
□ *Teacher as linguistic inquirer*
□ *Student generation of rules*

Typical techniques
□ *Language experience*
□ *Directed reading-thinking activity*
□ *Reading logs*

Conclusions About Type of Structures.   The diagnostic teacher thinks about the student's reading performance and the information he has collected. He asks, "What kind of mediated instruction, implicit or explicit, will facilitate learning for this student?" In other words, does the student want direction on how to complete the tasks. Does she appear to need direct, explicit information before she attempts a reading task or does she want to control her own learning? The teacher theorizes about the kind of mediated instruction the student needs in order to change her reading behavior. The diagnostic teacher predicts whether implicit (student-discovered strategies) or explicit (teacher-directed learning) instruction will result in a greater change in reading performance. The teacher matches this prediction with an appropriate technique using Table 8–7.

In order to learn this skill or strategy, what kind of mediated instruction (implicit or explicit) will be needed?

Diagnostic Hypothesis.   For Jenny, the decision is clear-cut. She prefers to control the decision making when she reads. During the retelling, for example, she stated, "I'm not saying this in order." She also made the self-evaluation about a statement that it "might not be right," which shows that she has control over her comprehension, although not over word recognition. Consequently, a more implicit technique to develop fluency is selected.

Classifying Techniques by Strengths in Cognitive Processing

Individual differences in problem solving influence how students build their models of meaning as they read. A multitude of theoretical frameworks exist for studying individual differences; however, recent attention has been focused on a model of dichotomous thinking referred to as simultaneous and successive cognitive processing (Das, Kirby, & Jarman, 1979; Luria, 1973). This model refers to *how* students solve problems, recognizing and restructuring information in a problem-solving situation like reading.

As students read, they vary their cognitive processing depending on the nature of the reading task, (i.e., they flexibly shift between simultaneous and successive processing). For example, when constructing a main idea from the text, readers organize important information (successive processing) while drawing relationships among this information (simultaneous processing). When reading requires a step-by-step analysis of text, readers use successive processing and sequentially order the information to solve the problem. Reading tasks such as phonic decoding and sequencing story events require that readers recognize and structure information in

Table 8–7
Classifying Techniques by Type of Structure

	Implicit	*Explicit*
Word Identification	Echo Reading Impress Method Language Experience Listening-Thinking Activity Predictable Language Secondary Reading Sequence Talking Books	Linguistic Method Multisensory Approach Sight Word Approach
Word Analysis	Analytic Phonics Message Writing Repeated Readings	Phonogram Approach Synthetic Phonics
Fluency	Echo Reading Impress Method Language Experience Readers Theatre Secondary Reading Sequence Talking Books	Chunking Repeated Readings (with teacher mediation)
Meaning Vocabulary	Cloze Instruction Direct Experience Motor Imaging Thematic Experience Approach Visualization Vocabulary Maps	Contextual Processing Experience-Text-Relationships Metaphors
Sentence Comprehension	Alternate Writing Cloze Instruction Story Writing	Contextual Processing Sentence Combining
Literal Comprehension	Alternate Writing Listening-Thinking Activity K-W-L Readers Theatre ReQuest Retelling Say Something Story Writing	Herringbone Technique Opinion-Proof Reciprocal Teaching Story Maps Summarization
Nonliteral Comprehension	Guided Imagery/Comprehension Literature Circles Readers Theatre Reading Logs Story Drama Visualization	Experience-Text-Relationships Prediction Maps Self-Directed Questioning
Study Skills	Guided Imagery/Comprehension Question-Generation Strategy SQ3R Thematic Experience Approach	Graphic Organizers Question-Answer Relationships Reciprocal Teaching Summarization Triple Read Outline

Note: 1) The lesson frameworks of strategy instruction, explicit teaching, implicit teaching, directed reading activity, directed reading-thinking activity, dialogue journals, and sustained silent reading are not classified. Of these, explicit teaching and the directed reading activity are explicit techniques. 2) Teacher implementation can change any technique to make it more or less explicit or implicit.

a step-by-step sequence. This problem-solving process is referred to as successive processing.

On the other hand, when reading requires the analysis of several ideas at the same time, readers use simultaneous processing; they relate ideas according to a general category to solve the problem. Reading tasks such as predicting the author's purpose and interpreting character motives draw heavily on organizing many aspects of information around their most important characteristics. This process is referred to as simultaneous processing.

Students can be identified as having strengths in one of these ways of processing information. A *simultaneous* preference refers to the propensity to think about multiple relationships among ideas relating the most important characteristics (Kaufman & Kaufman, 1983). Simultaneous students build their models of meaning using large, inclusive categories of meaning. A noticeable characteristic of these students is their well-developed ability to manipulate visual information. These readers often draw visual diagrams or pictures to organize information. Students with a strength in simultaneous processing look for the coherent patterns of text by tying together the underlying relationships implied by the author. They use a minimal amount of textual information and rely heavily on their background knowledge to interpret text. They often comment, "Oh, yeah, that's like a. . . ." Their language is noticeably less precise and characterized by a tendency to draw images with words rather than use specific definitional language.

At the word identification level, these readers prefer using the semantic cueing system over the grapho-phonic or syntactic cueing system because they have a high need to create meaning from what they read. Their reliance on top-down processing often precludes a careful analysis of the text.

Simultaneous strength means that the student thinks first about the overall meaning and then organizes the parts as they relate to the entire meaning.

A *successive* preference refers to the propensity for developing sequential, logical relationships with words. These students prefer to develop models of meaning by arranging information in a logical, hierarchical sequence (Kaufman & Kaufman, 1983). They develop meaning from precise words that are logically organized to form definitional language. Students with a successive processing strength look for the logical organization of the text to gain meaning. After reading a text, they can recall the sequence of story events but often cannot tie together events to form a main idea. Because they rely heavily on text information to fill in unstated meanings, their models seldom reflect personal application of the text. They organize information according to its function; therefore, their comments are flooded with precise text-based references.

At the word identification level, successive readers prefer using the graphophonic or syntactic cueing system because they rely on the logical relationships among and within words. Their reliance on a bottom-up process often precludes using the overall meaning of the text to decode words, creating a word-bound reader. They forget to think about the overall meaning of the selection and to relate the textual information to their previous experiences.

> *Successive strength means that the student thinks about the parts first and then orders the parts to form the general meaning.*

Instructional decision making is facilitated by knowing which cognitive process is used in the various techniques. The techniques in this book have been classified by their simultaneous or successive framework. Some techniques initially ask children to consider the overall meaning before analyzing the parts. Other techniques ask readers to learn and use the parts before constructing the general meaning.

Simultaneous Framework. When selecting approaches that mediate learning using a simultaneous framework, the diagnostic teacher identifies techniques that focus on the overall meaning of text. In using these techniques, the diagnostic teacher continually redirects attention by asking how things make sense within the entire passage. Specific facts are presented to show relationships to the overall meaning and to one another. These procedures require the synthesis of information characteristic of simultaneous processing. For example, the predictable language approach (see "Predictable Language Approach" in Chapter 9) requires students to move from understanding the whole (memorizing the story) to identifying the parts (single words). Selecting techniques that focus on simultaneous processing, the diagnostic teacher also evaluates whether learning is mediated through a visual array of the relationships, through tactile/kinesthetic experiences, or through visualization. Techniques that have this focus ask students to look at multiple relationships simultaneously.

Simultaneous Framework

Based on
☐ *Multiple relationships among pieces of information*
☐ *Visual display of information*
☐ *Overall generalization*

Typical techniques
☐ *Predictable language*
☐ *Vocabulary maps*
☐ *Guided imagery*

Successive Framework. When selecting approaches that mediate instruction using a successive framework, the diagnostic teacher identifies techniques that focus on discrete parts that form meaning when grouped together. In these techniques, the diagnostic teacher gradually presents the sequential parts of the task, leading students to an overall understanding (see "Story Maps" in Chapter 9). These procedures require that new bits of information are evaluated individually and gradually arranged in a sequence that forms meaning. For example, the instructional emphasis of synthetic phonics (see "Synthetic Phonics" in Chapter 9) moves from knowing the parts (single letter sounds) to sequencing these sounds into words (sound synthesis) and finally to reading the words in stories. Selecting techniques that focus on successive processing, the diagnostic teacher also evaluates whether learning is mediated through auditory/verbal information, functional analysis, or analysis of small amounts of information. Each of these techniques requires a successive processing of individual sections within the text.

Successive Framework

Based on
☐ *Small, discrete parts*
☐ *Step-by-step arrangement*
☐ *Verbalizing function*

Typical techniques
☐ *Synthetic phonics*
☐ *Self-directed questioning*
☐ *Question-answer relationships*

Conclusions About Strengths in Cognitive Processing.   Effective readers do not operate exclusively in either the simultaneous or the successive mode. What is necessary for fluent reading is a flexible interplay between simultaneous and successive processing of text. Efficient readers flexibly shift between a successive analysis of the textual elements and a simultaneous relating of textual and nontextual information to construct a model of meaning. However, inefficient readers often rely too much on their strength in cognitive processing, thus inhibiting fluent reading performance.

To develop a more flexible text processing, the diagnostic teacher begins instruction using readers' strengths in cognitive processing (teach new reading strategies using the strength) and gradually introduces a more integrated processing of text by showing them how to incorporate their weaknesses into their reading repertoires. Thus, the diagnostic teacher initially uses students' strengths in cognitive processing to mediate learning before introducing other strategies.

The sensitive teacher—understanding the problem-solving demands of the tasks of reading, readers' preferences, and the various ways to teach reading—can modify instruction to facilitate students' learning. In other words, if fluency is an identified inhibiting behavior in the initial assessment, a technique that develops fluency would be chosen. Furthermore, if the child's cognitive processing appears to proceed from the overall meaning to the isolated parts (simultaneous understanding), a technique that develops fluency from a simultaneous perspective would be selected. The teacher looks at the data he collected and asks, "Does the reader use top-down (simultaneous) or bottom-up (successive) strategies to regain meaning?" Using Table 8–8, he then selects a technique that matches the student's processing style and will remedy the inhibiting reading behaviors.

What processing sequence (simultaneous or successive emphasis) does the student seem to prefer?

Diagnostic Hypothesis.   Jenny appears to use simultaneous processing. She relates stories to what she already knows and often makes word substitutions that fit the overall meaning of the text. Although she has a successive strength in comprehension (excellent literal comprehension), she does not have these same successive strengths in word recognition. Her miscues often reflect letter and syllable reversals. Continued instruction using these techniques encourages integration of simultaneous and successive processing rather than an overreliance on a single process.

Table 8–8
Classifying Techniques by Sequence of Cognitive Processing (pp. 135–136)

	Simultaneous	*Successive*
Word Identification	Echo Reading Impress Method Language Experience Listening-Thinking Activity Predictable Language Secondary Reading Sequence Sight Words*	Linguistic Method Multisensory Approach Word Cards
Word Analysis	Echo Reading Guided Imagery/LEA Impress Method Language Experience Repeated Readings Secondary Reading Sequence	Analytic Phonics Linguistic Method Message Writing Multisensory Approach Synthetic Phonics
Fluency	Chunking Echo Reading Impress Method Language Experience Readers Theatre Repeated Readings	Cloze Instruction
Vocabulary	Direct Experience Metaphors Motor Imaging Thematic Experience Approach Visualization Vocabulary Maps	Contextual Processing Cloze Instruction Feature Analysis Grid

continued

Table 8–8
continued

	Simultaneous	*Successive*
Sentence Comprehension	Readers Theatre Story Writing	Contextual Processing Cloze Instruction Sentence Combining
Literal Comprehension	Experience-Text-Relationships Question-Generation Strategy Story Maps* Story Writing Visualization Vocabulary Maps	Herringbone Technique Question-Answer Relationships Reciprocal Teaching ReQuest Summarization
Nonliteral Comprehension	Experience-Text-Relationships Guided Imagery/Comprehension K-W-L Literature Circles Opinion-Proof Prediction Maps Reading Logs Story Drama	Question-Answer Relationships Reciprocal Teaching Self-Directed Questioning
Study Skills	Guided Imagery/Comprehension Graphic Organizer Question-Generation Strategy Thematic Experience Approach Triple Read Outline	Herringbone Technique Question-Answer Relationships Summarization

*These techniques are less simultaneous than the others in the list.

Note: 1) The lesson frameworks of strategy instruction, explicit teaching, implicit teaching, directed reading activity, directed reading-thinking activity, dialogue journals, and sustained silent reading are not classified. Of these, explicit teaching and the directed reading activity are more successive than simultaneous. 2) Teacher implementation can change any technique to make it more or less simultaneous.

SUMMARY

Putting the Parts Together for Jenny

Reviewing Jenny's case, the teacher reaches the following conclusions. Jenny needs instruction in fluency (a skill) and self-correction (a strategy). She likes expository text and has a high need for stories to make sense. She also attributes her poor fluency to forces outside her control, thus increasing her negative attribution of reading failure. However, she prefers to control her own learning (implicit instruction) whenever she can. She also has a tendency to prefer material presented with the overall theme first (simultaneous), before learning the details.

When the diagnostic teacher looks at all the hypotheses, he selects a text that contains expository passages of interest to the student (predominately science stories) to use during guided contextual reading. Prior to instruction, he introduces key vocabulary words, which allows Jenny to elaborate her knowledge about the concepts and reinforce it by making her own word cards (implicit instruction). After the lesson, Jenny presents science facts to the class. She is allowed to use the assigned reading or her own research efforts.

To help Jenny attribute her success to effective strategies and to lead her to more flexible strategies when reading errors occur, a program of repeated readings (see "Repeated Readings" in Chapter 9) is used in skill and strategy instruction. After the first reading, an intervention to talk about efficient strategies is used. The teacher models the following self-statement consistent with implicit instruction: "What would make sense and start with a _____?" This procedure allows Jenny to assume increasing responsibility for her own oral reading fluency, while permitting her to use the overall meaning (simultaneous strength) of the selection to correct her miscues, thus respecting her natural preference for using prior experience and context to self-correct. Charting the repeated readings also helps Jenny attribute her increasing fluency to her own efforts and ability, reversing her negative attribution in word recognition.

Reviewing Technique Selection

The teacher's selection of a technique reflects the diagnostic hypotheses about a student's learning at that particular time. Then he selects techniques. To select the most appropriate technique, the diagnostic teacher analyzes each technique according to its instructional features. First, the diagnostic teacher thinks about the instructional framework during guided contextual reading and selects techniques that will lead the student to meaningfully interpret whole stories. He thinks about the students' print and meaning processing skill and how he will advance their overall reading by supporting reading before, during or after instruction. He also thinks about the type of text they are using and selects techniques that are appropriate for that type of text. He thinks about the students' preferences and decides whether more writing or discussing will advance story understanding.

Next, the diagnostic teacher selects techniques to encourage the students to use areas of weakness that are inhibiting the reading process. He thinks about the element of strategy and skill instruction and selects techniques that remediate weaknesses by showing the students how to use their strengths to support their weaknesses.

Finally, the diagnostic teacher refines his selections by checking the selection against the students' strengths and needs so he can utilize these during instruction. He uses the following criteria: source of information, amount of direct instruction, and cognitive processing. He thinks about the sources of information the students rely upon: reader-based or text-based. He matches this with instructional techniques that show them how to integrate information sources while at the same time use their strength. Then he decides on the type of structure that is needed: explicit or implicit. Providing the appropriate type of structure in the learning situation enhances students' reading performance. The diagnostic teacher decides which technique matches the students' strengths in cognitive processing. Some techniques incorporate a successive, serial approach to instruction, while others incorporate a global, simultaneous approach. For hard-to-teach children, instruction using their processing strength facilitates the learning of new information.

Throughout his instruction, the diagnostic teacher makes instructional modifications that increase reading performance. To date, there has been no one instructional sequence or instructional framework that has proven effective for problem readers.

However, teachers vary in their preferences for teaching, and these preferences often dictate how they conduct the diagnostic session. Effective teachers remember that student learning is not accomplished "by a mindless enthusiasm for a given method . . . [but] by understanding the many moving variables in the process of learning to read . . ." (Finn, 1985, p. 150). Therefore, the diagnostic teacher needs to employ a variety of techniques to meet the individual needs of problem readers, identify the key features of these techniques, and evaluate how these features affect reading acquisition.

The Instructional Techniques

CHAPTER

9

In this chapter 60 instructional procedures are presented to help teachers design
programs for problem readers. The instructional procedures, or techniques,
include a variety of instructional formats, approaches, methods, and specialized
remedial techniques. These techniques represent a variety of ways to encourage
proficient reading. Each technique is discussed in two parts: (a) a simple procedural
description followed by (b) an explanation of specific diagnostic applications.

In field use, this chapter may be used in the following manner. First, the
diagnostic teacher consults the general description and its steps. In order to make
instructional modifications, the teacher needs to evaluate how she instructs the lesson.
As she instructs the lesson, therefore, she evaluates at what point she modified
instruction to mediate learning. Consequently, this chapter describes the steps in
implementing each technique, thus facilitating a comparison of how instruction
occurs when using various techniques. The teacher may then wish to turn to the
second part of the discussion, since the knowledge of learner patterns where the
technique produces success will be of assistance when matching an appropriate
instructional technique to the needs of an individual student. As shown in Figure 9–1,
the teacher uses this information to formulate her diagnostic hypotheses. Furthermore, the teacher uses diagnostic lessons to evaluate her hypotheses (see Chapter 7).

THE INFORMATION FOR EACH TECHNIQUE

Initially, the explanation is presented in simple terminology and is constructed to
assist the transition between prescription and implementation. The following topics
are included.

- **Description.** In an effort to simplify communication, a two- or three-sentence
description is presented. This description can be used in report writing or
communicating with parents.
- **Targeted Reading Levels.** Many techniques were developed for use with students at
a particular stage in reading development. This section will facilitate selecting a
technique that matches the reading level of the student.
- **Predominant Focus of Instruction.** This section delineates the critical focus of
each technique. Techniques can be placed on a continuum of various instructional
features that are stressed during implementation. For example, most techniques
have both an oral discussion and a written component, however, one of these will
predominate. It must be remembered that the significance of this emphasis

139

Figure 9–1
The Decision-
Making Cycle of
Diagnostic
Teaching

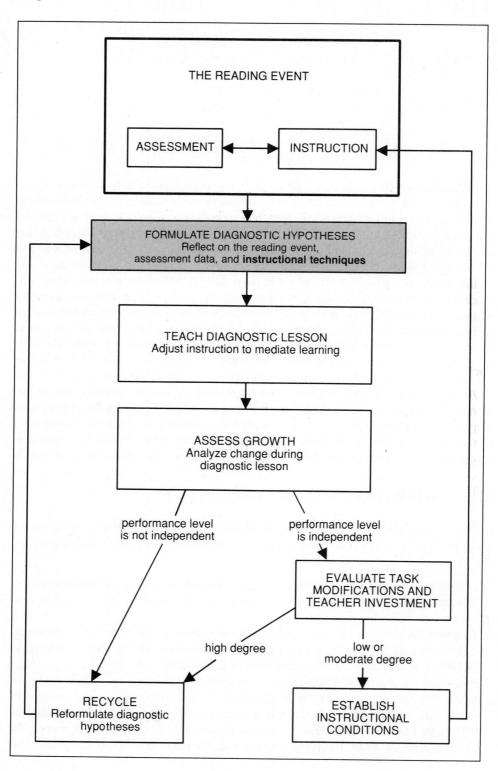

depends on the learner's strategies, his task knowledge, and the situational context. In this section, the predominant focus is delineated according to the charts in Chapter 8. The following list represents the selected areas:

1. Print or Meaning Processing
2. Instructional phase (before, during or after reading) in the lesson.
3. Response mode emphasized (oral or written)
4. Strategy emphasized (prediction, monitoring, or elaboration)
5. Skill emphasized (word identification, word analysis, fluency, sentence comprehension, word meaning, literal comprehension, non-literal comprehension, or study skills)
6. Source of information (text- or reader-based)
7. Type of instruction (explicit or implicit)
8. Type of cognitive processing (successive or simultaneous)

☐ *Procedures.* This section is a sequential enumeration of the process of instruction for each technique. This explanation serves two purposes. First, it facilitates implementation of the technique so experimenting with new methods of instruction is not overwhelming. Second, by delineating the steps of instruction, the diagnostic teacher can analyze in what part of the instruction the student has incorporated the desired reading behaviors. This knowledge facilitates modifying instruction to increase its efficiency.

The next section specifies the diagnostic applications of each technique and includes the following elements.

☐ *Basic View of Reading.* Techniques have developed from various views of learning. As individuals formulate views of how learning occurs in young children, they propose teaching techniques that support their views. Therefore, instructional techniques reflect theories about how children learn. It is an assumption of this chapter that the diagnostic teacher can match how a child is learning with a diagnostic technique that reflects that learning process. The major views are bottom-up, where instruction is focused on text-based processing; top-down, where instruction is focused on reader-based processing; and interactive, where instruction is focused on combining reader-based and text-based processing (see Chapter 1).

☐ *Patterns of Strengths and Strategies.* This section looks specifically at what the student is asked to do when the teacher implements the technique. The underlying strengths and strategies that are necessary to profit from this instructional technique are then presented.

☐ *Learner Patterns That Produce a High Success Rate.* Techniques can be used in different ways to produce success. This section analyzes the technique as it would be integrated into instruction with different learners. How the technique is implemented is matched to the corresponding learner patterns. Learner patterns (see Chapter 8 for further explanation) that are highlighted in this section are the following:

1. *Active readers,* who independently solve reading problems by reorganizing new information around its key features. They predict, monitor, and elaborate what they read, using both the text and what they know.

2. *Passive readers,* who rely heavily on cues from their environment to decide what is important to remember. They prefer to follow a teacher's model when predicting, monitoring, and elaborating what they read. When reading, they use either the text or what they know to solve the reading problem.
3. *Readers who have a simultaneous strength* and think first about the overall meaning, then organize the parts as they relate to the entire meaning.
4. *Readers who have a successive strength* and think about the parts first, then order the parts to form the general meaning.

Described first are the learner patterns that represent how the technique matches a learner strength. For these students, the technique can be used to modify the basic lesson during guided contextual reading or for skill and strategy instruction (see Chapter 4 for further explanation of these features of the diagnostic teaching session). The *starred* items, which appear second, represent how the technique would be used to remediate a weakness during skill and strategy instruction.

☐ ***Using the Technique as a Diagnostic Teaching Lesson.*** This section is a short checklist to focus the evaluation of a student's success when using this technique. If the answers are "yes," the technique facilitates learning for this particular student.

WAYS TO USE THIS CHAPTER

The techniques in this chapter are arranged alphabetically so they can be used as a resource rather than procedures to be memorized. The alphabetical arrangement facilitates locating a technique that was selected in Chapter 8.

These pages have been used by preservice teachers, inservice teachers, and school psychologists in many different ways. Preservice teachers follow the procedures step by step as they learn how to teach in different ways. Then they begin reading why they are doing what they are doing. When students do not succeed with a particular technique, these teachers analyze what they asked them to do by reading the second section. This helps preservice teachers understand how children are different. Inservice teachers use Chapter 8 extensively to choose several techniques. They use each of these techniques to help them decide what the students' strengths are. As they identify what technique works best, they also identify their students' strengths. The school psychologist, on the other hand, uses Chapter 8 to match test data with particular techniques. Then he looks up each technique to verify which might be the most beneficial. He then recommends the procedures to the appropriate teacher.

ALTERNATE WRITING

Description. Alternate writing is the composition of a story among a group of students and a teacher. By writing a specified time, each person alternately continues the development of a cohesive story line. Each person's contribution to the story line must build upon prior information in the composition and must lead to the next event.

Targeted Reading Levels: 4 – 8

Text: Students' and teacher's writing

Predominant Focus of Instruction

1. Processing focus: meaning
2. Instructional phase: during reading
3. Response mode emphasized: written discourse
4. Strategy emphasized: elaboration
5. Skill emphasized: sentence comprehension
6. Source of information: reader-based
7. Type of instruction: implicit
8. Type of cognitive processing: successive

Procedure

1. The teacher selects topics of interest to the students. As the procedure is used, an increasing variety of text types and subject areas needs to be included.
2. Using the story starter or topic selected, the teacher begins writing and continues developing the story line for 2 minutes. In a small group, an overhead can be used.
3. The story is passed to the next student. This student writes for 2 minutes.
4. In order to continue the story, each student must read the previous text and create text that maintains the story theme and moves the story to its conclusion.
5. When the story is completely written, the teacher reads the story as a whole.
6. The teacher revises her own parts of the story for coherence and grammatical clarity. As she is revising, she thinks out loud, "Will this make sense to my reader?"
7. The teacher encourages students to revise their writing for coherence and grammatical clarity.

Modifications

1. A story map can be developed prior to writing so that each student adds information that will fit the story map (see "Story Map" in this chapter).
2. A word processing program can be used, and students can write and revise the story on the computer.
3. Cartoons can be used as a framework for the story line.
4. This technique can be used in pairs, small groups, and tutoring situations.
5. This technique can be easily adapted to a writing center, where students add to the story when they attend that center. Students initial their additions.

Further Diagnostic Applications

Basic View of Reading.   Reading is an interactive process where the reader uses prior knowledge to construct and monitor understanding. Likewise, writing is an active-constructive process that requires reading, interpreting, and monitoring what was written. Through writing, the reader becomes sensitive to how stories are constructed so that they make sense.

Patterns of Strengths and Strategies.   Alternate writing is most appropriate for students who have facility with writing and prefer to communicate through writing rather than discussion. This approach helps students develop a sense of the story line and approach text as a communication between reader and writer.

Learner Patterns That Produce a High Success Rate

1. The successive learner who writes well but does not understand that reading is a communication process. This technique provides a tool for talking about the communicative intent of the author.
2. The simultaneous learner who writes and reads for self-understanding and meaning but does not realize that the text is a contractual agreement between reader and writer. This technique provides a tool for talking about what needs to be in a text in order to make it understandable to a reader.
*3. The nonverbal learner who needs to participate in writing a story to understand story structure. This technique provides an experience in developing writing fluency in a less threatening manner.

Using the Technique as a Diagnostic Teaching Lesson.   For alternate writing to be effective, a majority of the following statements must be answered in the affirmative.

Yes   No

——— ——— 1. The student writes fluently and can construct text that makes sense.
——— ——— 2. The student prefers to write what he thinks rather than contribute to a discussion.
——— ——— 3. The student can retell a cohesive story and has an intuitive sense of story structure.

For Further Reading

Harste, J. C., Short, K. G., & Burke, C. (1988). *Creating classrooms for authors* (336–339). Portsmouth, NH: Heinemann.

Tiedt, I. M., Bruemmer, S. S., Lane, S., Stelwagon, P., Watanabe, K. O., & Williams, M. Y. (1983). *Teaching writing in K–8 classrooms.* Englewood Cliffs, NJ: Prentice-Hall.

ANALYTIC PHONICS

Description.   Analytic phonics is an approach to teaching decoding based on drawing phonic relationships among words that have the same letter patterns. Using words the child already recognizes "at sight," the student identifies the sounds of letter groups by making analogies to known words. In other words, the child says, "I already know a word that looks like this new word. I will match the sounds in that word with the sounds in the new word."

---

*Indicates how a technique can be used to remediate a weakness.

Targeted Reading Levels: 1–2

Text: Known sight words and new words that have the same sound pattern

Predominant Focus of Instruction

1. Processing focus: print
2. Instructional phase: after reading
3. Response mode emphasized: oral discussion
4. Strategy emphasized: elaboration
5. Skill emphasized: word analysis
6. Source of information: text-based
7. Type of instruction: implicit
8. Type of cognitive processing: simultaneous to successive

Procedure

1. The teacher selects a text that contains an abundance of the letter sounds to be taught.
2. The teacher presents sight words that represent the targeted sound or sound cluster. For example, she places these words on the board.

   green
   grass
   grow

3. She asks the student to identify how these words are alike. The student responds, "They all have the letters *gr* at the beginning."
4. The teacher directs attention to the sounds by saying, "How does the *gr* sound in these words?"
5. If the student cannot figure out the sound, the teacher says, "Try the *gr-r-r* sound as in *green, grass,* and *grow*"
6. The student reads a text with words that have the *gr* sound.

   In the land of the gremlins, there were gobs of green grapes as big as Grandpa. One baby gremlin loved to eat the green grapes. He began to grow and grow and grow. So his mother said, "You cannot eat anymore. You have grown too big." This made the gremlin grumpy. He growled and growled. He grabbed a great big green grape and gobbled it up. Then he grabbed another green grape and gobbled it up. Then he grabbed another and another and another. He grew and grew and grew until he popped. That was the end of the gremlin.

7. The teacher draws attention to how the student used the strategy of decoding by analogy.

Further Diagnostic Applications

Basic View of Reading.   Learning to read is a process where the learner makes inferences about the phonic relationships within words. When a student can read an abundance of words that contain a consistent phonic relationship, he will infer the phonic rule for the target words and similar words. This is called implicit or analytic phonics.

Patterns of Strengths and Strategies.   Analytic phonics is most appropriate for students who can segment words into their sounds and readily make phonic inferences about the sound consistency of words. This technique matches their strategies and allows them to develop the strategy of decoding by analogy.

Learner Patterns That Produce a High Success Rate

1. A simultaneous learner who can segment words into their sounds and has established a sight word vocabulary. This technique matches his strengths in knowing the whole word before the parts and finding the patterns between what he knows and what is new.
2. An active reader who does not respond to the direct instruction of other decoding approaches. This technique allows him to develop his own rules for how phonics works.
3. A learner who has an overriding need for meaning and purpose in his learning. Minimal instruction in decoding by analogy makes sense and provides strategies for decoding.

Using the Technique as a Diagnostic Teaching Lesson.   For analytic phonics to be effective, a majority of the following statements must be answered in the affirmative.

Yes   No

____ ____ 1. The student is efficient at segmenting sounds.

____ ____ 2. The student has a well-established sight vocabulary, which facilitates making phonic inferences to new words.

____ ____ 3. The student can draw sound analogies between known words and new words.

For Further Reading

Aukerman, R. C. (1984). *Approaches to beginning reading* (2nd ed.). New York: John Wiley & Sons.

Anderson, R. C., Hiebert, E. H., Scott, J. A., & Wilkinson, I. A. G. (1985). *Becoming a nation of readers: The report of the commission on reading.* Washington, DC: National Institute of Education.

CHUNKING

Description.   Chunking is a technique to encourage the student to read phrases of language that represent meaning rather than separate words. It focuses on reading phrases of text that represent a thought. Chunking facilitates comprehension and fluency by using thought units rather than word-by-word reading.

Targeted Reading Levels: 4–8

Text: All kinds

Predominant Focus of Instruction

1. Processing focus: print and meaning
2. Instructional phase: during reading
3. Response mode emphasized: oral production
4. Strategy emphasized: prediction
5. Skill emphasized: fluency and sentence comprehension
6. Source of information: text-based and reader-based
7. Type of instruction: explicit
8. Type of cognitive processing: successive to simultaneous

Procedure

1. The teacher chooses a passage at an instructional reading level that will take about 3 minutes to read.
2. The teacher tapes the student reading the passage.
3. The teacher and the student echo read (see "Echo Reading" in this chapter) the passage using meaningful phrases. In other words, the teacher reads a sentence modeling appropriate chunks of the sentence, and the student repeats the same sentence using the phrasing. The example that follows illustrates the sequence.

   Text: The bright girl liked to read stories about horses.
   Student reading: The / bright / girl / liked / to / read / stories / about / horses.
   Teacher modeling: The bright girl / liked to read / stories about horses.
   Student echoing: The bright girl / like to / read stories / about horses.
   Teacher comment: I liked the way you chunked "read stories." Did it make more sense to you to read it that way?

4. The teacher and student continue reading the entire passage. When possible, the teacher increases the number of sentences chunked before the student repeats the model.
5. As the student's ability to chunk thought units increases, the teacher ceases to model the chunking, and the student reads the passage on her own.
6. The teacher tapes the reading of the passage again.
7. The teacher and the student compare fluency, intonation, and phrasing.

Modifications

1. For the extremely slow reader, the teacher may incorporate oral chunking experiences as an intervention with multiple timed, silent readings.
2. For the beginning reader, chunking a language experience story by writing phrases from the story on 3″ × 5″ cards is an effective technique.

Further Diagnostic Applications

Basic View of Reading.   Reading is an interactive process whereby a reader thinks about how the words of the text are combined to form the ideas the author intended to convey.

Patterns of Strengths and Strategies.   Chunking is most appropriate for students who have facility with word identification and reflect a sequential, bottom-up processing of text. Chunking of text encourages these students to connect the underlying thought with the text as they are reading.

Learner Patterns That Produce a High Success Rate

1. A successive learner who has difficulty relating what is written in the text to his own thoughts. When chunking, the student must use his understanding of the meaning to group the words together.
2. The passive reader who reads words without thinking of their meaning. Chunking uses recognizing the words (a strength) to understand how the words create meaning (a weakness).
*3. A learner who is word-bound because of an overemphasis on phonics or oral accuracy. Chunking increases his fluency and speed.
*4. An extremely slow reader who thinks about every word. Chunking encourages thinking about groups of words rather than individual words.

Using the Technique as a Diagnostic Teaching Lesson.   For chunking to be effective, a majority of the following statements must be answered in the affirmative.

Yes   No

_____ _____ 1. The student has accurate word identification skills.
_____ _____ 2. The student can model the teacher's chunking of words.
_____ _____ 3. The student transfers the chunking to new text.

For Further Reading

Allington, R. L. (1983). Fluency: The neglected reading goal. *Reading Teacher, 36,* 556–561.

Ekwall, E. E., & Shanker, J. L. (1983). *Diagnosis and remediation of the disabled reader* (2nd ed.). Boston: Allyn and Bacon.

Guszak, F. J. (1985). *Diagnostic reading instruction in the elementary school.* New York: Harper & Row.

CLOZE INSTRUCTION

Description.   The instructional cloze is a technique that develops comprehension by deleting target words from a text. This encourages the student to think about what word would make sense in the sentence and in the context of the entire story.

Targeted Reading Levels: 4–12

Text: Paragraphs and stories that are coherent

Predominant Focus of Instruction

1. Processing focus: meaning
2. Instructional phase: after reading
3. Response mode emphasized: written
4. Strategy emphasized: prediction and monitoring

5. Skill emphasized: sentence comprehension and word meaning
6. Source of information: text-based with some reader-based
7. Type of instruction: implicit
8. Type of cognitive processing: successive

Procedure

1. The teacher selects a text of 200–400 words.
2. The teacher decides on the target words.
3. The teacher systematically deletes the words from the paragraph and inserts a blank for the deleted word.
4. The student is instructed to read the entire passage to get a sense of the entire meaning.
5. The student is then instructed to fill in the blanks in the passage.
6. When the student finishes filling in the blanks, the answers are evaluated as to the similarity of meaning between the deleted word and the supplied word.
7. The student reviews his choices and talks about what strategies he used to decide on the word choices.

Modifications

1. An oral cloze can be used to develop predictive listening in the young child.
2. A cloze exercise can be constructed from language experience stories in order to develop the ability to predict a word by using prior knowledge (what I said) and the text (how I said it).
3. Cloze can be adapted so that pairs of students work together to decide what word fits in the text. This causes a discussion and justification of word choices.

Further Diagnostic Applications

Basic View of Reading. Reading is an interactive process of verifying text expectation by using knowledge of how language works (sentence structure) and what the passage means (overall contextual meaning).

Patterns of Strengths and Strategies. The cloze procedure relies on a well-developed sense of the redundancy of language and a manipulation of sentence structure. For students who have verbal fluency, this technique facilitates comprehension by encouraging the combination of text and meaning cues.

Learner Patterns That Produce a High Success Rate

1. The successive learner who has become word-bound during the process of initial reading instruction and needs to increase the use of context to decode meaning. This technique increases the ability to guess what words are from context.
2. The successive learner who tends to read isolated words rather than using the context and asking what would make sense. This technique helps the reader think about what groups of words mean.
*3. The simultaneous learner who needs to use both sentence structure and overall meaning to read text effectively. The technique focuses attention on sentence meaning.

Using the Technique as a Diagnostic Teaching Lesson.   For cloze instruction to be effective, a majority of the following statements must be answered in the affirmative.

Yes   No

____ ____ 1. The student fills in the blanks with some degree of certainty.

____ ____ 2. The student has verbal facility, which supplements his performance on the cloze.

____ ____ 3. The student begins to use not only *word* knowledge but also *world* knowledge to complete the cloze.

For Further Reading

Jongsma, E. A. (1980). *Cloze instruction research: A second look.* Newark, DE: International Reading Association and ERIC/RCS.

Weaver, G. C. (1979). Using the cloze procedure as a teaching technique. *Reading Teacher, 32,* 632–636.

CONTEXTUAL PROCESSING

Description.   Contextual processing is a technique used to develop new word meanings as they are found in the context of a selected story. This technique shows the student how to use context to figure out what new vocabulary words mean.

Targeted Reading Levels: 2–12

Text: Paragraphs three to four sentences long, where the meaning of new vocabulary is apparent from the surrounding context.

Predominant Focus of Instruction

1. Processing focus: meaning
2. Instructional phase: before or after reading
3. Response mode emphasized: oral discussion
4. Strategy emphasized: monitoring and elaboration
5. Skill emphasized: word meaning and sentence comprehension
6. Source of information: text-based
7. Type of instruction: explicit
8. Type of cognitive processing: successive

Procedure

1. The teacher selects unfamiliar key vocabulary words to teach.
2. The teacher finds a passage in the text where the meaning of the word is apparent when using the surrounding context. If not available, she creates her own three-sentence paragraph.
3. She writes the paragraph on the overhead or chalkboard.
4. She reads the paragraph aloud to the students.

5. The students reread the paragraph silently.
6. The teacher asks the students about the meaning of the word found in the paragraph, asking, for example, "What does the paragraph tell you about the word . . . ?"
7. The teacher uses the students' answers to probe further understanding, asking, "Why did you think that?"
8. The teacher asks students to write down what the new word might mean.
9. The teacher has students think of other similar situations where they could use the word. She asks, "Who else might be . . . ? Where else might you . . . ?"
10. The students think of other words with similar meanings.
11. The students record target words and a personal definition in their word notebooks.

Modification

The teacher can increase the explicitness of the technique by modeling how to figure out the meaning of the word using the surrounding words in the paragraph. The teacher models Steps 6 (what the paragraph told her), 7 (why she thought that), and 8 (how she came up with the meaning).

Further Diagnostic Applications

Basic View of Reading.   Reading is an interactive process where the readers use what they know about how the words in the story are used to interpret what the author is saying.

Patterns of Strengths and Strategies.   Contextual processing has students figure out unfamiliar word meanings from the context; therefore, it is most appropriate for students who have facility with sentence meaning but do not use this strength to figure out what new words mean. This is often the pattern of successive learners who have facility with sentence structure but do not combine this strength with what they already know to expand their understanding of word meanings.

Learner Patterns That Produce a High Success Rate

1. A successive learner who has the ability to use sentences to figure out new words but does not use his background knowledge to expand word meanings. This technique starts with his strength and then asks him to use background knowledge to tie the meaning to other events in his life.
2. A passive learner who reads the words without actively thinking about what they mean in the new context or other contexts. This technique encourages him to think actively about what words mean. The modification of modeling may be needed.
*3. A simultaneous learner who does not use the sentence context to figure out word meanings. This technique encourages him to use context as well as what he knows to figure out new word meanings.

Using the Technique as a Diagnostic Teaching Lesson.   For contextual processing to be effective, a majority of the following statements must be answered in the affirmative.

Yes   No

—— —— 1. The student can use sentence comprehension to facilitate learning new word meanings.

—— —— 2. The student learns to use information from two sentences to define the word easily.

—— —— 3. The student can use words to define new meanings and does not need a direct experience.

For Further Reading

Gipe, J. P. (1978–1979). Investigating techniques for teaching word meanings. *Reading Research Quarterly, 14,* 624–644.

McKeown, M. (1985). The acquisition of word meaning from context by children of high and low ability. *Reading Research Quarterly, 20,* 482–496.

Tierney, R. J., Readence, J. E., & Dishner, E. K. (1990). *Reading strategies and practices: A compendium* (3rd ed.). Boston: Allyn and Bacon.

DIALOGUE JOURNALS

Description.   Dialogue journals use writing as a communication device between the students and the teacher. In small notebooks, the students write about ideas that they want to communicate to the teacher. The teacher responds to these ideas with questions, comments, and personal reactions. Through multiple journal entries, students and teacher carry on a conversation.

Targeted Reading Levels: All levels

Text: Self-generated dialogue

Predominant Focus of Instruction

1. Processing focus: meaning
2. Instructional phase: after reading
3. Response mode emphasized: written discourse
4. Strategy emphasized: elaboration
5. Skill emphasized: non-literal comprehension
6. Source of information: reader-based
7. Type of instruction: implicit
8. Type of cognitive processing: simultaneous

Procedures

1. The teacher secures writing notebooks. She can use bound composition notebooks, student-made books of stapled pages, or loose-leaf notebooks.
2. The teacher explains that a dialogue journal is like writing a letter to someone.
   a. She talks about how exciting it feels to get a letter from someone.
   b. She explains that the dialogue journal is like writing important things about your life to your teacher.
   c. She tells the students she will comment personally on what is written.

3. The teacher shows the students an example from another journal. (The teacher first secures permission from the writer and reader.)
4. She reminds the students that they can write about any topic.
5. The teacher designates a time for writing and then sets the timer.
6. The students and teacher write in their journals.
7. The teacher reads what the students write.
8. The teacher responds with questions or comments: "Can you describe . . . ? I have felt like that, too."
9. The students read the teacher's comments.
10. The students write a response or choose another topic.
11. The writing cycle continues.

COMMENT: Although this technique is more effective for some students than others, it is recommended as part of the diagnostic teaching session because it releases the structured format of directed and guided instruction.

Further Diagnostic Applications

Basic View of Reading.   Reading is a top-down process where readers' personal interpretations focus comprehension. Both reading and writing are constructive processes that are influenced by the desire to communicate.

Patterns of Strengths and Strategies.   Dialogue journals are most appropriate for simultaneous, nonverbal students who enjoy communicating ideas through writing rather than talking. In this technique, personal ideas are communicated without an oral explanation or eye contact.

Learner Patterns That Produce a High Success Rate

1. A simultaneous learner who needs time to express his ideas in words. Writing allows him to think through ideas without noticeably lengthy pauses.
2. A nonverbal reader who prefers to communicate his ideas through writing rather than talking. Dialogue journals allow him to put his thoughts into words without talking.
*3. A passive reader who does not realize that reading and writing are constructive processes. This technique allows him to experience reading and writing as communication.
*4. A text-bound reader who does not use his personal understanding of the world to interpret information. Dialogue journals show him how a writer uses personal understanding to compose text.

Using the Technique as a Diagnostic Lesson.   For dialogue journals to be effective, a majority of the following statements must be answered in the affirmative.

Yes   No

_____ _____ 1. The student can write (produce letters) fairly easily.
_____ _____ 2. The student likes to communicate his ideas in writing.
_____ _____ 3. The student uses the teacher's model to correct his own writing errors.

For Further Reading

Gambrell, L. B. (1985). Dialogue journals: Reading-writing interaction. *Reading Teacher, 38,* 512–515.
Glazer, S. M. (1984). Liberating students to write. *Early Years, 15*(1), 67–69.
Harste, J. C., Short, K. G., & Burke, C. (1988). *Creating Classrooms for Authors* (pp. 336–339). Portsmouth, NH: Heinemann.

DIRECT EXPERIENCE APPROACH

Description.   Direct experience is an approach where actual situations are used to develop word meanings. The actual object is manipulated or the event is enacted in order to develop an understanding of the concept. During the activity, the teacher and students use the new word (label) as they actually experience the concept. This associates the word label with the word concept.

Targeted Reading Levels: All levels. Necessary for young children.

Text: The object or event in a situational context.

Predominant Focus of Instruction

1. Processing focus: meaning
2. Instructional phase: before reading
3. Response mode emphasized: oral discussion
4. Strategy emphasized: elaboration
5. Skill emphasized: word meaning
6. Source of information: reader-based
7. Type of instruction: implicit
8. Type of cognitive processing: simultaneous

Procedure

1. The teacher makes a list of target words that are not well developed in the students' meaning vocabularies.
2. She secures the objects that these words represent or plans an excursion for the event. To develop an understanding of the word *sour,* for example, the teacher brings lemons to the class.
3. The teacher constructs a situation in which to use the object. In the example, the students would taste the lemons.
4. The students use the objects in the situation and describe the experience. In the example, students could describe how the lemons tasted.
5. The students identify other objects that are similar and tell how they are alike and then how they are different. In the example, students could contrast the taste of the lemon with a pickle, a doughnut, and a hamburger.
6. The students identify other objects that are different and tell how they are different and then how they may be alike. In the example, the students would think of other fruits that are sour and those that are not sour.

7. The teacher writes the words on a card or the chalkboard so that meaning can be associated with what the words look like.

Modifications

1. Science experiments use activities to develop a concept and follow the activity with a labeling and recording of the information; therefore, they develop meaning through a direct experience.
2. Simulation of social studies concepts provides an activity where words describing a concept are used in a social-interactive context and, therefore, develop meaning through a direct association between the concept and the label.

Further Diagnostic Applications

Basic View of Reading.   Reading is a top-down process where a conceptual understanding of words is based on generalizations from specific events that the reader has encountered. Therefore, word meanings are based not only on categorical relationships but also on the knowledge of specific events each person has had. Definitions are developed as the child uses language in social situations.

Patterns of Strengths and Strategies.   Direct experience is appropriate for students who learn through sensory motor involvement in their learning. Concrete objects build a store of specific instances from which to develop definitional language. For these students, the approach matches their underlying preference for developing meaning within the context of situations rather than by verbal descriptions devoid of actions.

Learner Patterns That Produce a High Success Rate

1. A simultaneous learner who uses past experiences rather than specific definitional knowledge to comprehend text. Direct experience shows him how to label his environment.
2. A kinesthetic learner who needs to touch and feel concrete objects in order to develop word meanings. The direct experience helps him to develop verbal and concept meaning simultaneously.
*3. A passive but verbal learner who uses word labels without understanding the underlying conceptual meaning of the words. Direct experience makes the connections between the words he uses and their underlying conceptual meaning.

Using the Technique as a Diagnostic Teaching Lesson.   For the direct experience approach to be effective, a majority of the following statements must be answered in the affirmative.

Yes   No

_____ _____ 1. The student uses specific examples when defining words.
_____ _____ 2. The student uses *like a* statements rather than definitional language.
_____ _____ 3. The student finds manipulative activities meaningful and not boring.

For Further Reading

Dale, E. (1969). *Audiovisual methods in teaching* (3rd ed.). New York: Holt, Rinehart & Winston.

Johnson, D. D., & Pearson, P. D. (1984). *Teaching reading vocabulary* (2nd ed.). New York: Holt, Rinehart & Winston.

May, F. (1986). *Reading as communication: An interactive approach* (2nd ed.). Columbus, OH: Merrill.

DIRECTED READING ACTIVITY

Description.   A directed reading activity (DRA) is an instructional format for teaching reading where the teacher assumes the major instructional role. She develops background knowledge, introduces new words, and gives the students a purpose for reading. Then she directs the discussion with questions to develop reading comprehension. Finally, she reinforces and extends the skills and knowledge developed in the story.

Targeted Reading Levels: All levels

Text: Graded stories in basal readers or content area textbooks

Predominant Focus of Instruction

1. Processing focus: print and meaning
2. Instructional phase: before and after reading
3. Response mode emphasized: oral discussion
4. Strategy emphasized: elaboration
5. Skill emphasized: word identification and literal comprehension
6. Source of information: text-based
7. Type of instruction: implicit
8. Type of cognitive processing: successive

Procedure

1. The teacher develops readiness for reading:
   a. She presents new vocabulary words in oral and written context. Children are asked what these new words mean and directed to remember the words by their distinctive visual features.
   b. She develops appropriate background knowledge so that students will understand the general setting of the story.
   c. She gives the students a purpose for reading by telling them to read to find out a particular thing or concept. She develops purposes that require students to read the entire story before an answer is resolved.
2. The students read the story silently.
   a. If necessary, the teacher divides the story into sections. After reading a section, the teacher asks a variety of questions emphasizing literal and nonliteral story understanding.

   b. The teacher asks the students to support their answers by reading the appropriate sections in the text.
3. The teacher reinforces and extends concepts introduced in the story.
   a. Activities to reinforce word recognition and word meanings are used to develop independence in reading.
   b. Activities that develop a creative response to the story are assigned.
   c. Activities that require students to relate the story to their own experiences and to other stories are used.

Further Diagnostic Applications

Basic View of Reading.   Reading requires recognizing words and then associating meaning with these new words. Initially, therefore, reading is a text-based process. However, when new words have been learned and purposes have been set, students can read with comprehension.

Patterns of Strengths and Strategies.   A directed reading activity is a flexible approach for instructing young children to read stories. Following this format, the text can be narrative or expository, short or long, interrupted or read as a whole. However, it must be remembered that the directed reading activity is just that, reading directed by the teacher and not the student. Therefore, it is most appropriate for young readers who need a substantial amount of teacher direction in order to understand stories.

Learner Patterns That Produce a High Success Rate

1. The active reader who needs new words presented before she reads so that word recognition does not interfere with story comprehension. This approach introduces new words to facilitate story comprehension.
2. The passive reader who needs the teacher to direct his attention to important word recognition and comprehension cues. The teacher can begin with this format but should phase as quickly as possible to strategies that require a more active stance from the reader.

Using the Technique as a Diagnostic Teaching Lesson.   For directed reading to be effective, a majority of the following statements must be answered in the affirmative.

Yes   No

_____ _____ 1. The student comprehends the story and is fairly active when he reads.
_____ _____ 2. The student needs his attention directed to recognizing words in isolation and context.
_____ _____ 3. The student is more comfortable answering questions than retelling the story.

For Further Reading

Anderson, R. C., Hiebert, E. H., Scott, J. A., & Wilkinson, I. A. G. (1985). *Becoming a nation of readers: The report of the commission on reading.* Washington, DC: National Institute of Education.

Betts, E. A. (1946). *Foundations of reading instruction.* New York: American Book.

Tierney, R. J., Readence, J. E., & Dishner, E. K. (1990). *Reading strategies and practices: A compendium* (3rd ed.). Boston: Allyn and Bacon.

DIRECTED READING-THINKING ACTIVITY (DRTA)

Description.   A directed reading-thinking activity is an instructional format for teaching reading that includes three stages: readiness for reading, active reading comprehension, and reacting to the story (Stauffer, 1975).

Targeted Reading Levels: All levels

Text: Can be applied to all narrative and expository texts

Predominant Focus of Instruction

1. Processing focus: meaning
2. Instructional phase: during and after reading
3. Response mode emphasized: oral discussion
4. Strategy emphasized: prediction and monitoring
5. Skill emphasized: non-literal comprehension
6. Source of information: reader-based and text-based
7. Type of instruction: implicit
8. Type of cognitive processing: simultaneous

Procedure

1. The teacher asks the students to predict what will happen in the story using the title and any available pictures.
2. She continues her questioning by asking the students why they made their predictions.
3. The students read to a turning point in the story.
4. The teacher asks the students if their predictions were confirmed or not.
5. The teacher asks the students to support their answers using the information in the text and explaining their reasoning.
6. The teacher then asks the following questions:
   a. What do you think is going to happen next?
   b. Why do you think that?
7. The students read to the next turning point in the story.
8. The teacher repeats steps 4, 5, 6, and 7.
9. When they are finished reading, the teacher and the students react to the story as a whole.
10. The teacher leads the students to analyze the story in relation to other stories, personal experiences, and the author's purpose.
11. The teacher discusses the strategies that were used to understand the story.
12. The teacher reviews the meaning of any key vocabulary words.

Further Diagnostic Applications

Basic View of Reading.   Reading is an active thinking process where a reader predicts, confirms, and revises his interpretation using important textual information. The reflective thought process focuses on not only what was understood about the story but also how it was understood.

Patterns of Strengths and Strategies.   A DRTA is appropriate for students who readily engage in constructing meaning as they read. They use what they already know to predict what will happen in the story and then select important information from the text to justify their answers. The teacher matches these active strategies by discussing not only what the students think but also how the students think.

Learner Patterns That Produce a High Success Rate

1. The active reader who uses what he already knows and the text to construct meaning. A DRTA allows this reader to construct meaning with the guidance of the teacher.
2. The simultaneous reader who uses what he already knows to understand stories but has difficulty justifying his answers with information from the text. This technique requires the reader to justify his thinking with information from the text.

Using the Technique as a Diagnostic Teaching Lesson.   For a directed reading-thinking activity to be effective, a majority of the following statements must be answered in the affirmative:

Yes   No

_____ _____ 1. The student directs and monitors his own learning when reading.
_____ _____ 2. The student uses appropriate text-based and reader-based inferences when evaluating predictions.
__✗__ _____ 3. The student is more comfortable summarizing the story than answering questions.

For Further Reading

May, F. (1986). *Reading as communication: An interactive approach* (2nd ed.). Columbus, OH: Merrill.
Stauffer, R. (1975). *Directing the reading-thinking process.* New York: Harper & Row.
Tierney, R. J., Readence, J. E., & Dishner, E. K. (1990). *Reading strategies and practices: A compendium* (3rd ed.). Boston: Allyn and Bacon.

ECHO READING

Description.   Echo reading is a form of modeling oral reading where the teacher reads a line of a story and the student echos her model by reading the same line, imitating her intonation and phrasing.

Targeted Reading Levels: 1–4

Text: Any text that is well written

Predominant Focus of Instruction

1. Processing focus: print
2. Instructional phase: during reading
3. Response mode emphasized: oral
4. Strategy emphasized: prediction
5. Skill emphasized: fluency
6. Source of information: reader-based
7. Type of instruction: implicit
8. Type of cognitive processing: successive

Procedure

1. The teacher selects a text around 200 words long that is near frustration level reading.
2. The teacher reads the first line of the text, accentuating appropriate phrasing and intonation.
3. Immediately, the student reads the same line, modeling the teacher's example.
4. The teacher and the student read in echo fashion for the entire passage, increasing the amount of text when the student can imitate the model.

Modifications

1. Echo reading is an effective intervention when using repeated readings (see "Repeated Readings" in this chapter). After the first reading, the teacher and student can echo read those sentences where there were a string of miscues or errors.
2. Echo reading can also be used in conjunction with chunking (see "Chunking" in this chapter) so the student can hear the way the teacher chunks language into thoughts.

Further Diagnostic Applications

Basic View of Reading.   Reading is a top-down process where a reader matches what he hears with the text. The reader must read fluently to integrate the meaning with the text on the page.

Patterns of Strengths and Strategies.   Echo reading is most appropriate for the student who needs the teacher to model fluent oral reading and needs to repeat that model immediately in order to remember how the text sounded.

Learner Patterns That Produce a High Success Rate

1. A passive and successive reader who has become word-bound and lost the flow of language. This technique allows him to hear fluent oral reading and immediately imitate the model.

2. A simultaneous learner who has become extremely word-bound by an overemphasis in decoding. Echo reading shows him how to use sentence meaning as well as the model to increase oral reading fluency.
3. An extremely slow reader who needs to hear language read fluently. The teacher reads each sentence rapidly and in thought units so this reader can read fluently with intonation.
4. A learner who refuses to follow the teacher when using the impress method or simultaneous reading. Echo reading provides a clear model for this student to follow.

Using the Technique as a Diagnostic Teaching Lesson. For echo reading to be effective, a majority of the following statements must be answered in the affirmative.

Yes   No

_____ _____ 1. The student imitates the model of the teacher.
_____ _____ 2. The student follows the line of print as he reads the text.

For Further Reading

Aulls, M. (1982). *Developing readers in today's elementary school.* Boston: Allyn and Bacon.
Tierney, R. J., Readence, J. E., & Dishner, E. K. (1990). *Reading strategies and practices: A compendium* (3rd ed.). Boston: Allyn and Bacon.

EXPLICIT TEACHING

Description. Explicit teaching is a lesson framework that directly instructs a student in the skills and strategies of reading. The lesson framework is based on making the task relevant to the student and directly teaching the task through examples and modeling. The teacher systematically plans activities to increase independent application of the skill or strategy.

Targeted Reading Levels: Depends on the skill being taught

Text: Text chosen or constructed to teach the targeted task.

Predominant Focus of Instruction

1. Processing focus: print or meaning
2. Instructional phase: before and during reading
3. Response mode emphasized: oral discussion
4. Strategy emphasized: monitoring
5. Skill emphasized: depends on task
6. Source of information: depends on task, most often the text
7. Type of instruction: explicit
8. Type of cognitive processing: successive

Procedure

1. The teacher selects the skill or strategy to be taught.
2. The teacher selects a series of texts to illustrate the skill or strategy.
3. The teacher introduces the skill or strategy. For example, she may choose finding the main idea in paragraphs.
4. She explains the reason why learning this skill or strategy will facilitate reading performance. In this example, she may say that finding the main idea is important because it helps us remember facts using one idea rather than many different facts.
5. She asks students how this is like other skills or strategies that they have learned. This helps them understand the reasons for learning a particular skill. In this example, she may say, "We already studied how to identify key vocabulary words. How did this help us?" The students and teacher discuss how these words were often what the text was mainly about.
6. The teacher explains the process of the skill. For example, he may say, "When deciding on a main idea, you think to yourself, 'What does each sentence tell about and how is the information alike?' How the information is alike becomes the main idea."
7. The teacher demonstrates how to think when using the skill. A sample demonstration might include the steps that follow.
   a. The teacher puts a three- or four-sentence paragraph on an overhead or the chalkboard.
   b. She summarizes each sentence aloud.
   c. She tells how they are related to the main idea.
   d. She explains that the way the sentences are alike is what the paragraph is mostly about, or the main idea.
8. The students and the teacher do the next example together. The students talk through the new example, explaining what they are doing, why they are doing it, and how they are doing it. The teacher explains her thinking to clarify any steps in the process.
9. The students do the next example by talking through how they complete the task. Then the students tell how this will help them read.
10. The teacher provides feedback about what the students say by modeling how she would have completed the task.
11. The students read more paragraphs and use the newly learned task on their own.

Further Diagnostic Applications

Basic View of Reading.   Reading is an interactive process where the reader monitors his reading using both skills and strategies. Reading instruction, therefore, should explicitly teach the student to use reading skills and strategies independently.

Patterns of Strengths and Strategies.   Introducing the new skill or strategy, the approach systematically leads students through the reasoning process relating to the skill or strategy. It takes the separate parts, explains them, and then integrates the parts into the whole task. It is most efficient for the passive or successive learner who profits from seeing how to fit the parts of reading into the whole process.

Learner Patterns That Produce a High Success Rate

1. A passive learner who does not actively use a particular skill or strategy when reading stories independently. Explicit instruction teaches the skill by showing him how to use it when he is reading.
2. A successive learner who needs to be shown exactly how the strategies of reading affect the entire reading process. Explicit instruction shows him how the parts fit into the whole.
3. An inattentive learner who approaches reading in a trial-and-error fashion, not understanding the exact skills and strategies necessary for consistent reading performance. Explicit instruction gives him a system for approaching learning.
*4. A simultaneous learner who needs to be shown how to control his own learning. (Mediation would be very short.)

Using the Technique as a Diagnostic Teaching Lesson. For explicit teaching to be effective, a majority of the following statements must be answered in the affirmative.

Yes	No	
_____	_____	1. The student learns from the examples what the process is and how it works.
_____	_____	2. The student improves his ability to do the skill or strategy.
_____	_____	3. The student can explain how the process works in new situations.

For Further Reading

Garcia, G. E., & Pearson, P. D. (1990). *Modifying reading instruction to maximize its effectiveness for all students* (Technical Report No. 489). Champaign, IL: University of Illinois, Center for the Study of Reading.

Tierney, R. J., & Cunningham, J. (1984). Research on teaching reading comprehension. In P. D. Pearson (Ed.), *Handbook of reading research* (pp. 609–656). New York: Longman.

Tierney, R. J., Readence, J. E., & Dishner, E. K. (1990). *Reading strategies and practices: A compendium* (3rd ed.). Boston: Allyn and Bacon.

EXPERIENCE-TEXT-RELATIONSHIP (ETR)

Description. Experience-text-relationship is specifically designed to use children's experiences to teach new concepts and new words in the story. In this technique, the teacher spends time showing students the relationships between what they know and what they are reading, both before and after reading the story. It is specifically designed for use with multiculture students (Au, 1979).

Targeted Reading Levels: All levels

Text: Stories with an interesting theme or plot that can sustain an in-depth discussion

Predominant Focus of Instruction

1. Processing focus: meaning
2. Instructional phase: before and after reading
3. Response mode emphasized: oral discussion
4. Strategy emphasized: elaboration
5. Skill emphasized: non-literal and literal comprehension
6. Source of information: reader-based phasing to text-based
7. Type of instruction: implicit
8. Type of cognitive processing: simultaneous

Procedure

1. The teacher chooses an appropriate text.
2. The teacher reads the selected passage to decide the theme, topic, and important points.
3. The teacher thinks about what the students know related to the theme, topic, and important points.
4. The teacher formulates general questions that will initiate a discussion about what the students know.
5. The teacher begins the instruction with a general discussion of what the students know. (This step is the *experience phase* of the lesson and is student-initiated.)
6. The teacher uses the information that is generated to tie the students' experiences directly to the story. She uses pictures and information that come directly from the story. (This step is teacher-directed.)
7. She asks the students to make a prediction based on the discussion (student input).
8. Then, if necessary, the teacher sets other purposes for reading (teacher input).
9. The students read a portion of the story to see if their predictions are right. This begins the *text phase* of the lesson.
10. The teacher returns to predictions and asks the students what they have learned so far about these predictions.
11. The teacher sets additional purposes.
12. The teacher calls attention to important information in the text if necessary.
13. The teacher alternates periods of silent reading and discussion until the entire story has been read.
14. When the entire story has been read, the teacher directs a discussion of the key ideas in the story.
15. She then compares the key ideas in the text to the key experiences of the students. To do this, she returns to the information gained during the experience phase of the lesson. This is called the *relationship phase* and is teacher-directed.
16. She then contrasts the key ideas in the text with the students' experiences.
17. The teacher summarizes the main relationships after the discussion is complete.
18. Finally, the teacher recommends that the students use the ETR steps when they read on their own.

Further Diagnostic Applications

Basic View of Reading.   Reading is an interactive process where the learners use what they know to interpret what the text says. Readers need assistance learning how to figure out what they know that is useful to interpret the text. They also need assistance in making connections between this information and what the text says.

Patterns of Strengths and Strategies.   The ETR technique is appropriate for students who need assistance in bringing their background knowledge to the text. It is especially useful for multiculture students who experience a gap between the way they talk about their experiences and the way an author describes those same experiences. This technique helps these students relate their own language and experiences to the text.

Learner Patterns That Produce a High Success Rate

1. A passive learner who reads text without relating what he knows. ETR focuses on the student's experience during every step of the lesson.
2. A passive learner who will not venture a guess while reading. ETR gives him the tools to make a guess.

Using the Technique as a Diagnostic Teaching Lesson.   For experience-text-relationship to be effective, a majority of the following statements must be answered in the affirmative:

Yes   No

____ ____ 1. The student can express what he knows.
____ ____ 2. The student can make a prediction.
____ ____ 3. With teacher assistance, the student can see the relationship between his experience and what the text says.

For Further Reading

Au, K. (1979). Using the experience-text-relationship method with minority children. *Reading Teacher, 32,* 677–679.

McNeil, J. D. (1987). *Reading comprehension: New directions for classroom practice.* Glenview, IL: Scott, Foresman.

Mason, J. M., & Au, K. H. (1990). *Reading instruction for today* (2nd ed.). Glenview, IL: Scott, Foresman.

FEATURE ANALYSIS GRID

Description.   A feature analysis grid is a technique to develop word meanings by graphing the major characteristics of target words. Key words are compared as to how they are alike and how they are different (Johnson & Pearson, 1984).

Targeted Reading Levels: All levels

Text: Isolated words that are associated in categories.

Predominant Focus of Instruction

1. Processing focus: meaning
2. Instructional phase: before reading
3. Response mode emphasized: oral discussion
4. Strategy emphasized: elaboration
5. Skill emphasized: word meaning
6. Source of information: reader-based
7. Type of instruction: explicit
8. Type of cognitive processing: successive

Procedure

1. The teacher selects categories and words to analyze.
2. The teacher makes a feature analysis grid with a column of words to analyze.

CATEGORY: LANDSCAPES

New and Known Words	Important Characteristics			
	Trees	Water	Rocks	Snow
Mountains	+	+	+	+

3. The teacher and the students discuss the characteristics of the first word.
4. The teacher adds the characteristics across the top of the grid, indicating the important characteristics with a plus in the respective squares of the grid.
5. The teacher and the students then discuss the second target word.
6. The teacher and the students evaluate this word according to the important features on the grid. The teacher puts a plus on those characteristics that the second target word has and a minus on those that it does not have.

CATEGORY: LANDSCAPES

New and Known Words	Important Characteristics				
	Trees	Water	Rocks	Snow	Sand
Mountains	+	+	+	+	−
Deserts	−	+	−	?	+

7. The teacher adds any new important characteristics, indicating those with a plus in the appropriate square on the grid. The teacher and the students discuss any uncertain responses. In the example, deserts consist mainly of sand, but there are some snow deserts.
8. The teacher and the students discuss how the two words are alike and how they are different.
9. The procedure is repeated for other words. The teacher adds important characteristics as needed.
10. The teacher adds other words that are prevalent in the students' oral vocabularies to make comparisons between what is new and what is already known.

Modifications

1. Use a rating scale (1–3) to show the relative importance that each characteristic contributes to the meaning of the words.
2. Use as a prewriting activity for a comparison paragraph among words and concepts.

Further Diagnostic Applications

Basic View of Reading.   Reading is an interactive process that is based on what the reader already knows about the words used in the text. Comprehension is facilitated by understanding the specific attributes of the words used in a passage.

Patterns of Strengths and Strategies.   The feature analysis grid is most appropriate for students who have a well-developed background of experiences but who overgeneralize word meanings, failing to see the likenesses and differences between specific definitional meanings. For these students, the graphic representation of important characteristics organizes the prior knowledge into specific linguistic categories.

Learner Patterns That Produce a High Success Rate

1. A successive learner who has difficulty drawing comparisons among word meanings but has verbal fluency and analyzes individual words by their major features. This technique allows him to compare and contrast the major features of words at the same time.
2. A divergent thinker who notices features other than the major characteristics but easily understands the grid and the relationships among word meanings. This technique focuses his attention on the key features of the words.
*3. A passive learner who does not think about the differences among words. This technique helps him think and talk about how words are alike and different.

Using the Technique as a Diagnostic Teaching Lesson.   For a feature analysis grid to be effective, a majority of the following statements must be answered in the affirmative.

Yes   No

_____ _____ 1. The student understands the purpose of the grid and can visualize the negative and positive aspects of the grid.

_____ _____ 2. Using the grid, the student develops a clear understanding of the attributes of the target words.

_____ _____ 3. The student understands likenesses and differences.

For Further Reading

Anders, P., Bos, C., & Filip, D. (1984). The effects of semantic feature analysis on the reading comprehension of learning disabled students. In J. Niles & L. Harris, (Eds.), *Changing perspectives on research in reading/language processing and instruction* (pp. 62–166). Rochester, NY: National Reading Conference.

Johnson, D. D. (1982). *Three sound strategies for vocabulary development* (Ginn Occasional Papers No. 3). Lexington, MA: Silver, Burdett & Ginn.

Johnson, D. D., & Pearson, P. D. (1984). *Teaching reading vocabulary* (2nd ed.). New York: Holt, Rinehart & Winston.

GRAPHIC ORGANIZERS

Description.   The graphic organizer technique is designed to provide a visual representation of the main concepts in content areas. By arranging the key words in a chapter, the teacher and students develop an idea framework for relating unfamiliar vocabulary words and concepts.

Targeted Reading Levels: 3–12

Text: Expository text

Predominant Focus of Instruction

1. Processing focus: meaning
2. Instructional phase: before reading
3. Response mode emphasized: oral discussion with written responses
4. Strategy emphasized: elaboration
5. Skill emphasized: word meaning and literal comprehension
6. Source of information: text-based
7. Type of instruction: explicit
8. Type of cognitive processing: simultaneous

Procedure:

1. The teacher chooses a chapter from the textbook.
2. The teacher selects key vocabulary words and concepts.
3. The teacher arranges the key words into a diagram that shows how the key words interrelate.
4. The teacher adds a few familiar words to the diagram so students can connect their prior knowledge with the new information.
5. The teacher presents the graphic organizer on the chalkboard or an overhead transparency. As she presents the organizer, she explains the relationships.

6. Students are encouraged to explain how they think the information is related.
7. The students read the chapter referring as needed to the graphic organizer.
8. After reading the selection, the students may return to the graphic organizer to clarify and elaborate concepts.

Modifications: Students can generate their own graphic organizers after they read the chapter. In this situation, graphic organizers are an implicit instructional technique.

Further Diagnostic Applications

Basic View of Reading.   Reading is an active process where learners use what they know to elaborate and extend what the text says. By constructing a visual map of word relationships, the teacher helps create an idea framework prior to reading the information.

Patterns of Strengths and Strategies.   The Graphic Organizer technique is appropriate for students who profit from a visual framework relating unfamiliar words and ideas to known information. It is especially useful for the highly visual students who profit from seeing relationships in order to tie them to what they are reading.

Learner Patterns That Produce a High Success Rate

1. A simultaneous reader who thinks in visual images relating patterns of information. Graphic Organizers help relate and elaborate topic knowledge.
*2. A reader who reads without relating what he knows to the text. Graphic Organizers help him relate what he knows to unfamiliar concepts.
*3. The passive reader who reads words without defining their underlying meaning. Graphic Organizers help focus on new word meanings.

Using the Technique as a Diagnostic Teaching Lesson.   For Graphic Organizers to be effective, a majority of the following statements must be answered in the affirmative:

Yes   No

_____ _____ 1. The student can easily see the visual pattern.
_____ _____ 2. The student refers to the organizer as he reads.
_____ _____ 3. The student can organize the information learned.

For Further Reading

Alvermann, D. E. (1989). Effects of spontaneous and induced lookbacks on self-perceived high- and low-ability comprehenders. *Journal of Educational Research, 81,* 325–331.

Tierney, R. J., Readence, J. E., & Dishner, E. K. (1990). *Reading strategies and practices: A compendium* (3rd ed.). Boston, MA: Allyn & Bacon.

GUIDED IMAGERY/COMPREHENSION

Description. Guided imagery uses sensory images related to the story line to increase active comprehension and activate background knowledge about (a) situations and characters in a story or (b) key concepts in expository text (Walker, 1985).

Targeted Reading Levels: 2–Adult

Text: Narrative text or concepts in expository text

Predominant Focus of Instruction

1. Processing focus: meaning
2. Instructional phase: before reading
3. Response mode emphasized: oral discussion
4. Strategy emphasized: prediction and monitoring
5. Skill emphasized: non-literal comprehension
6. Source of information: reader-based
7. Type of instruction: implicit (can be adapted to explicit)
8. Type of cognitive processing: simultaneous

Procedure

1. The teacher selects a text.
2. She identifies key events and characters or key concepts, depending on the type of text.
3. The teacher writes a guided journey that uses these key items. In the journey, the teacher intersperses calming statements with the story events and character descriptions or the key concepts. The following (Walker, 1985, p. 140) is an example that might be used prior to reading a narrative story.

"Close your eyes . . . and relax in your chair. . . . Now listen to the noises in the room. . . . Can you hear them? Feel the temperature of the room. . . . Now turn the noises of this room into the sounds of a meadow. . . . What kind of day is it? You are at the foot of a mountain in China . . . begin walking up . . . up . . . up . . . the mountain. . . . As you climb higher . . . and higher . . . you see a lake. . . . Walk toward the lake. . . . Your village needs the water in this lake. . . . Looking for a way to release the water, you walk around . . . and around . . . and around the lake. . . . A wild goose soars toward you. . . . Listen to the goose. . . . She says that you will need the golden key. . . . It will open the gate of the lake. . . . Looking around . . . you see the keyhole in the stone gate . . . but there is no key. . . . You begin searching . . . and searching for the golden key. . . . Something is flying toward you. . . . It says to find the third daughter of the Dragon King. . . . She will help you. . . . I will leave you now to continue searching for the golden key. . . . When you have finished your search . . . you may return to this room . . . and open your eyes."

4. For narrative text, the teacher uses the key events to develop the guided imagery, but she leaves the problem in the story unresolved. The students are to finish the story in their minds.
5. For expository text, the teacher develops a guided imagery that illustrates the attributes of the key concepts.
6. To begin the lesson, the teacher has the students relax in their chairs and think of sounds and smells like the setting. Then she reads the journey in a calm, serene voice, interspersing action statements with calming statements.
7. She tells the students to return to the classroom when they have completed their journeys in the mind.
8. The teacher and students share their images. The students can share their stories in pairs.
9. Students read the selection to compare their journeys with the text.

Modifications

1. The guided imagery can form the basis for a dictated language experience story. The teacher uses targeted sight words to compose the guided imagery.
2. In narrative text, the use of images facilitates comprehension by activating what students already know (images) so they can use this information to understand how the author resolved the problem.
3. In expository text, the use of images helps students remember the key concepts in the text so they can elaborate or compare those images with the text as they read.

Further Diagnostic Applications

Basic View of Reading.   Reading is a top-down process that uses personal images (reader-based inferencing) to create meaning. As the student reads, he forms an expectation for meaning that is represented by images of specific events. He refines his model of meaning (basically images) when he reads.

Patterns of Strengths and Strategies.   Guided imagery/comprehension is a technique for students who store information in images. It is appropriate for the reflective, simultaneous thinker who refers to specific events and images when discussing text. Using guided imagery prior to discussion helps this learner translate his images into a verbal response.

Learner Patterns That Produce a High Success Rate

1. The simultaneous thinker who uses images to construct meaning that often results in changing the story line to fit his model of meaning. This technique helps him see how his own ideas and images affect his comprehension.
2. An extremely imaginative thinker who enjoys sharing his images and comparing them to the text. This technique allows him to use this strength when comprehending.
3. A simultaneous reflective thinker who uses images instead of words when thinking. This allows images to be connected with words.

*4. The passive reader who does not check what he knows while he reads. Learning to image can increase his elaboration and monitoring of what he is reading.

*5. The extremely literal thinker who seldom constructs images. The guided image technique provides a process for the student to use images when reading.

Using the Technique as a Diagnostic Teaching Lesson.   For guided imagery/comprehension to be effective, a majority of the following statements must be answered in the affirmative.

Yes   No

____ ____ 1. The student constructs a coherent and logical ending to the guided journey.

____ ____ 2. The student reads with increased involvement comparing his journey with the text.

____ ____ 3. The student does not overly rely on the guided journey and make the text fit his predictions.

For Further Reading

Gambrell, L. B., & Bales, R. J. (1986). Mental imagery and the comprehension-monitoring performance of fourth and fifth grade poor readers. *Reading Research Quarterly, 21,* 454–465.

Vacca, R., & Vacca, J. (1986). *Content area reading* (2nd ed.). Boston: Little, Brown.

Walker, B. J. (1985). Right-brained strategies for teaching comprehension. *Academic Therapy, 21,* 133–141.

Walker, B. J. (1985). *Using guided fantasy to teach reading.* Paper presented at the Second Ruperstsland Regional Reading Conference of the International Reading Association, Regina, Saskatchewan, Canada. (ERIC Document Reproduction Service No. ED 253 850)

HERRINGBONE TECHNIQUE

Description.   The herringbone technique develops comprehension of the main idea by plotting the *who, what, when, where, how* and *why* questions on a visual diagram of a fish skeleton. Using the answers to the *wh* questions, the student writes the main idea across the backbone of the fish diagram (Tierney, Readence, & Dishner, 1990).

Targeted Reading Levels: 5 – 12

Text: Particularly suited for expository text. Can be used for narrative text.

Predominant Focus of Instruction

1. Processing focus: meaning
2. Instructional phase: during and after reading
3. Response mode emphasized: written response and oral discussion
4. Strategy emphasized: elaboration
5. Skill emphasized: literal comprehension

6. Source of information: text-based
7. Type of instruction: implicit with some explicit
8. Type of cognitive processing: successive, but is written in a visual display (simultaneous)

Procedure

1. The teacher selects a text at the appropriate reading level.
2. The teacher constructs a visual diagram of the herringbone.
3. The teacher tells the student to record the answers to the questions on the diagram (see Figure 9–2). He will look for answers to:
   a. Who is the author talking about?
   b. What did they do?
   c. When did they do it?
   d. Where did they do it?
   e. How did they do it?
   f. Why did they do it?
4. The student reads to find the answers and records the answers on the diagram.
5. After the information is recorded, the teacher shows the student how each answer fits into a slot in a main idea sentence.
6. The student writes a main idea, using the information from the herringbone diagram.
7. The teacher duplicates sheets with the herringbone diagram, and students complete the diagram on their own.
8. The diagram becomes a tool for story discussion. During the discussion, the teacher and students compare their answers and their rationales.

Modification.   The implementation of the herringbone can be changed from finding the facts first to writing the main idea and then looking for the facts that support this main idea.

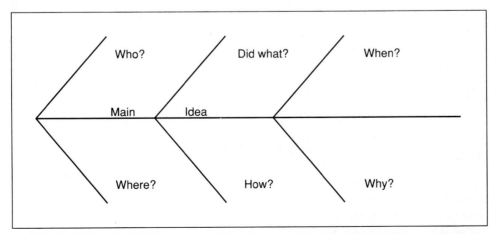

Figure 9–2
Herringbone
Technique

Note: From Robert J. Tierney, John E. Readence, and Ernest K. Dishner, *Reading Strategies and Practices: A Compendium.* Third Edition. Copyright © 1990 by Allyn and Bacon, Inc. Reprinted with permission.

Further Diagnostic Applications

Basic View of Reading.   Reading is a bottom-up process where the reader uses the facts in the text to construct a main idea.

Patterns of Strengths and Strategies.   The herringbone technique is most appropriate for students who need a visual structure to draw relationships between the facts in a text and the main idea. For these students, the technique records the information so that it can be organized into a whole.

Learner Patterns That Produce a High Success Rate

1. A successive learner who has difficulty organizing factual information to form a main idea. This technique shows him how the facts fit together to form the main idea.
2. A passive learner who has difficulty identifying the important facts that are used to form a main idea. This technique gives him an active strategy to use while he is reading.
3. A simultaneous learner who has difficulty identifying the factual information that he used to construct a main idea. This technique can be modified so that first the student writes the main idea and then rereads the text to find the facts that support the main idea.

Using the Technique as a Diagnostic Teaching Lesson.   For the herringbone technique to be effective, a majority of the following statements must be answered in the affirmative.

Yes   No

_____ _____ 1. The student can find the facts in the text and record them on the diagram.

_____ _____ 2. The student can construct a main idea from the facts.

_____ _____ 3. The student is more active in a group discussion after using the herringbone diagram.

For Further Reading

Herber, H. L. (1978). *Teaching reading in content areas* (2nd ed.). Englewood Cliffs, NJ: Prentice-Hall.

Tierney, R. J., Readence, J. E., & Dishner, E. K. (1990). *Reading strategies and practices: A compendium* (3rd ed.). Boston: Allyn and Bacon.

IMPLICIT TEACHING

Description.   Implicit teaching is a nondirective approach to instruction where the teacher creates an instructional environment that stimulates thinking about specific reading tasks. The teacher participates only as a cognitive inquirer, asking the student, "How did you know that?" The student makes generalizations because he is immersed in a literate environment.

Targeted Reading Levels: All levels

Text: Authentic texts selected to demonstrate the skill or strategy that is targeted for instruction

Predominant Focus of Instruction

1. Processing focus: print and meaning
2. Instructional phase: after reading
3. Response mode emphasized: oral discussion
4. Strategy emphasized: elaboration
5. Skill emphasized: depends on child, environment, and scaffolds
6. Source of information: reader-based phasing to text-based
7. Type of instruction: implicit
8. Type of cognitive processing: depends on child and task

Procedure

1. The teacher decides on the targeted learning outcome.
2. The teacher strategically arranges the physical environment so that students can discuss with the teacher what they read in a relaxed atmosphere.
3. The teacher arranges attractive books or printed materials that incorporate the skill or strategy in prominent places in the room.
4. The teacher creates a social activity that causes the students to use the targeted skill or strategy in a meaningful way.
5. When the students use print to make sense of their environment, the teacher asks, "How did you know that?"
6. The teacher creates the expectation of the learning outcome by discussing informally the learning outcome. She says, "Did you notice . . . ?"
7. When appropriate, the teacher models reading the text for meaning and enjoyment. She says, "When I read that I thought. . . . "
8. The teacher creates a similar experience that causes the students again to use the targeted skill or strategy in a meaningful way.

COMMENT: Implicit instruction is an instructional format where the teacher takes a more indirect role in mediating learning. This type of instruction is associated with a whole language environment where the children are more actively involved in directing their own learning. Techniques fall along a continuum, ranging from *less teacher intervention* to *more teacher intervention.* Implicit instruction has less teacher intervention and more student participation in the learning activity.

Further Diagnostic Applications

Basic View of Reading.   Reading is a top-down process where the reader uses what he knows to make sense of his environment. Reading instruction, therefore, should consist of creating a literate environment where a child can use print to make sense of his environment.

Patterns of Strengths and Strategies.   This format presents skills and strategies in the whole learning context. The teacher asks the student what he did to make sense of his environment. The student who actively restructures his environment so that it makes sense learns easily through this method.

Learner Patterns That Produce a High Success Rate

1. An active learner who needs learning activities to make sense. This method allows him to use his thinking strategies in natural learning environments.
2. An active learner who prefers to learn without teacher direction. This method allows him to direct his own learning.
3. A simultaneous learner who needs to experience the whole before understanding the parts. This method allows him to use the social-interactive experience to understand the parts of reading.

Using the Technique as a Diagnostic Teaching Lesson.   For implicit teaching to be effective, a majority of the following statements must be answered in the affirmative.

Yes   No

_____ _____ 1. The student actively explores the context to make sense of his reading.

_____ _____ 2. The student can explain his reasons for the way language works.

For Further Reading

Duffy, G. G., & Roehler, L. R. (1986). *Improving classroom reading instruction.* New York: Random House.

Harste, J. C., Short, K. G., & Burke, C. (1988). *Creating classrooms for authors* (336–339). Portsmouth, NH: Heinemann.

Haussler, M. M. (1985). A young child's developing concepts of print. In A. Jaggar & M. T. Smith-Burke (Eds.), *Observing the language learner* (pp. 73–81). New York: International Reading Association & National Council of Teachers of English.

IMPRESS METHOD

Description.   The impress method uses unison oral reading between the teacher and the student. The teacher and student sit side by side, with the teacher reading out loud slightly louder and ahead of the student, modeling fluent and expressive oral reading (Heckelman, 1969).

Targeted Reading Levels: K – 5

Text: Self-selected text is recommended

Predominant Focus of Instruction

1. Processing focus: print
2. Instructional phase: during reading
3. Response mode emphasized: oral production
4. Strategy emphasized: prediction

5. Skill emphasized: fluency and word identification
6. Source of information: reader-based
7. Type of instruction: implicit
8. Type of cognitive processing: simultaneous

Procedure

1. The student and the teacher select a text that is near frustration-level reading and around 200 words long.
2. The teacher and the student read the text in unison. The teacher reads slightly ahead of and slightly louder than the student.
3. The teacher sits on the right side of the student and reads into the right ear to impress the language structure on the left side of the brain.
4. The teacher moves her finger along the line of print so that the student's eyes can follow his reading.
5. The student's eyes follow the line of print as he reads.
6. As the student gains success through understanding the context, the teacher gradually lets him take the lead.
7. At this time, the teacher releases her lead in reading; however, she supplies difficult words when needed.

Modification.   The textual characteristics seem to influence the effectiveness of impress reading. Rhythmic and repetitive texts seem to increase the student's participation. A good source is Shel Silverstein's *Where the Sidewalk Ends*.

Further Diagnostic Applications

Basic View of Reading.   Reading is a process of accurate word identification, where automatic word identification precedes understanding. Therefore, reading is a bottom-up process. An abundance of reading errors contributes to an incorrect visual form being imprinted in memory. Therefore, accurate word identification is increased by unison reading, with the teacher modeling fluent oral reading.

Patterns of Strengths and Strategies.   Impress method is most appropriate for students who make a series of word identification errors without using passage meaning to self-correct the errors. This is often the result of reading at frustration level for an extended period of time. In the impress method, the student follows the teacher's model and imitates her fluent, accurate oral reading.

Learner Patterns That Produce a High Success Rate

1. A simultaneous learner who relies heavily on background knowledge when orally reading and who does not attend to the graphic cues. The impress method establishes accurate identification of words using overall textual meaning.
2. A nonfluent reader who is word-bound because of a heavy emphasis on phonic instruction. This method can rapidly increase oral reading fluency.
*3. A nonreader who has not established a sight vocabulary. Using high interest material, this technique develops a sight vocabulary.

Using the Technique as a Diagnostic Teaching Lesson.   For the impress method to be effective, a majority of the following statements must be answered in the affirmative.

Yes   No

_____ _____ 1. The student is sufficiently motivated to read along with the teacher.
_____ _____ 2. The student begins to track with the teacher and follows the model.
_____ _____ 3. There is an increase in sight word accuracy as a result of using the method.

For Further Reading

Heckelman, R. G. (1969). A neurological-impress method of remedial reading instruction. *Academic Therapy, 4,* 277–282.
Memory, D. M. (1981). The impress method: A status report of a new remedial reading technique. *Journal of Research and Development in Education, 14,* 102–114.

K-W-L

Description.   K-W-L is a technique used to direct students reading and learning from content area text. Before the text is read students write what they already know about the topic and questions that they would like to explore. After the text is read, students write what they learned about the topic (Ogle, 1986).

Targeted Reading Levels: 3–12

Text: Especially suited for expository text, but can be applied to all text.

Predominant Focus of Instruction:

1. Processing focus: meaning
2. Instructional phase: before and after reading
3. Response mode emphasized: written with some discussion
4. Strategy emphasized: prediction and elaboration
5. Skill emphasized: literal and non-literal comprehension
6. Source of information: reader-based phasing to text-based
7. Type of instruction: implicit
8. Type of cognitive processing: simultaneous

Procedure:

1. The teacher chooses an appropriate topic and text.
2. The teacher introduces the K-W-L worksheet (see Figure 9–3).
3. The students brainstorm ideas about the topic.
4. The teacher writes this information on a chart or chalkboard.
5. Students write what they know under the K ("What I Know") column.
6. Together, the teacher and students categorize the K column.

What I Know	What I Want to Learn	What I Learned

Figure 9–3
K-W-L Technique

Note. Adapted from "K-W-L: A teaching model that develops active reading of expository text" by Donna Ogle, 1986, *The Reading Teacher, 39*, pp. 564–570. Copyright 1986 by International Reading Association. Adapted by permission.

7. Students generate questions they would like answered about the topic and write them in the W ("What I Want to Learn") column.
8. Students silently read the text and add new questions to the "What I Want to Learn" column.
9. Students also add information to the L ("What I Learned") column.
10. After reading the selection, the students complete the "What I Learned Section."
11. The students and teacher review the first two columns to tie together what students knew and the questions they had with what they learned.

Modifications:

1. The K-W-L Plus technique extends the after phase to include organizing the learned information through mapping (a graphic outline) and then writing a summary.
2. The information known and learned can be combined to form a book about the topic.

Further Diagnostic Applications

Basic View of Reading. Reading is an active process where learners use what they know to elaborate and extend what the text says. Readers need experience relating what they know, the questions they have, and what they have learned from text in order to improve their active reading process.

Patterns of Strengths and Strategies. The K-W-L technique is appropriate for students who need to talk and write about the topic prior to reading. It is especially useful for the highly visual students who need to see concretely what they know in order to tie it to what they are reading.

Learner Patterns That Produce a High Success Rate

1. A self-directed reader who does not readily elaborate what he learns as he reads. K-W-L helps this student expand and elaborate topic knowledge.

*2. A reader who reads without relating what he knows to the text. K-W-L helps tie together what he knows and the text.

*3. A passive reader who needs to see what he has learned in relation to what he knows. The K-W-L helps him assess the understanding he has developed through reading.

Using the Technique as a Diagnostic Teaching Lesson.   For K-W-L to be effective, a majority of the following statements must be answered in the affirmative:

Yes   No

_____ _____ 1. The student easily writes what he knows.
_____ _____ 2. The student develops at least one question that he wants answered.
_____ _____ 3. The student can organize the information learned.

For Further Reading

Carr, E., & Ogle, D. (1987). K-W-L plus: A strategy for comprehension and summarization. *Journal of Reading, 30,* 626–631.

Ogle, D. (1986). K-W-L: A teaching model that develops active reading of expository text. *The Reading Teacher, 39,* 564–570.

Ogle, D. (1989). The know, want to know, learn strategy. In K. D. Muth (Ed.), *Children's comprehension of text* (pp. 205–223). Newark, DE: International Reading Association.

LANGUAGE EXPERIENCE APPROACH (LEA)

Description.   The language experience approach is a technique that is used for beginning reading instruction where the child dictates a story to the teacher. The story becomes the text for instruction and a collection of the stories becomes the child's first reader (Stauffer, 1970).

Targeted Reading Levels: K – 3

Text: The child's own language

Predominant Focus of Instruction

1. Processing focus: print
2. Instructional phase: before and during reading
3. Response mode emphasized: oral discussion
4. Strategy emphasized: prediction and monitoring
5. Skill emphasized: word identification
6. Source of information: reader-based
7. Type of instruction: implicit
8. Type of cognitive processing: simultaneous

Procedure

1. The teacher engages students in dialogue about a particular topic. A stimulating, engaging, and concrete topic tends to elicit more language from the students.

2. The students dictate a story while the teacher serves as secretary for the class.

3. Using leading questions, the teacher guides the students to develop a story line by using questions like these: "What happened next? Is this what you wanted to say? How can you make a story using this information?"

4. The students and the teacher read the story simultaneously to revise any statements or phrases that are unclear to the students. The story is to follow the natural language patterns of the students.

5. Then the teacher and the students read the story *repeatedly* so that repetition of the entire story will encourage a predictive set for the story.

6. The students are asked to read the story independently.

7. Activities to reinforce word identification are constructed from the story.

8. Word cards or chunk cards are developed using the words in the story. It is recommended that chunk cards (made by dividing the entire story into meaningful phrases) be used.

9. Initially, these chunk cards are flashed in the order in which they appear in the story. Later, they are mixed up. This activity maintains the sense of the whole while the whole is being broken into parts.

10. Stories are collated into anthologies that create the initial reading material for the student.

11. As words are learned, progress is monitored by checking the words off a word list.

Modifications

1. The teacher can design a guided imagery journey that incorporates targeted sight words. For instance, if the targeted sight words are *balloon, climb, sky,* and *wind,* the journey might contain the events that follow.

   Close your eyes and imagine that you are walking on a narrow pathway. . . . The wind is blowing gently as you walk softly down the path. . . . You come to an open meadow, and there is a hot air balloon. . . . A wise teacher offers to take you on a ride in the sky. . . . You climb into the basket. . . . You soar up . . . up . . . up . . . in the sky. I will leave you now. . . . You can finish the journey in your mind. . . . When you have finished your journey . . . you may return to the classroom and open your eyes.

2. When all the students have opened their eyes, they share their journeys in pairs. This allows them to verbalize the images.

3. The students dictate the journey while the teacher serves as secretary for the class (or individual student).

4. The students are reminded that the stories represent what happened in their imaginations. Their stories represent their images, just like a published story represents an author's images.

Further Diagnostic Applications

Basic View of Reading.   Reading is a top-down process. By reading his own story, the child will infer the consistency of printed language patterns. Since the story is based on his own experience, he continually uses this experience to remember the words in the story.

Patterns of Strengths and Strategies.   Language experience is most appropriate for students who have facility with language and are simultaneous, top-down thinkers. If a student predicts from his own experiences rather than the words in the text, then language experience matches his strategies (using what he knows); therefore, this technique facilitates word learning by asking the student to identify words using his own experiences.

Learner Patterns That Produce a High Success Rate

1. A simultaneous thinker who uses prior knowledge to construct meaning, often resulting in overpredicting or guessing without identifying words by how they are written. LEA uses the student's strength (using prior knowledge) to facilitate word identification.
2. An extremely verbal, creative student whose verbalization interferes with the mundane task of looking at words. LEA uses the strength (verbalization) to facilitate word identification.
3. A student who is unwilling to take a guess unless very certain that the response will be correct. LEA provides a text that allows the student to take a safe guess, using both what is on the page and what he remembers was written.
4. A learner who has had an overemphasis on phonics. Language experience can increase his fluency and the predictive set.

Modifications

1. The extremely imaginative, creative learner can use guided imagery as a medium for creating stories.
2. The extremely concrete learner can use field trips and science activities as a medium for creating stories.
3. The student who deals most effectively in visual-spatial relationships can use mapping as a medium for developing a story.
4. The shy, simultaneous learner who has difficulty developing a coherent story can use wordless picture books to boost his confidence in developing a story.

Using the Technique as a Diagnostic Teaching Lesson.   For LEA to be effective, a majority of the following statements must be answered in the affirmative.

Yes   No

_____ _____ 1. The student can remember the story he told.
_____ _____ 2. The student focuses on the words and story line.
_____ _____ 3. The student tells a fairly coherent story.
_____ _____ 4. The student remembers the story well enough to predict the words he does not remember.
_____ _____ 5. The student responds correctly when prompted using the preceding context and story theme.

For Further Reading

Aukerman, R. C. (1984). *Approaches to beginning reading* (2nd ed.) (pp. 368–371). New York: John Wiley & Sons.

Stauffer, R. G. (1970). *The language experience approach to the teaching of reading.* New York: Harper & Row.

Walker, B. J. (1982). A new approach to language experience. *Journal of Language Experience, 5,* 25–30.

LINGUISTIC METHOD

Description. The linguistic method is an approach for instructing a beginning reader that is based on word patterns. The word families have a minimal contrast in the word patterns. Therefore, this approach emphasizes decoding by visual analogy.

Targeted Reading Levels: K – 2

Text: Isolated words that have the same word patterns and designated text that introduces the word patterns.

Predominant Focus of Instruction

1. Processing focus: print
2. Instructional phase: before reading
3. Response mode emphasized: oral discussion
4. Strategy emphasized: elaboration
5. Skill emphasized: word analysis
6. Source of information: text-based
7. Type of instruction: implicit (can be adapted to explicit)
8. Type of cognitive processing: successive

Procedure

1. The teacher introduces a word pattern by presenting three new words in the word family. For example:

   cat
   mat
   fat

2. The teacher spells each word. Then she says each word. For example:

   c-a-t spells *cat*
   m-a-t spells *mat*
   f-a-t spells *fat*

3. The teacher asks the students how the words are alike. He elicits the response that the words have the same ending pattern of *at.*
4. The teacher asks the students how the words are different. She elicits the response that the words are different because they have a different letter at the beginning.
5. The students read the text that uses the word pattern.

   The cat is fat.
   The cat is on the mat.
   The fat cat is on the mat.

Further Diagnostic Applications

Basic View of Reading.   Reading is a bottom-up process where the reader masters a set of word patterns that have a minimal visual contrast. Meaning is stressed after the code is broken. Since the student comes to school with a well-developed oral language, initial reading instruction should focus on decoding.

Patterns of Strengths and Strategies.   The linguistic word structure approach to reading is most appropriate for students who have extremely high visual discrimination skills and need a directed approach to word learning.

Learner Patterns That Produce a High Success Rate

1. A successive learner who visually discriminates difference among wholes and has a well-developed visual memory. This technique shows him the parts in whole words.
2. A student who has good visual memory but needs his attention drawn to the patterns in words. This technique shows him how to form decoding analogies.

Using the Technique as a Diagnostic Teaching Lesson.   For the linguistic method to be effective, a majority of the following statements must be answered in the affirmative.

Yes   No

_____ _____ 1. The student can visually discriminate the differences in words.
_____ _____ 2. The student recognizes letter names and patterns easily and transfers visual patterns to new words.
_____ _____ 3. The student finds the simple stories exciting because he is breaking the code.

For Further Reading

Bloomfield, L., & Barnhart, C. (1961). *Let's read: A linguistic approach.* Detroit: Wayne State Press.

Ray, D. D. (1971). Specificity in remediation. In B. Batemen (Ed.), *Learning Disorders* (pp. 180–191). Seattle, WA: Special Child Publications.

LISTENING-THINKING ACTIVITY

Description.   A listening-thinking activity (LTA) is an instructional format for teaching children how to listen to stories. It involves predicting what will happen, talking about what happened, and talking about how you know what is happening. As the teacher reads aloud, he communicates the message by adding intonation and gestures to facilitate understanding.

Targeted Reading Levels: All levels

Text: An interesting, well-written text. Picture storybooks are excellent.

Predominant Focus of Instruction

1. Processing focus: meaning
2. Instructional phase: before and during reading
3. Response mode emphasized: oral discussion
4. Strategy emphasized: prediction and monitoring
5. Skill emphasized: listening comprehension
6. Source of information: reader-based
7. Type of instruction: implicit
8. Type of cognitive processing: simultaneous

Procedure

1. Using the title, the teacher has the students brainstorm what the story might be about.
2. She reads to a turning point.
3. The teacher models her questions about what is happening thus far in the story: "I wonder why the author said . . . ?"
4. The teacher summarizes what she has read so far, relating it to the *I wonder* statements.
5. From the summary, she develops a prediction or bet. She says, "Oh, I know, I bet. . . ."
6. Then the students make predictions or bets.
7. The teacher continues reading to the next turning point in the story.
8. She asks the students to talk about what they are thinking using *I wonder* statements. The teacher models her thinking also.
9. The teacher asks the students to tell what has happened so far to make them curious. The teacher adds her own interpretation.
10. The teacher and the students review previous predictions. Then they decide if they still want to keep all the predictions.
11. The students revise or make a new prediction.
12. The teacher alternates reading and discussing until the end of the story.
13. The teacher uses nonverbal cues from the students to check their understanding. When students are confused, the teacher stops to discuss the story line and how they arrived at their interpretations.
14. The teacher and the students discuss the story as a whole, relating various interpretations.

Further Diagnostic Applications

Basic View of Reading.   Reading is an interactive process where the student thinks about what he reads, using what he knows and the text. Listening is also an active process where the student interprets the story as he listens. In a listening activity, there is the interpersonal communication during reading, where the teacher can use nonverbal cues and intonation to convey the author's message.

Patterns of Strengths and Strategies.   A listening-thinking activity is appropriate for developing readers who need the added input of social interaction to learn either the strategy of predicting or monitoring comprehension. This technique allows the

teacher to model these active reasoning strategies and to check students' understanding.

Learner Patterns That Produce a High Success Rate

1. A passive reader who needs to learn how to make predictions. The LTA provides a short lesson where the student can be involved in making predictions.
2. A passive reader who needs to check his understanding. The LTA provides a short lesson where the teacher can model comprehension monitoring.
3. The severely reading disabled student. This technique allows the student to practice active thinking strategies without having to read the words. The LTA leads the student to more active thinking strategies that he can use when he can read the words.
*4. A simultaneous reader who needs to experience the steps of active thinking to clarify his thinking.

Using the Technique as a Diagnostic Teaching Lesson. For LTA to be effective, a majority of the following statements must be answered in the affirmative:

Yes   No

_____ _____ 1. The student listens to stories and can remember what was read.
_____ _____ 2. The student can construct an oral response after listening.
_____ _____ 3. The student likes listening to stories that are read orally.

For Further Reading

Baker, L., & Brown, A. (1984). Metacognitive skills and reading. In P. D. Pearson (Ed.), *Handbook of reading research* (pp. 353–394). New York: Longman.

Gillet, J. W., & Temple, C. (1986). *Understanding reading problems* (2nd ed.). Boston: Little, Brown.

LITERATURE CIRCLES

Description. Literature circles are used to develop personal response to literature by having students share their interpretations in a discussion group. By talking about the literature, students integrate the author's ideas and concepts with their own (Harste, Short & Burke, 1988).

Targeted Reading Levels: K – 12

Predominant Focus of Instruction:

1. Processing focus: meaning
2. Instructional phase: after reading
3. Response mode emphasized: oral discussion
4. Strategy emphasized: elaboration
5. Skill emphasized: non-literal comprehension

6. Source of Information: reader-based phasing into text-based
7. Type of Instruction: implicit
8. Type of Cognitive Processing: simultaneous

Procedure:

1. The teacher introduces several books by giving short summaries or book talks.
2. The students choose a book to read for the next two days or a week.
3. After the books are read, the students reading the same book gather into a literature circle.
4. The discussion is open-ended with the teacher beginning with an invitation like: "Tell me about this book" or "What was your favorite part?"
5. At the end of the discussion time, the group decides what they will talk about the next day.
6. As the students become familiar with this format, the teacher becomes less involved in the discussion and lets the students take the lead.
7. At the conclusion of the discussion, group members can present their interpretation to the class as a "book talk."

Modifications:

1. To add a writing component, students can keep a literature log (See Reading Log in this chapter) so they can more easily share their ideas.
2. For some groups, the teacher may continue in the literature circle as a group member.

Further Diagnostic Applications

Basic View of Reading.   Reading is a social-interactive process where the social context affects individual interpretation of text. Through sharing ideas in a peer group, students define and elaborate their ideas.

Patterns of Strengths and Strategies.   The Literature Circle technique is appropriate for students who can discuss their ideas freely in a group. The dialogue helps these students elaborate their understanding of literature and connect that understanding to their experiences.

Learner Patterns That Produce a High Success Rate

1. A self-directed reader who profits from sharing his ideas in a group. Literature circles help this student verify and create interpretations.
2. A self-directed reader who likes to share personal feelings about text but needs time to reflect on ideas before discussing. Literature circles help this student connect his personal feelings with the text.
*3. A reader who is bound by the text and believes that reading means getting right answers. Literature circles allow this student to verbalize ideas in a safe environment.

Using the Technique as a Diagnostic Teaching Lesson.   For Literature Circles to be effective, a majority of the following statements must be answered in the affirmative:

Yes   No

——— ——— 1. The student can share interpretations in a group.
——— ——— 2. The student likes narrative text so that he finds it engaging enough to make a response.

For Further Reading

Harste, J. C., Short, K. G., & Burke, C. (1988) *Creating classrooms for authors* (pp. 336–339). Portsmouth, NH: Heinemann.
Routman, Regie (1988). *Transitions: From literature to literacy.* Portsmouth, NH: Heinemann.

MESSAGE WRITING

Description.   Message writing is a technique to develop prediction and monitoring of print processing. The student writes a message, usually a sentence, by slowly saying the words. The student predicts and then writes the letters in the words.

Targeted Reading Levels: 1–4

Text: Student generated

Predominant Focus of Instruction:
1. Processing focus: print
2. Instructional phase: after reading
3. Response mode emphasized: written and oral production
4. Strategy emphasized: prediction and monitoring
5. Skill emphasized: word identification
6. Source of Information: reader-based information
7. Type of Instruction: implicit
8. Type of cognitive processing: simultaneous phasing to successive

Procedure
1. The teacher provides a blank writing book where each page is divided in half. The top half is practice writing and the bottom half is the sentence writing.
2. Assisted by the teacher, the student composes a brief message (one or two sentences).
3. The sentence is written word by word.
4. If the student is unfamiliar with the printed form of a word, he uses the practice page.

5. The teacher assists by drawing boxes for each letter of the unfamiliar word. For example, the word dog would look like this:

6. The student slowly says the sounds and places the letters he knows in the appropriate boxes.

7. The teacher supplies any unknown letters in the appropriate boxes. In the example, the teacher places an "o" in the middle box.
8. The teacher asks, "Does this look right?"
9. The student evaluates the word and places it in his sentence.
10. After the sentence is written, the teacher writes it on a sentence strip and then cuts it apart.
11. The student reconstructs the sentence, matching the words in his writing book.
12. The sentence is always read in its entirety.

Modification: When working with an unfamiliar word, the teacher may want to use magnetic letters before using the writing book. In that case, the student constructs a familiar part and then the teacher supplies other letters.

Further Diagnostic Applications

Basic View of Reading.   Reading is a top-down process where the reader predicts what words will look like by using his understanding of printed words.

Patterns of Strengths and Strategies.   The Message Writing approach is most appropriate for students who write with facility and can predict some letters in a word. By predicting and writing the letters, the student creates his own system for recognizing words.

Learner Patterns That Produce a High Success Rate

1. A simultaneous learner who uses only what he knows when comprehending text, therefore, he guesses wildly when he comes to an unknown word. Sentence writing helps this student focus on the details of printed words as he communicates a message.
*2. The passive learner who does not attempt to figure out unknown words. By writing a message, the student actively predicts letters in words.

Using the Technique as a Diagnostic Teaching Lesson.   For message writing to be effective, a majority of the following statements must be answered in the affirmative:

Yes   No

____ ____ 1. The student can form letters.
____ ____ 2. The student can predict letter sounds in words.
____ ____ 3. The student wants to communicate a message.

For Further Reading

Pinnell, G. S., Fried, M. D., & Estice, R. M. (1990). Reading recovery: Learning how to make a difference. *Reading Teacher, 43,* 282–295.

Clay, M. (1985). *The early detection of reading difficulties* (2nd ed.). Exeter, NH: Heinemann.

METAPHORS

Description. Metaphors are used to relate words and concepts to already known objects by identifying their likenesses and differences. For young children, common concrete objects can be used to develop metaphors.

Targeted Reading Levels: 4–8

Text: Isolated words or concepts

Predominant Focus of Instruction

1. Processing focus: meaning
2. Instructional phase: after reading
3. Response mode emphasized: oral discussion
4. Strategy emphasized: elaboration
5. Skill emphasized: word meaning
6. Source of information: reader-based
7. Type of instruction: implicit
8. Type of cognitive processing: simultaneous

Procedure

1. The teacher selects a key word or concept from the assigned text.
2. The teacher creates a metaphor which would describe the key attributes of the word or concept.
3. The teacher describes how the metaphor is like the key word and how it is different from the key word. For example, "A cloud is a puddle in the sky. It is like a puddle because a cloud is made of water droplets. It is not like a puddle because the water droplets have become water vapor."
4. Then the students create a metaphor within a particular class. For example, "What can you think of that is like a volcano? What animal is like a volcano?"
5. The students decide on a metaphor. For example, "A dragon is like a volcano."
6. The students explain the similarity. For example, "A dragon is like a volcano because they are both hot and spit fire."
7. The students explain how it is different from the metaphor. For example, "A dragon is not like a volcano because it has four legs, and can run very, very fast."
8. The students discuss the meaning of the words.

Modification.   A brainstorming or listing of options in group situations can facilitate understanding. In this situation, students would justify their metaphors and decide on one or two metaphors to use as the concept is developed in class.

Further Diagnostic Applications

Basic View of Reading.   Reading is an interactive process where a reader's prior knowledge influences his comprehension of the text. Word knowledge is based on conceptual knowledge that is related by analogous relationships among prior experiences.

Patterns of Strengths and Strategies.   Metaphors are most appropriate for students who have facility with verbal language but draw unspecific relationships among concepts. The words *like a* are often prevalent in their conversations. For these students, creating metaphors elaborates the relationships they draw between what they already know and the new information.

Learner Patterns That Produce a High Success Rate

1. A simultaneous learner who relates many concepts at once but is often unaware of the relationship or the precise words used to associate them. This technique helps him label and categorize word relationships.
2. A highly verbal student whose facility with words needs to elaborate the analogous relationships between what he already knows and new words. This technique helps him relate what he knows into more inclusive categories.
*3. A successive learner who uses words without drawing relationships between the word concepts and the word label. This technique helps him explain relationships among words and experiences.

Using the Technique as a Diagnostic Teaching Lesson.   For metaphors to be effective, a majority of the following statements must be answered in the affirmative.

Yes   No

____ ____ 1. The student understands how a metaphor is constructed and can readily draw analogous relationships.

____ ____ 2. The student can rationally explain the similarities and differences of the metaphors he creates.

____ ____ 3. The student creates more elaborate definitions of words as a result of explaining the relationships.

For Further Reading

Delain, M. T., Pearson, P. D., & Anderson, R. C. (1985). Reading comprehension and creativity in black language use: You stand to gain by playing the sounding game! *American Educational Research Journal, 22,* 155–173.

Johnson, D. D., & Pearson, P. D. (1984). *Teaching reading vocabulary* (2nd ed.). New York: Holt, Rinehart & Winston.

Readence, J. E., Baldwin, R. S., & Rickelman, R. J. (1983). Instructional insights into metaphors and similes. *Journal of Reading, 27,* 109– 112.

MOTOR IMAGING

Description.   The Motor Imaging technique is specifically designed to develop word meanings by using images of movements related to the key attributes of a word. This technique ties together actions, images, and words. (Casale, 1985)

Targeted Reading Levels: All levels.

Text: Any kind, but specially helpful in content areas.

Predominant Focus of Instruction

1. Processing focus: meaning
2. Instructional phase: before reading
3. Response mode emphasized: oral and kinesthetic
4. Strategy emphasized: elaboration
5. Skill emphasized: word meaning
6. Source of information: reader-based
7. Type of instruction: implicit
8. Type of cognitive processing: simultaneous

Procedure:

1. The teacher selects target words from the passage to be read.
2. The word is written on the chalkboard.
3. The teacher explains what the word means.
4. Then, the teacher asks the students to visualize a pantomime for the word meaning. ("How could you demonstrate without words what this word means?")
5. At the teacher's indication, the students do their "pantomimes" all at the same time.
6. The teacher selects the most frequent, sensible occurrence.
7. The teacher demonstrates this action to the class.
8. Then, the students say the word and make the same gesture.
9. This procedure is continued with each new and difficult vocabulary word.
10. The students read the assigned text.

Further Diagnostic Application

Basic View of Reading.   Reading is a top-down process where the reader uses his own understanding of words to predict and confirm textual meaning. Word meaning is developed through concrete experiences and revisiting those experiences connects new meanings to experiences.

Patterns of Strengths and Strategies.   The motor imaging technique is most appropriate for less verbal students who rely on their prior experiences when interpreting text. By acting out word meanings, they can tie their experiences to verbal information.

Learner Patterns That Produce a High Success Rate:

1. A simultaneous thinker who draws patterns from experiences. Motor imaging uses this strength to develop word meanings.
2. This technique has been used with Bilingual students to increase their understanding of English as a second language. Through their actions, they code the experience in both languages.
*3. A text-based reader who needs to connect what he reads with his own experiences. Motor imaging helps the student make these connections.

Using the Technique as a Diagnostic Teaching Lesson.   For the Motor Imaging technique to be effective, a majority of the following statements must be answered in the affirmative:

Yes   No

____ ____ 1. The student can act out images.
____ ____ 2. The student can readily image actions.
____ ____ 3. The student ties actions, images, and words together.

For Further Reading

Casale, U. (1985). Motor imaging: A reading-vocabulary strategy. *Journal of Reading, 28,* 619–621.

Manzo, A., & Manzo, U. (1990). *Content area reading: A heuristic approach* (pp. 160–163). Columbus, OH: Merrill.

MULTISENSORY APPROACHES

Description.   Multisensory approaches or VAKT (visual/auditory/kinesthetic-tactile) techniques reinforce learning by tracing the letters and words to develop mastery. Relying on tactile-kinesthetic reinforcement, these techniques provide a multisensory stimulation for word learning.

Targeted Reading Levels: K – 3

Text: Varies with approach; however, a generic VAKT can be used to reinforce any word that is difficult to learn.

Predominant Focus of Instruction

1. Processing focus: print
2. Instructional phase: before reading
3. Response mode emphasized: written production
4. Strategy emphasized: elaboration
5. Skill emphasized: word identification
6. Source of information: text-based

7. Type of instruction: explicit
8. Type of cognitive processing: successive

Procedure

1. The teacher selects the key words to be learned and writes them with a crayon on cardboard or large paper. (A rough surface is better for the tactile reinforcement.)
2. The teacher models writing the word one letter at a time, saying the letter name, syllable, or letter sound.
3. The student traces each word letter by letter, saying either the letter name or letter sound. Then the student says the entire word.
4. The procedure is repeated with each word until the word can be written (not copied) from memory.
5. At any point that an error is made, the procedure is stopped and the teacher models the correct form of writing and saying the word.
6. This structured presentation continues until the student has mastered a sight vocabulary sufficient to read the stories.

Modifications.   Many variations of the generic VAKT exist. The following approaches are a few examples of how the variations can be used to differentiate instruction.

1. The Fernald Technique moves from self-selected word learning to creating personal stories from individual word banks. Words are presented by syllables, maintaining more of a sense of the whole than other VAKT procedures. Therefore, the technique is highly personalized and motivational for students who like to structure their own language.
2. The Orton-Gillingham-Stillman Method, the Herman Method, the Cooper Method, and the Spaulding Method use the generic VAKT to reinforce the sounds of letters and require the student to blend sounds of letters to form words. Therefore, words are selected that are decodable and follow an extremely structured presentation of phonic generalizations. This variation is most appropriate for a student who guesses at words and has poor visual memory but can blend sounds to form words.

Further Diagnostic Applications

Basic View of Reading.   Reading is a bottom-up process where the reader learns a basic sight vocabulary through repetitious, multisensory reinforcement of letters in words before reading complete stories.

Patterns of Strengths and Strategies.   Multisensory approaches are most appropriate for students who have strong tactile-kinesthetic preferences for learning and exhibit difficulty in initial word learning. This approach focuses the attention of the learner to the key features of each word.

Learner Patterns That Produce a High Success Rate

1. A successive learner with tactile-kinesthetic preferences who has difficulty remembering sight words that have been taught. This technique reinforces those words that are difficult to learn.

2. An extremely passive learner with tactile-kinesthetic preferences who does not attend to the key features of words but instead makes wild guesses. This technique draws attention to what words look like and the key features of the words.
3. The simultaneous learner who has difficulty remembering key sight words. Multisensory techniques reinforce words that are difficult for her to remember.

Using the Technique as a Diagnostic Teaching Lesson. For multisensory techniques to be effective, a majority of the following statements must be answered in the affirmative.

Yes   No

____ ____ 1. The student guesses at words without using their graphic or phonic cues.

____ ____ 2. Tracing the word facilitates recognition of sight words or sounds.

____ ____ 3. Tracing the words focuses attention on the key features of words.

For Further Reading

Fernald, G. (1943). *Remedial techniques in basic school subjects*. New York: McGraw-Hill.

Orton, J. (1966). The Orton-Gillingham approach. In J. Money (Ed.), *The disabled reader* (pp. 119–146). Baltimore: Johns Hopkins University Press.

OPINION-PROOF APPROACH

Description. The Opinion-Proof Approach is a technique designed to engage students in higher level thinking skills by asking students to write opinions and supporting evidence about a selection. This emphasizes evaluative thinking, verification and persuasive argument (Santa, Daily, and Nelson, 1985).

Targeted Reading Levels: 4–12

Text: Any kind where various points of view can be taken.

Predominant Focus of Instruction

1. Processing focus: meaning
2. Instructional phase: after reading
3. Response mode emphasized: written discourse to oral discussion
4. Strategy emphasized: monitoring and elaboration
5. Skill emphasized: non-literal comprehension
6. Source of information: reader-based information supported by text-based
7. Type of instruction: implicit
8. Type of cognitive processing: simultaneous

Procedure:

1. The students read a selected text usually in the content area.
2. The teacher guides the silent reading using an appropriate technique (see Table 8–2).
3. After the text is read, the teacher provides the students with an "Opinion-Proof" guide either on the chalkboard or a handout.
4. She explains that on the left side of the page the students are to write opinions about characters or events.
5. The teacher further explains that on the right side of the page, the students are to write proof for their opinions. This proof is to be derived directly from the text.
6. When students have completed their Opinion-Proof guide, they are to write an essay using their opinions with the supporting evidence they collect.
7. The teacher and students develop specific criteria for evaluating the essay. Some examples are: "Is the evidence found in the text?" "Does this evidence support my opinion?"
8. The teacher divides the class into groups or pairs.
9. The students share their essays and revise unclear ideas.

Modification: If writing an essay is difficult, the teacher may provide "framed paragraphs" where leading lines introduce the opinion followed by the support. For example, "In this story, I believe . . . The reason I think this is . . . ."

Further Diagnostic Applications

Basic View of Reading. Reading is an interactive process where the reader predicts and interprets information using his own ideas based on information in the text. This interactive process begins by using the reader's own knowledge and then support is found in the text.

Patterns of Strengths and Strategies. The opinion-proof approach is most appropriate for students who need time to write and think about their ideas prior to discussion. The writing helps elaborate their ideas integrating both the text and background knowledge.

Learner Patterns That Produce a High Success Rate:

1. Readers who use reader-based inferencing and are quiet and reflective. The opinion-proof allows them to have time to think through their ideas before discussion.
*2. Readers who are highly verbal and can write with ease but who are text-based. This approach uses their writing strength to lead them to tie the text to reader-based inferencing.
*3. Readers who use reader-based inferencing when comprehending text. The opinion-proof approach helps them return to the text to support, revise and modify their thinking based on textual information.

Using the Technique as a Diagnostic Teaching Lesson. For Opinion-Proof to be effective, a majority of the following statements must be answered in the affirmative:

Yes   No

_____ _____ 1. The student readily writes information.
_____ _____ 2. The student can generate at least one opinion.
_____ _____ 3. The student listens to ideas from his peers and refines his thinking.

For Further Reading

Manzo, A., & Manzo, U. (1990). *Content area reading: A heuristic approach* (pp. 228–230). Columbus, OH: Merrill.

Santa, C. M., Dailey, S. C., & Nelson, M. (1985). Free-response and opinion-proof: A reading and writing strategy for middle grade and secondary teachers. *Journal of Reading, 28,* 346–352.

PHONOGRAM APPROACH

Description.   The phonogram approach is a structured program to introduce phonic principles by using sound clusters within whole words. As whole words are introduced, the student is directed to look at the sound clusters in the words. Then the student finds similar letter clusters in new words and associates them with the known cluster words (Glass, 1973).

Targeted Reading Levels: 1–3

Text: Isolated words only; purchased materials or teacher-made word cards

Predominant Focus of Instruction

1. Processing focus: print
2. Instructional phase: after reading
3. Response mode emphasized: oral discussion
4. Strategy emphasized: elaboration
5. Skill emphasized: word analysis
6. Source of information: text-based
7. Type of instruction: explicit
8. Type of cognitive processing: generally successive, but does look at patterns (simultaneous)

Procedure

1. The teacher presents isolated words that contain the letter cluster. For the *an* sound cluster, these words could be presented:

fan	can	candy
man	pan	fancy
ran	Stan	candle

2. The teacher pronounces the whole word and identifies letter names and letter sounds of that target cluster. For example:

   "In the word *fan,* the letter *f* goes *f-f-f* and the letters *a-n* go *an.*"

3. The teacher pronounces the letter sound or cluster sounds and asks the student for its name. For example:

   "In the word *fan,* what letter goes *f-f-f?*"
   "In the word *fan,* what letters go *an?*"

4. The teacher pronounces the letter name or cluster and asks the student for its sound. For example:

   "In the word *fan,* what sound does the *f* make?"
   "In the word *fan,* what sound do *a-n* make?"

5. The teacher asks the student, "What is the word?"
6. Steps 2, 3, 4, and 5 are continued until the pattern is learned.
7. The teacher presents the words in sentences, and the student reads the sentences. For example:

   The man canned the fancy candy.
   Stan ran to fan the candle.

8. If a word cannot be decoded, the teacher directs the student to the letter cluster and asks for its name and sound. For example:

   "Look at the word. Where is the *a-n?* What sound does it make?
   What's the first letter? What sound does it make?"

9. The teacher returns to the list of words and asks the student, "How are *can, candy,* and *canopy* alike and how are they different?"

Modifications

1. The target words can be selected to teach the word patterns that are causing the student difficulty.
2. The target words can be selected to teach a particular letter sound. For example, if short *a* words are difficult for the student, the teacher can choose the patterns of *an, at, am, ab,* and *ap* so he can generalize the concept of short *a* without separating the individual letter sound from its pattern.

Further Diagnostic Applications

Basic View of Reading.   Reading is a bottom-up process where the student must learn to decode printed words before he can read for meaning. As such, the learner is explicitly taught the analogous sound relationships to enhance decoding.

Patterns of Strengths and Strategies.   Looking for sound clusters in whole words is most appropriate for a simultaneous learner. For this student, the approach facilitates word identification using the similarity among sounds in already known words.

Learner Patterns That Produce a High Success Rate

1. A simultaneous learner who needs direct instruction in forming phonic analogies among the words he already knows and new words. This technique uses his strength in identifying patterns.

2. An older student who needs to add a decoding strategy to supplement contextual analysis. This technique helps him use what he knows about context and word identification.

Using the Technique as a Diagnostic Teaching Lesson. For the phonogram approach to be effective, a majority of the following statements must be answered in the affirmative.

Yes   No

____ ____ 1. The student can segment sounds.

____ ____ 2. The student applies the analogies to both known and unknown words.

____ ____ 3. The student applies the strategy when reading connected text and encountering an unknown word.

For Further Reading

Glass, G. (1973). *Teaching decoding as separate from reading.* Garden City, NY: Adelphi University Press.

Glass, G., & Burton, E. (1973). How do they decode: Verbalization and observed behaviors of successful decoders. *Education, 94,* 58–63.

PREDICTABLE LANGUAGE APPROACH

Description. The predictable language approach uses the rhythmic, repetitive language structures of young children's stories to develop a predictive set for facilitating word identification.

Targeted Reading Levels: K – 2

Text: Predictable books with patterned language like:
Run, run, as fast as you can
You can't catch me; I'm the Gingerbread Man.

Predominant Focus of Instruction

1. Processing focus: print
2. Instructional phase: during reading
3. Response mode emphasized: oral
4. Strategy emphasized: prediction and monitoring
5. Skill emphasized: word identification
6. Source of information: reader-based and text-based
7. Type of instruction: implicit
8. Type of cognitive processing: simultaneous

Procedure

1. The teacher chooses a predictable book or story.
2. The teacher and the students talk about the story to develop a predictive set.

3. The teacher reads the first few pages or lines to the child. The teacher uses her finger above the line of print to mark the flow of language.
4. The teacher asks the student to join her. The teacher and student read together.
5. The teacher continues to read using an oral cloze. The student supplies the missing word in the language pattern.
6. When the student knows the language pattern, he reads the rest of the story on his own.
7. The student reads the whole story again on his own. The teacher assists him when necessary.
8. Using the predictable pattern, the student writes his own story, changing the characters and the setting.

Modifications: When the student does not predict the omitted word readily, the teacher reads the entire book orally. Then the teacher and students discuss the book. The second reading of the book is conducted using steps 4, 5, and 6.

Further Diagnostic Applications

Basic View of Reading: Reading is a top-down process where the reader's knowledge of language structures drives the word recognition process. Through rhythmic, repetitious language patterns, the student recognizes the printed forms of words and infers the graphophonic rule system.

Patterns of Strengths and Strategies. The predictable language approach encourages the student to associate printed words with the predictive patterns of language; therefore, it is most appropriate for students who laboriously try to decode words to derive meaning from text. Because a repetitive sentence pattern is used in this technique, the student can easily predict both what the words are and what they mean at the same time.

Learner Patterns That Produce a High Success Rate

1. A simultaneous thinker who has facility with verbal language but does not attend to the key features of short similar words found in basal readers. This technique allows him to identify words using the repetitive pattern.
2. A learner who needs a sense of the whole story before reading. The predictable language approach provides him with a brisk, paced reading of the entire story prior to word identification.
*3. An extremely slow, laborious letter-by-letter reader. The predictable language approach can restore his sense of the whole and the predictive nature of reading.
*4. The learner who reads in a monotone. This approach can restore his sense of rhythm and cadence in reading.

Using the Technique as a Diagnostic Teaching Lesson. For the predictable language approach to be effective, a majority of the following statements must be answered in the affirmative.

Yes   No

_____ _____ 1. The student identifies the language patterns easily and can complete the oral cloze.

_____ _____ 2. The student models the teacher's fluent reading and intonations readily.

_____ _____ 3. The student enjoys repetitive language and does not find it boring.

For Further Reading

Leu, D. J., DeGroff, L. C., & Simons, H. D. (1986). Predictable texts and interactive-compensatory hypotheses: Evaluating individual differences in reading ability, context use, and comprehension. *Journal of Educational Psychology, 78,* 347–352.

McClure, A. A. (1985). Predictable books: Another way to teach reading to learning disabled children. *Teaching Exceptional Children, 17,* 267–273.

Routman, Regie (1988). *Transitions: From literature to literacy.* Portsmouth, NH: Heinemann.

PREDICTION MAPS

Description.   The prediction map uses a conceptual, flowchart to visually map the comprehension process of prediction and revision. In using the map, teacher questioning focuses on what the reader is understanding about the text and the sources of information he is using. The teacher suggests that he can revise or expand his prediction according to what he has read and what he already knows (Walker, 1985).

Targeted Reading Levels: 4–8

Text: Short narrative stories

Predominant Focus of Instruction

1. Processing focus: meaning
2. Instructional phase: during reading
3. Response mode emphasized: written
4. Strategy emphasized: prediction and monitoring
5. Skill emphasized: literal and non-literal comprehension
6. Source of information: reader-based with some text-based
7. Type of instruction: explicit
8. Type of cognitive processing: simultaneous, but is an interrupted story (successive)

Procedure

1. The teacher selects a narrative text at the appropriate reading level.
2. The teacher identifies the key turning points in the story. (A story map can help.)
3. The teacher designates the story intervals that reveal enough of the story line to encourage logical inferences, but not enough to draw exact conclusions.

Figure 9–4
Prediction Map-
ping

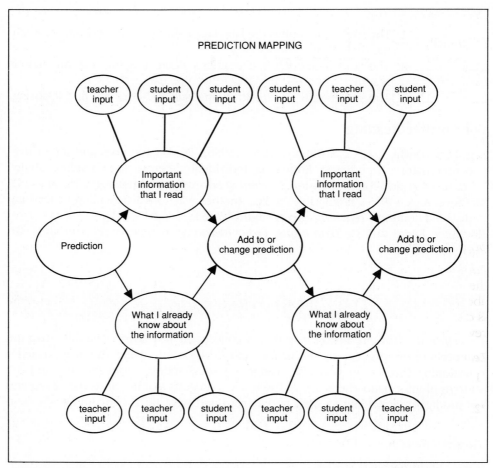

Note. From "Right-Brained Strategies for Teaching Comprehension" by Barbara J. Walker, 1985, *Academic Therapy, 21,* p. 137. Copyright 1985 by PRO-ED. Reprinted by permission.

4. Using the title, the student makes a prediction and places it in the center of the circle on the left side of the page (see Figure 9.4).
5. The teacher and the student record important information and what he already knows about it as illustrated.
6. The student reads the first section.
7. The student is asked to evaluate his prediction and to revise or change it if needed. The new prediction is written in the center circle.
8. The teacher asks, "What in the text made you think that?" The student records important information to support or revise the prediction.
9. The teacher asks, "What do you know about the important information that made you think that?" The student writes what he knows about the important information on the map to support the revised prediction.
10. The prediction/revision process is mapped at the designated intervals in the story,

using important information from the text and what is already known about the important information.

11. Initially, the teacher takes an active role by mapping her own process of comprehending as the story is read.
12. The predictions, important textual information, and personal interpretations are mapped interchangeably in the flowchart, with the teacher modeling how the comprehending process is restructured during the reading of a story. (Walker, 1985, pp. 136–138)

Further Diagnostic Applications

Basic View of Reading.   Reading is an interactive process where a reader uses both textual and nontextual information to build a model of meaning. The reader actively builds his model of meaning by predicting what the author is going to say, selecting important information from the text, and evaluating his interpretation of the text using prior knowledge (reader-based inferencing) and the text (text-based inferencing).

Patterns of Strengths and Strategies.   Prediction mapping is most appropriate for the simultaneous nonverbal student who tends to overrely on what he already knows about the text rather than the textual information. In this technique, the information is displayed in a spatial orientation and offers the reader more flexibility of options, revisions, and additions during the reading of a story.

Learner Patterns That Produce a High Success Rate

1. A nonverbal reader who needs to see a map of how to use the information he knows and the text. The map provides a tool for verbalizing how he is thinking.
*2. A passive reader who maintains his initial prediction without revising it even when conflicts develop between the prediction and important new information from the text and what he already knows about it. The map helps him see when he needs to revise a prediction because of new information presented in the text.
*3. A text-bound reader who does not use background knowledge when reading a story. The map helps him see how he can use what he knows to interpret what he is reading.

Using the Technique as a Diagnostic Teaching Lesson.   For prediction maps to be effective, a majority of the following statements must be answered in the affirmative.

Yes   No

_____ _____ 1. The student will make a prediction and fill in the circle.
_____ _____ 2. The student responds to the teacher model and adds information of his own.
_____ _____ 3. The student retells the story in more detail, relating important information and background knowledge.

For Further Reading

Walker, B. J. (1985). Right-brained strategies for teaching comprehension. *Academic Therapy, 21,* 133–141.

QUESTION-ANSWER RELATIONSHIPS (QAR)

Description.   The question-answer relationships (QAR) technique is used to identify the type of response necessary to answer a question. Questions are the most prevalent means of evaluating reading comprehension; therefore, knowledge about sources of information required to answer questions facilitates comprehension and increases a student's ability to participate in teacher-directed discussion and answer questions in textbook exercises (Raphael, 1982).

Targeted Reading Levels: 4 – 8

Text: Any text with accompanying questions

Predominant Focus of Instruction

1. Processing focus: meaning
2. Instructional phase: after reading
3. Response mode emphasized: oral discussion
4. Strategy emphasized: monitoring and elaboration
5. Skill emphasized: literal and non-literal comprehension
6. Source of information: text-based with some reader-based
7. Type of instruction: explicit
8. Type of cognitive processing: successive

Procedure

1. The teacher selects a text that represents different kinds of questions.
2. She introduces "right there" and "on my own" sources of information.
   a. "Right there" means that the answers are "right there" on the page and the words from the text can be used to answer the question. This source must often be used in answering a teacher's questions and in completing textbook exercises.
   b. "On my own" means that the students must fill in missing information using what they know about what is in the text to answer the question. In this instance, the students must realize that they are "on their own" and use their own experience when they answer the question.
3. The teacher completes an example lesson identifying the kind of answer that is required by the question as well as the answer. She models the strategy of finding answers to questions and identifying the sources of information used.
4. The teacher introduces the "think and search" question-answer relationship. Here the student must read the text carefully and then "think and search" different parts of the text to find the answers that fit together to answer the question.
5. Then the teacher introduces "author and you" sources of information. In this response, the students need to think about what they know, what the author tells them, and how this information fits together.
6. The teacher completes an example lesson, identifying the kind of answer that is required by the questions as well as the answer. She models by using all four sources of information and telling why and how the answers were obtained.

7. The students complete a third example lesson using a paragraph, the questions, and the answers. The students as a group identify the question-answer relationships. The students talk about reasons for a particular answer and the strategy used to obtain the answer.
8. The students complete a fourth example lesson using a paragraph, the questions, and the answers. Individually, the students identify the question-answer relationship. Then the students tell why they chose an answer, based on textual and nontextual information and the strategy used to obtain the answer.
9. Steps 5, 6, and 7 are extended to longer passages in progressive steps until the procedure can be used with basal readers or content area text.

Further Diagnostic Applications

Basic View of Reading.   Reading is an interactive process where a reader's interpretation of text is based on textual and nontextual information. Readers shift between the text and what they already know to construct answers to questions. Therefore, not only do students figure out answers to questions, but they also know the source of information they are using to construct the answer.

Patterns of Strengths and Strategies.   QAR is most appropriate for students who rely heavily on one source of information to answer questions or who cannot answer questions. For these students, the technique requires them to distinguish when it is appropriate to use their background knowledge and/or textual information to answer questions.

Learner Patterns That Produce a High Success Rate

1. A passive learner who is unaware of the various sources of information used when answering questions. This technique increases his active reading by asking him to evaluate how he got an answer.
2. A simultaneous learner who relies heavily on background knowledge about the subject to answer questions. This technique shows him when and how he can use background knowledge effectively and when he needs to use the text.
3. A successive text-bound learner who does not use what he already knows to answer questions. This technique shows him how to fill in missing information using what he knows.

Using the Technique as a Diagnostic Teaching Lesson.   For QAR to be effective, a majority of the following statements must be answered in the affirmative.

Yes   No

_____ _____ 1. The student can understand the differences between reader-based answers and text-based answers.

_____ _____ 2. The student can explain which source of information was used when he answered the question.

_____ _____ 3. The student elaborates his responses to questions.

For Further Reading

Pearson, P. D., & Raphael, T. E. (1985). Increasing student's awareness of sources of information for answering questions. *American Educational Research Journal, 22,* 217–235.

Raphael, T. E. (1982). Question-answering strategies for children. *Reading Teacher, 36,* 186–190.

Raphael, T. (1986). Teaching question-answer relationships, revisited. *The Reading Teacher, 39,* 516–522.

QUESTION-GENERATION STRATEGY

Description. Writing postreading questions uses student-generated questions to develop an understanding of the important information in the text. By deciding what to ask in their questions, students think about what is important in the text.

Targeted Reading Levels: 4 – 12

Text: Narrative or expository

Predominant Focus of Instruction

1. Processing focus: meaning
2. Instructional phase: after reading
3. Response mode emphasized: written
4. Strategy emphasized: elaboration
5. Skill emphasized: literal and non-literal comprehension
6. Source of information: reader-based because the student writes the question, but can be text-based if the student uses only the text
7. Type of instruction: initially explicit, then rapidly moves to implicit
8. Type of cognitive processing: simultaneous

Procedure

1. The teacher selects a text at the appropriate level.
2. She discusses how to write questions:
   a. A question has an answer.
   b. A good question begins with a question word like *who, what, when, where,* or *why.*
   c. A good question can be answered using information in the story.
   d. A good question asks about important information in the story.
3. The teacher selects a short paragraph and models writing questions about the important information in the text.
4. The students write questions after they read a short paragraph.
5. The students answer their questions.
6. The students compare their questions and answers with the teacher's questions and answers.
7. The teacher gives feedback about the importance of the questions.

8. The students write questions about the important information in their assigned text.
9. The students answer their questions.
10. The students compare their questions and answers with the teacher's questions and answers.

Modifications

1. Instead of Step 2, the teacher uses story grammar questions (e.g., "Who was the leading character?"). Then, she has the students make story-specific questions (see "Story Map" in this chapter).
2. Instead of Step 10, the teacher allows the students to share their questions and answers in small groups.
3. The teacher uses postgenerated questioning with book reports. After reading a book, the student writes his questions on cards. Then other students who have read the same book can use the cards to answer questions for their book reports.

Further Diagnostic Applications

Basic View of Reading.   Reading is an interactive process where the reader selects important textual information by constructing questions using his background knowledge and selected information.

Patterns of Strengths and Strategies.   Postgenerated questioning is most appropriate for students who have facility with word identification and word meaning but have difficulty studying for tests. For these students, this approach requires them to read text in order to formulate questions about the important information in the text or important parts of the story organization.

Learner Patterns That Produce a High Success Rate

1. A successive learner who knows the meanings of words but depends on teacher questioning to interpret the important information. This technique helps the student become more independent by having him write the questions before comparing them with the teacher's questions.
2. A simultaneous learner who has not learned to ask himself questions to monitor what he needs to remember when he reads. This technique encourages him to monitor his understanding by asking himself questions.
*3. A passive learner who tries to remember all the details rather than focusing on the important facts. By writing and comparing questions, he thinks about what is important to remember.

Using the Technique as a Diagnostic Teaching Lesson.   For question-generation strategy to be effective, a majority of the following statements must be answered in the affirmative.

Yes   No

_____ _____ 1. The student can recognize and understand the individual words in the text.

_____ _____ 2. The student begins to ask himself what information is important enough to remember.

_____ _____ 3. The student rehearses important information.

For Further Reading

Barr, R., & Sadow, M. (1985). *Reading diagnosis for teachers.* White Plains, NY: Longman.

Cohen, R. (1983). Self-generated questions as an aid to reading comprehension. *Reading Teacher, 36,* 770–775.

King, J. R., Biggs, S., & Lipsky, S. (1984). Student's self-questioning and summarizing as reading study strategies. *Journal of Reading Behavior, 15,* 205–218.

READERS THEATRE

Description.   Readers theatre is a dramatic interpretation of a play script through oral interpretive reading. The story theme and character development are conveyed through intonation, inflection, and fluency of oral reading.

Targeted Reading Levels: 2 – 5

Text: Scripts designed for the appropriate number of readers

Predominant Focus of Instruction

1. Processing focus: print and meaning
2. Instructional phase: after reading
3. Response mode emphasized: oral
4. Strategy emphasized: elaboration
5. Skill emphasized: non-literal comprehension and fluency
6. Source of information: reader-based and text-based
7. Type of instruction: implicit
8. Type of cognitive processing: simultaneous

Procedure

1. The teacher selects a narrative text at the appropriate reading level and constructs a play script.
2. The teacher presents a brief description of the characters, setting, events, and problem.
3. The students select or are assigned appropriate parts to read.
4. The students preview the scripts silently.
5. Standing in a line in front of a seated audience, the students read the scripts orally.
6. No props or costumes are used.
7. The students convey the story line by their intonation and phrasing.
8. Listeners must use their imaginations to interpret the story line.

Modifications

1. A readers theatre can be developed from the text that the student is reading. This provides additional reinforcement for word recognition. For example, when deciding how to write a script from a preprimer, the students and teacher reread parts of the text numerous times as they write the scripts on chart tablets.
2. Writing a readers theatre script from a story can also improve comprehension. The students must decide what important dialogue and narration are necessary to understand the story.
3. Different reading levels can be included in a script to allow readers of varying reading abilities to participate in the same activity.

Further Diagnostic Applications

Basic View of Reading.   Reading is a top-down process where the reader interprets the author's intended meaning through dramatic oral interpretative reading.

Patterns of Strengths and Strategies.   Readers theatre is most appropriate for students who have a dramatic flair and when given the stage will perform. Often a quiet, nonverbal student will perform in a readers theatre because the expectation is performance.

Learner Patterns That Produce a High Success Rate

1. A simultaneous learner who communicates through drama and needs to develop oral reading fluency. This is a natural way to develop fluency for this reader.
*2. The highly efficient decoder who is word-bound and does not identify with characters. This student benefits from the naturalness of character identification forced by the readers theatre script.
*3. A student who has difficulty tracking. He develops a purposeful reason to track when reading *short* readers theatre scripts.

Using the Technique as a Diagnostic Teaching Lesson.   For readers theatre to be effective, a majority of the following statements must be answered in the affirmative.

Yes   No

_____ _____ 1. The student has enough oral reading fluency to convey the message.
_____ _____ 2. The student likes to perform.
_____ _____ 3. The student becomes more fluent as he identifies with the character.

For Further Reading

Aulls, M. (1982). *Developing readers in today's elementary school.* Boston: Allyn and Bacon.
Sloyer, S. (1982). *Readers theatre: Story dramatization in the classroom.* Urbana, IL: National Council of Teachers of English.
Wertheimer, A. (1974). Story dramatization in the reading center. *English Journal, 64,* 85–87.

READING LOGS

Description.   Reading logs are written journals of students' thoughts as they are reading. At designated points, the students write a summary, make a prediction, and construct a reason for their prediction. As they read and write about the story, they evaluate new information in relation to their previous predictions. The written record of their previous thoughts allows the students to analyze how they construct meaning.

Targeted Reading Levels: 4 – 12

Text: Narrative text

Predominant Focus of Instruction

1. Processing focus: meaning
2. Instructional phase: during reading
3. Response mode emphasized: written discourse
4. Strategy emphasized: elaboration
5. Skill emphasized: non-literal comprehension
6. Source of information: reader-based
7. Type of instruction: implicit
8. Type of cognitive processing: simultaneous

Procedure

1. The teacher selects interesting stories so that the readers can make predictions.
2. He decides on key turning points in the story and marks them for the students.
3. The teacher prepares log sheets with the following information:

Name of story: _____

Author: _____

Segment: _____

Summary:

Prediction:

Reason for prediction:

How my comprehension is happening:

4. After the story is read, the reading logs are used as a basis for discussing the story.
5. The students discuss how their interpretation developed through the story.
6. The students discuss the influence of personal understanding on comprehension.

[handwritten: Background Knowledge]

Further Diagnostic Applications

Basic View of Reading.   Reading is an interactive process where the reader builds a model of meaning based on textual and nontextual information. As the reader builds his model of meaning, he predicts, monitors, and evaluates his interpretation in relation to the context of the situation.

Patterns of Strengths and Strategies.   Reading logs are most appropriate for the reflective student who needs to evaluate how he forms his model of meaning. He often does not realize what information he uses from the text and what he already knows. Furthermore, he has difficulty thinking about how he forms his conclusions about a story. Reading logs provide a method for analyzing how he constructs meaning.

Note

Learner Patterns That Produce a High Success Rate

1. A simultaneous, reflective learner who understands the story but does not understand how he constructs a response. Reading logs provide a record of his thoughts so that he can analyze them.
2. A successive learner who cannot tie story events together using what he already knows and the story events. Reading logs provide written summaries of events so that he can relate events to one another.
*3. A passive learner who needs actively to engage in forming and revising his model of meaning. Reading logs have the student elaborate his understanding during the reading of the story.

Using the Technique as a Diagnostic Teaching Lesson.   For reading logs to be effective, a majority of the following statements must be answered in the affirmative.

Yes   No

____ ____ 1. The student can write a summary selecting important information.
____ ____ 2. The student profits from the self-directed approach.
____ ____ 3. The student passively reads the story, recalling events but not relating those events to one another.

For Further Reading

Harste, J. C., Short, K. G., & Burke, C. (1988). *Creating classrooms for authors* (pp. 336–339). Portsmouth, NH: Heinemann.

Smith-Burke, M. T. (1982). Extending concepts through language activities. In J. Langer & M. T. Smith-Burke (Eds.), *Reader meets author/bridging the gap* (pp. 163–180). Newark, DE: International Reading Association.

RECIPROCAL TEACHING

Description.   Reciprocal teaching is a technique to develop comprehension of expository text by modeling and practicing how to read and understand the text. The teacher and students take turns leading a discussion about sections of the text. The teacher provides the initial model by thinking aloud about *how* she constructs a summary, makes up questions, clarifies what is difficult, and predicts what else the text will discuss (Palincsar & Brown, 1984).

Targeted Reading Levels: 5 – 12

Text: Expository text is preferred

Predominant Focus of Instruction

1. Processing focus: meaning
2. Instructional phase: during reading
3. Response mode emphasized: oral discussion
4. Strategy emphasized: elaboration
5. Skill emphasized: literal comprehension
6. Source of information: text-based
7. Type of instruction: explicit
8. Type of cognitive processing: successive

Procedure

1. The teacher selects a text from a content area.
2. The teacher explains the four tasks: (a) question generating, (b) summarizing, (c) clarifying the difficult parts, and (d) predicting what the next section will discuss.
3. Both the students and the teacher read silently the first section of the text.
4. The teacher talks about the four tasks of reading for that section.
   a. She constructs several good questions.
   b. She constructs a summary of the section using the main idea and supporting details.
   c. She clarifies difficult parts by stressing vocabulary and organization.
   d. She predicts what the next section will discuss by using the title and headings.
5. The students help revise the summary, answer the questions, clarify unclear parts of the summary and the text, and evaluate the prediction (agree or disagree and add a rationale for doing so).
6. After a few models by the teacher, a student takes the turn of teacher. He thinks aloud using the four steps.
7. The teacher becomes a student and assumes the student's role.
8. Students take turns playing "teacher."
9. Periodically the teacher reviews the four activities with the student.
   a. Rule for good questions: They should be clear and stand by themselves.
   b. Rule for summaries: Look for the topic sentence, make up a topic sentence if there is none, name lists, and delete what is unimportant.
   c. Rule for clarifying: Look for difficult vocabulary, incomplete information, unclear references, and unusual expressions.
   d. Rule for predictions: Use the title and headings, use questions in the text if present, and use text structures (references to *two kinds, four levels,* etc.).
10. As the students play "teacher," the teacher does the following:
    a. She provides feedback about the quality of summaries or questions. When necessary, she models her thinking for the student. For example, she might comment, "That was a start on a summary, but I would summarize by adding. . . ."
    b. She provides encouragement to the student playing "teacher." For example, she may say, "I liked the way you identified the important information."

Further Diagnostic Applications

Basic View of Reading.   Reading is an interactive process where a reader's interpretation of the text is based on textual and nontextual information. By thinking aloud, the student becomes more aware of how to integrate knowledge sources when reading.

Patterns of Strengths and Strategies.   Reciprocal teaching is most appropriate for students who have verbal fluency and experiential knowledge of the topics but need to focus on their understanding of text. These students read and retain information, but the complexities of content area reading often produce an overload of unorganized facts rather than important related information.

Learner Patterns That Produce a High Success Rate

1. A passive yet verbally fluent learner who needs to organize the information read. By leading the discussion, the student actively thinks about his section of the text. He also can follow the teacher's model.
2. A sequential learner who tries to memorize a string of unrelated facts rather than focus on the important points and how the facts relate to these points. This technique encourages him to use only the important information in his summary.
*3. A passive reader who does not monitor information learned and relate it to an organized whole. This technique helps him actively summarize text and clarify the difficult parts.

Using the Technique as a Diagnostic Teaching Lesson.   For reciprocal teaching to be effective, a majority of the following statements must be answered in the affirmative.

Yes   No

____ ____ 1. The student has enough expressive language that constructing a summary is not terribly time-consuming.
____ ____ 2. The student increases his ability to ask good questions.
____ ____ 3. The student increases his ability to summarize information.

For Further Reading

Palincsar, A. S., & Brown, A. L. (1984). Reciprocal teaching of comprehension-fostering and comprehension-monitoring activities. *Cognition and Instruction, 1,* 117–175.
Pearson, P. D. (1985). Changing the face of reading comprehension instruction. *Reading Teacher, 38,* 724–738.

REPEATED READINGS

Description.   The repeated readings technique is the oral rereading of a self-selected passage until accuracy and speed are fluent and represent the natural flow of language. Students must be able to read the selection with some degree of accuracy at the beginning of instruction.

Targeted Reading Levels: 1 – 4

Text: Self-selected

Predominant Focus of Instruction

1. Processing focus: print
2. Instructional phase: after reading
3. Response mode emphasized: oral production
4. Strategy emphasized: monitoring
5. Skill emphasized: fluency and word identification
6. Source of information: text-based phasing to reader-based
7. Type of instruction: implicit, but can be adapted to explicit
8. Type of cognitive processing: initially successive, but rapidly moves to simultaneous

Procedure

1. The student selects a text that he wants to read. The teacher segments the text into manageable passages for oral reading.
2. The teacher makes a copy of the text so she can mark errors as the student reads.
3. The teacher explains that rereading a passage is like practicing a musical instrument or practicing a football play. The repetition helps us read more smoothly and automatically.
4. The student reads the passage orally while the teacher records errors and speed.
5. The errors and speed are charted on a graph.
6. The student practices silently rereading the passage while the teacher listens to other students.
7. The student rereads the passage to the teacher while she records errors with a different colored pen.
8. The errors and speed are charted on a graph for the second reading. Progress toward the reading goals is discussed.
9. The procedure is continued until a speed of 85 words per minute is reached.
10. Steps 6, 7, and 8 are repeated as needed.

Modifications

1. The teacher can select a text that corresponds to instructional needs.
2. Instead of Step 4, the following interventions have been successfully used.
   a. Discussion of the errors and process of self-correction. The teacher suggests that the student say to himself, "Did that make sense? Can we say it that way?"
   b. Echo reading (see "Echo Reading") of sentences where the most errors occur.
   c. Discussion of the author's use of language and intended meaning of the paragraph.
   d. Tape-recording the readings. Then the student listens to the recording, marks errors, and records his time.
   e. Chunking (see "Chunking") the selection to improve fluency and the interaction of thought and language.
3. Only one or two rereadings are used. All readings are charted.

Further Diagnostic Applications

Basic View of Reading.   Reading is both a decoding and a comprehension process. Comprehension is dependent on the automatic decoding of printed language. Therefore, fluent and accurate decoding are necessary for efficient comprehension. Thus initially, reading is a bottom-up process.

Patterns of Strengths and Strategies.   Repeated readings are most appropriate for students who read word by word and do not use contextual clues to confirm anticipated words as they read. For this learner, the repeated readings encourage the use of overall contextual meaning and sentence structure to predict words and correct mistakes.

Learner Patterns That Produce a High Success Rate

1. A simultaneous learner who has a great deal of difficulty with word recognition because of an overemphasis on isolated word drill. This technique uses the overall textual meaning to increase word recognition accuracy.
2. A simultaneous learner who cannot blend sounds and must rely, therefore, on the context for word recognition accuracy. If progressively difficult text is used, this technique allows the student to read more complex text, where words can be recognized by using context rather than what the word looks or sounds like.
*3. A successive learner who has become word-bound with a heavy phonics instruction and needs to develop fluency and use of contextual cues for word identification. This technique emphasizes using context to identify words rather than sounding out individual words.

Using the Technique as a Diagnostic Teaching Lesson.   For repeated readings to be effective, a majority of the following statements must be answered in the affirmative.

Yes   No

_____ _____ 1. The student's errors decrease on a second reading.
_____ _____ 2. The student's speed increases on a second reading.
_____ _____ 3. The student's pattern of errors includes more self-corrections as fluency increases.
_____ _____ 4. Over several interventions, the student decreases the number of errors on an initial at-sight reading.

For Further Reading

Dowhower, S. (1989). Repeated reading: Research into practice. *The Reading Teacher, 42,* 502–507.

Kahn, R. (1983). The method of repeated readings: Expanding the neurological impress method for use with disabled readers. *Journal of Learning Disabilities, 16,* 90–92.

Moyer, S. B. (1982). Repeated reading. *Journal of Learning Disabilities, 15,* 619–623.

Samuels, S. J. (1979). The method of repeated readings. *Reading Teacher, 32,* 403–408.

REQUEST (RECIPROCAL QUESTIONING TECHNIQUE)

Description. The ReQuest technique develops comprehension by having the teacher and the student take turns asking and answering questions. At turning points in the text, the teacher models effective question-asking strategies. The student, in turn, asks appropriate questions by following the model. The goal is to develop self-questioning strategies for the student (Manzo, 1969).

Targeted Reading Levels: 4 – 12

Text: Particularly suited for narrative text but can be used with expository text

Predominant Focus of Instruction

1. Processing focus: meaning
2. Instructional phase: during reading
3. Response mode emphasized: oral discussion
4. Strategy emphasized: prediction and elaboration
5. Skill emphasized: literal and non-literal comprehension
6. Source of information: reader-based
7. Type of instruction: implicit
8. Type of cognitive processing: successive

Procedure

1. The teacher selects a text that is at the student's reading level and that is predictive in nature.
2. The teacher identifies appropriate points for asking questions.
3. The teacher introduces the ReQuest procedure in terms the student will understand. She tells him that they will be taking turns asking questions about the sentence and what it means. The student is to ask questions that a teacher might ask. Then the teacher emphasizes that questions must be answered fully and that they sometimes require support from the text.
4. The student and teacher read silently the first sentence.
5. When the teacher closes her book, the student asks questions. The teacher answers the question, integrating background knowledge and textual information. She also tells how she decided on her answer.
6. The procedure continues for the next sentence. This time the teacher asks the questions, modeling integrating information and the predictive nature of the reading by using questions like the following: "What do you think will happen next? Why do you think so?"
7. The teacher provides feedback about the student's questioning behavior during the procedure.
8. The procedure is used to develop purposes for reading and employs only the first three paragraphs.
9. The student reads the rest of the story silently to see if he answers his questions.
10. Follow-up discussion and activities can be used.

Further Diagnostic Applications

Basic View of Reading.   Reading is an interactive process that requires the reader to monitor his behavior by asking himself questions about the important information in the text and answering these questions, using both textual and nontextual information.

Patterns of Strengths and Strategies.   The ReQuest procedure is most appropriate for the sequential learner who likes to ask questions but does not always attend to the text for answers. For these students, the approach matches their desire to ask questions, but it focuses on the relevant information in a story and develops an active question-asking role rather than a passive role.

Learner Patterns That Produce a High Success Rate

1. A successive learner who asks questions and enjoys breaking a story into parts, reading only sections at a time. This technique uses his strength to show him how to elaborate his understanding using the text and what he knows.
2. A successive learner who asks irrelevant questions when reading and fails to comprehend the main points of the story. This technique focuses his attention on asking important questions and justifying answers.
*3. A passive learner who reads words fluently but does not ask himself, "What does this mean?" This technique develops self-questioning and monitoring of comprehension.
*4. A passive reader who reads words fluently but does not use his prior knowledge to interpret text. This technique asks the student to use both textual and nontextual information to ask and answer questions.

Using the Technique as a Diagnostic Teaching Lesson.   For the ReQuest technique to be effective, a majority of the following statements must be answered in the affirmative.

Yes   No

____   ____   1. The student likes to ask questions.
____   ____   2. The student can answer questions.
____   ____   3. The student can follow the teacher's model in question-answering behavior.

For Further Reading

Manzo, A. V. (1969). The request procedure. *Journal of Reading, 2,* 123–126.
Tierney, R. J., Readence, J. E., & Dishner, E. K. (1990). *Reading strategies and practices: A compendium* (3rd ed.). Boston: Allyn & Bacon.

RETELLING

Description.   Retelling is a technique to develop an oral recounting of a story. The student talks about the story by stating the characters, setting, problem, main episodes, and resolution.

Targeted Reading Levels: 1–5

Text: Narrative, but can be applied to all kinds.

Predominant Focus of Instruction

1. Processing focus: meaning
2. Instructional phase: after reading
3. Response mode emphasized: oral production
4. Strategy emphasized: elaboration
5. Skill emphasized: literal comprehension
6. Source of information: both reader-based and text-based
7. Type of instruction: implicit
8. Type of cognitive processing: simultaneous

Procedure

1. Before reading, the teacher explains to the students that she is going to ask them to retell the story when they have finished reading.
2. If the teacher is expecting the students to include specific information, she should tell the students before reading.
3. The teacher asks the students to retell the story as if they were telling it to a friend who has never heard it before.
4. The students tell the story noting the important parts: story setting, theme, plot, sequence, and resolution.
5. If the student is hesitant, the teacher uses prompts at the beginning, middle, and end (See Step 6).
6. If the student is unable to tell the story, the retelling is prompted step by step: "Once there was . . . who did . . . in the . . . (the character) had a problem . . . to solve the problem (the character) . . . first . . . second . . . third . . . and finally, the problem was solved by . . . and then. . . ."
7. When the retelling is complete, the teacher can ask direct questions about important information omitted.
8. The teacher can also refer to the text to reread omitted important information.

Modifications:

1. Retelling can be enhanced through the use of feltboards, role playing, and puppets.
2. Retelling can be easily adapted to small group or partner activities in the classroom.

Further Diagnostic Applications

Basic View of Reading.   Reading is a process where the reader interprets text using his own perceptions of what is important to remember. He makes a mental representation of the story and uses this to reconstruct the story.

Patterns of Strengths and Strategies.   The Retelling approach is most appropriate for students who have verbal strengths and remember the story long enough to internalize it and retell it. Retelling uses their strength to elaborate textual information.

Learner Patterns That Produce a High Success Rate

1. Readers who like to tell stories but fail to recount the most important events in the passage. Retelling uses their strength to draw attention to important textual information.

*2. Readers who are hesitant to communicate their ideas. Retelling increases the students' confidence by having them practice reformulating the information they read.

*3. Bilingual readers who become confused because they represent text in two language codes. Retelling helps these learners use the text and classroom language to express their ideas.

Using the Technique as a Diagnostic Teaching Lesson. For retelling to be effective, a majority of the following statements must be answered in the affirmative:

Yes   No

_____ _____ 1. The student verbalizes some ideas about the story.

_____ _____ 2. The student organizes a response that is fairly similar to the actual text.

For Further Reading

Glazer, S. M., & Searfoss, L. W. (1988). *Reading diagnosis and instruction: a C-A-L-M approach.* Englewood Cliffs, NJ: Prentice Hall.

Morrow, L. M. (1989) Retelling stories as a diagnostic tool. In S. M. Glazer, L. W. Searfoss, & L. M. Gentile (Eds.), *Reexamining reading diagnosis: New trends and procedures* (pp. 128–149). Newark, DE: International Reading Association.

SAY SOMETHING

Description. Say Something is a technique to develop personal response to literature by having students take turns saying something at intervals during the reading of the story (Harste, Short, & Burke, 1988).

Targeted Reading Levels: 2–12

Text: Especially suited for engaging, narrative text but can be applied to all text.

Predominant Focus of Instruction

1. Processing focus: meaning
2. Instructional phase: during reading
3. Response mode emphasized: oral discussion
4. Strategy emphasized: elaboration
5. Skill emphasized: non-literal comprehension
6. Source of information: reader-based
7. Type of instruction: implicit
8. Type of cognitive processing: sequential because story sections are used initially

Procedure

1. The teacher and students choose an engaging text.
2. The teacher demonstrates reading with a partner and making a personal response about the text read.
3. The teacher encourages students to challenge and extend the ideas of their partner.
4. The students choose partners for reading.
5. The partners decide if the reading will be oral or silent.
6. The partners take turns reading and saying something about what they have read.
7. After the students have finished, the teacher leads a group discussion.
8. The teacher puts a central topic in the middle of an overhead or on the chalkboard.
9. The students generate ideas about the topic and discuss how they fit with the author's ideas.
10. After reading several selections in this fashion, the teacher engages students in a discussion of how they use this strategy as they read.

Further Diagnostic Applications

Basic View of Reading.   Reading is a social-interactive process where interpretations develop through communicating ideas to others. This sharing enhances and extends text understanding.

Patterns of Strengths and Strategies.   The Say Something technique is appropriate for students who like to talk about what they read as they are reading the text. This dialogue helps social students refine their ideas using their strength.

Learner Patterns That Produce a High Success Rate:

1. A self-directed reader who needs to talk aloud about his personal feelings related to the story. Say Something allows him to talk about his personal responses to the story.
2. A quiet student who needs to verbalize ideas in a safe environment before discussing those ideas in a large group. The Say Something technique gives him a chance to try out ideas with a partner.

Using the Technique as a Diagnostic Teaching Lesson.   For Say Something to be effective, a majority of the following statements must be answered in the affirmative:

Yes   No

_____ _____ 1. The student can talk about the text read.
_____ _____ 2. The student can attend to the meaning while reading so he can make a response.
_____ _____ 3. The student can relate personally to his partner.

For Further Reading

Harste, J. C., Short, K. G., & Burke, C. (1988) *Creating classrooms for authors* (pp. 336–339). Portsmouth, NH: Heinemann.

SECONDARY READING SEQUENCE (SRS)

Description.   SRS is designed to integrate story understanding with word recognition. The teacher develops background knowledge by reading the story aloud and discussing its main points prior to the student's reading the story. The lesson sequence involves four comprehensive steps: listening comprehension, choral reading, oral reading, and review (Faas, 1980).

Targeted Reading Levels: 2 – 5; content level 6 – 12

Text: Adaptable to all contents. Particularly useful for content area reading. The newspaper and magazines are also good sources.

Predominant Focus of Instruction

1. Processing focus: print and meaning
2. Instructional phase: during reading
3. Response mode emphasized: oral discussion
4. Strategy emphasized: prediction and monitoring
5. Skill emphasized: word identification
6. Source of information: reader-based
7. Type of instruction: implicit
8. Type of cognitive processing: simultaneous

Procedure

1. The teacher selects a text that matches the student's listening comprehension level.
2. The teacher follows a listening comprehension sequence:
   a. The teacher reads the passage aloud. If the passage is long, an interrupted predictive listening format may be followed (See Listen-Thinking Activity in this chapter).
   b. The teacher either asks questions or has the student retell what was read to assess comprehension. Both literal and nonliteral information needs to be stressed.
   c. The teacher asks interpretative questions like these: "What would happen if? How is this character or idea similar to another character?" (VARIATION: Vocabulary maps or story maps of listening comprehension can be used.)
3. The teacher and the student chorally read the same passage. The teacher models correct intonation and phrasing. Errors are ignored as the teacher continues to read fluently.
4. Then the student reads the same passage orally. The teacher records errors on a copy of the text. Errors are reviewed and skill activities developed around these errors.
   The steps are as follows:
   a. The student reads the passage orally.
   b. The teacher records errors.
   c. The teacher and student review the errors, making a list of target words.
   d. Sentences are reread in an echo format. The teacher reads the correct form. The student reads following the teacher's model.

e. The student rereads the passage.

f. The teacher records errors in different colored pens.

g. A comparison is made of the errors.

5. The teacher makes a collection of the passages and target words. This booklet provides the text for weekly review and independent reading.

Modifications

1. During Step 4, the teacher uses the repeated readings format. This would involve charting progress toward the goal of fluent reading.

2. During Step 4, the teacher tape-records the student's reading. She then has the student listen to the tape and mark his errors on a copy of the text.

Further Diagnostic Applications

Basic View of Reading. Reading is a top-down process where the reader's background knowledge assists the recognition of words and fluent reading. Comprehension precedes decoding. The ultimate goal is a reader who will simultaneously apply the decoding skills of reading while comprehending text.

Patterns of Strengths and Strategies. SRS is most appropriate for adolescent readers who are simultaneous and have a high drive for meaning when reading. For these students, the approach uses their strengths of listening and thinking; then it transfers these strengths to word identification.

Learner Patterns That Produce a High Success Rate

1. A simultaneous learner with a high listening comprehension and minimal (second grade) word identification skills. This technique uses his strength in listening to develop an anticipation of what the text will say. This facilitates word identification.

*2. A passive learner with adequate listening comprehension skills and minimal word identification skills. The teacher needs to emphasize self-talk in error correction.

*3. An extremely word-bound, successive reader who lacks fluency. This technique uses what the student hears to develop expectations for what words will be in the text.

Using the Technique as a Diagnostic Teaching Lesson. For SRS to be effective, a majority of the following statements must be answered in the affirmative.

Yes   No

____ ____ 1. The student can listen and comprehend.

____ ____ 2. The student follows the teacher's model when choral reading.

____ ____ 3. The student discusses errors with the teacher.

For Further Reading

Chomsky, C. (1978). When you still can't read in third grade: After decoding what? In J. Samuels (Ed.), *What research has to say about reading instruction* (pp. 13–30). Newark, DE: International Reading Association.

Faas, L. A. (1980). *Children with learning problems: A handbook for teachers.* Boston: Houghton Mifflin.

SELF-DIRECTED QUESTIONING

Description.   Self-directed questioning uses student-generated questions to develop active reading. By following the sequence of self-directed questions, the student learns to monitor his understanding as he reads (Walker & Mohr, 1985).

Targeted Reading Levels: All levels but most appropriate for 4–12

Text: Narrative text is most appropriate

Predominant Focus of Instruction

1. Processing focus: meaning
2. Instructional phase: during reading
3. Response mode emphasized: oral discussion
4. Strategy emphasized: prediction and monitoring
5. Skill emphasized: non-literal comprehension
6. Source of information: reader-based
7. Type of instruction: initially explicit, but moves rapidly to implicit
8. Type of cognitive processing: simultaneous, but is an interrupted story (successive)

Procedure

1. The teacher selects a text at the appropriate level that has a fairly cohesive story line.
2. She decides on key prediction points. A story map (see "Story Map" in this chapter) can facilitate this process.
3. The teacher models the steps below with a short passage.

STEP A: Problem Definition
"What must I do? . . . I must guess what the author is going to say. . . . A good strategy is to use the title. . . . From the title, I bet that . . ."

STEP B: Plan of Action
"Now, let's see what's my plan for betting. . . . To make my bet, I already know that . . . To prove my bet, I must look for hints in the text. . . ."

STEP C: Self-Instruction in the Form of Self-Questioning
"I wonder how it fits? . . . The _____ must be important because the author keeps talking about it. . . . It fits because _____ ."

STEP D: Ways of Coping with Frustration and Failure
"Oops, that doesn't make sense. . . . I need to check the hints. . . . So far, I'm right about . . . but wrong about . . ."
"Oops, I was wrong. . . . It's OK to make a mistake. . . . I can change my bet as I get more information."

"From the new information, I bet that . . . or I wonder if . . ." The student then recycles to Step A.

STEP E: Self-Reinforcement
"I knew it, that sure fits. . . . So far I'm right!"
"Now I bet the author. . . ." The student then returns to Step A.*

4. The teacher emphasizes self-correcting behavior and self-reinforcement.
5. The student reads another example passage, talking aloud using the steps.
6. When comprehension breaks down, the teacher models her own thinking rather than asking questions. She says, "When I read that I thought . . ."
7. The teacher phases in and out of the story discussion as necessary, using questions like these: "Have you defined your problem? What is your plan? Does that make sense?"
8. At the end of the story, the student and the teacher discuss the story content and how they constructed meaning.

Modification: A chart of active reading behaviors can be kept by the teacher or student. In the chart they assess how many predictions or bets were revised and what sources of information were used.

Further Diagnostic Applications

Basic View of Reading. Reading is an interactive process where the reader builds a model of meaning based on textual and nontextual information. As the reader builds his model of meaning, he predicts, monitors, and reinforces his own learning.

Patterns of Strengths and Strategies. Self-directed questioning is most appropriate for students who overrely on what they know, failing to monitor reading comprehension and to relate textual information to prior knowledge. For these students, the approach matches their strength of prior knowledge and helps them revise their understanding based on textual information.

Learner Patterns That Produce a High Success Rate
1. A passive learner who needs to actively engage in forming and revising his interpretations of the text. This technique gives him a plan for thinking and checking his understanding.
2. A successive learner who knows the meanings of words but depends on teacher questioning to interpret the important information in the text. This technique gives him the steps to develop his own questions.
3. A successive learner who cannot tie story events together using what he already knows and these events. This technique asks the student to check both the text and what he knows to see if they fit together.

---

*Procedure 3 (steps A-E) adapted from *The Effects of Self-Questioning on Reading Comprehension* (pp. 9–10) by B. J. Walker and T. Mohr, 1985. Paper presented at the Washington Organization for Reading Development—Research Conference, Seattle, WA. (ERIC Document Reproduction Service No. ED 262 392) Adapted by permission.

*4. A simultaneous learner who understands the story but cannot recall the textual information used to construct his answer. The technique has him check the text. This will facilitate memory.

*5. A simultaneous learner who does not use self-talk to monitor the sources of information used to construct his answers. This technique encourages the internal dialogue that accompanies effective comprehension.

Using the Technique as a Diagnostic Teaching Lesson. For self-directed questioning to be effective, a majority of the following statements must be answered in the affirmative.

Yes   No

____ ____ 1. The student can make a prediction.
____ ____ 2. The student can follow the oral discussion of strategic reading.
____ ____ 3. The student does not use background knowledge when reading.
____ ____ 4. The student does not use key events to predict outcomes.

For Further Reading

Helfeldt, J. P., & Lalik, R. (1979). Reciprocal student-teacher questioning. In C. Pennock (Ed.), *Reading comprehension at four linguistic levels* (pp. 74–80). Newark, DE: International Reading Association.

Meichenbaum, D. (1977). *Cognitive-behavior modification: An integrative approach.* New York: Plenum Press.

Walker, B. J., & Mohr, T. (1985). *The effects of self-questioning on reading comprehension.* Paper presented at the Washington Organization for Reading Development—Research Conference, Seattle, WA. (ERIC Document Reproduction Service No. ED 262 392)

SENTENCE COMBINING

Description. Sentence combining is a technique designed to help students write and understand complex sentences. The student is shown how to combine short sentences to make increasingly more complex sentences.

Targeted Reading Levels: 3–7

Text: Structured programs of short sentences, the student's own writing, or short sentences from the text

Predominant Focus of Instruction

1. Processing focus: meaning
2. Instructional phase: after reading
3. Response mode emphasized: oral discussion and written discourse
4. Strategy emphasized: elaboration
5. Skill emphasized: sentence comprehension

6. Source of information: text-based
7. Type of instruction: implicit
8. Type of cognitive processing: successive, but using manipulatives adds a simultaneous aspect

Procedure

1. The teacher introduces the concept of combining sentences by using short sentences which the student can read.
2. The teacher explains that simple sentences can be combined and still have the same meaning.
3. She begins by writing sentences on the board. For example:

The dog is brown.
The dog is in the park.
The dog bit the man.

4. Then she shows the students how to delete repeated words or phrases. For the example in Step 3, the following process would take place.
   a. The teacher might say, "If the dog is brown, we can call it a brown dog." On the board, the teacher would write
   brown + dog = brown dog.
   b. The teacher explains that the sentence can be expanded by adding a phrase to tell where the dog is—"in the park." The teacher then shows the change: *The brown dog + in the park = The brown dog in the park.*
   c. She also explains that sentences can be further combined by telling what the dog did as the action in the sentence. Therefore, she adds *bit the man* as the action. The teacher writes: *The brown dog in the park + bit the man = The brown dog in the park bit the man.*
   d. The teacher states that here the combined sentences would be "the brown dog in the park bit the man."
5. The teacher points out to the student that by combining ideas into one sentence, reading and writing become more interesting.

Modifications

1. Phrases can be placed on cards and then combined and recombined to form new sentences.
2. Closed sentence combining, where cued words are provided to indicate how the sentence is combined, can be used to increase sensitivity to a particular sentence structure. For example, the following two sentences might be combined.

I know _____.
Chris stole the cookie.

The teacher supplies the cue word *that,* and the sentences are combined with the following result.

I know that Chris stole the cookie.

Further Diagnostic Applications

Basic View of Reading.   Reading is a text-based process that involves the action of constructing meaning with words in sentences. The sequence of how words are linked in sentences affects reading comprehension; therefore, learning how the words are related in sentences facilitates both reading and writing.

Patterns of Strengths and Strategies.   Sentence combining is most appropriate for students who can read short sentences but have difficulty following sentence order in longer sentences. Usually these students have verbal skills but lack the ability to link information in more complex frameworks.

Learner Patterns That Produce a High Success Rate

1. A successive learner who speaks in short choppy sentences without signal words to combine ideas. The technique shows him how short sentences are combined to form longer sentences.
*2. A simultaneous learner who has difficulty with sentence order as exhibited by continued failure with a cloze activity. Using sentence cards helps this student because he can visually manipulate the words in the sentence.

Using the Technique as a Diagnostic Teaching Lesson.   For sentence combining to be effective, a majority of the following statements must be answered in the affirmative.

Yes   No

_____ _____ 1. The student can easily see the connection between the short sentences and the complex sentences.
_____ _____ 2. The student likes to manipulate words.

For Further Reading

Combs, W. (1980). Sentence-combining practice aids in reading comprehension. In D. Sawyer (Ed.), *Disabled readers—Insight, assessment, instruction* (pp. 104–112). Newark, DE: International Reading Association.

O'Hare, F. (1973). *Sentence-combining* (NCTE Report No. 15). Urbana, IL: National Council of Teachers of English.

Straw, S. B., & Schreiner, R. (1982). The effect of sentence manipulation on subsequent measures of reading and listening comprehension. *Reading Research Quarterly, 17,* 339–352.

SIGHT WORD APPROACH

Description.   The sight word approach is a technique for beginning reading instruction that uses what words mean to develop what the word looks like. By using pictures and oral context, meaning is associated with isolated sight words. After a sight vocabulary is learned, decoding by analogy is taught to expand reading acquisition.

Targeted Reading Levels: K – 2

Text: The basic preprimers and primers of published reading series that contain a regular and controlled introduction of sight words in simple text. Decoding by analogy is taught through known sight words.

Predominant Focus of Instruction

1. Processing focus: print
2. Instructional phase: before reading
3. Response mode emphasized: oral discussion
4. Strategy emphasized: prediction
5. Skill emphasized: word identification
6. Source of information: text-based
7. Type of instruction: implicit
8. Type of cognitive processing: successive, but has a simultaneous quality

Procedure

1. The teacher selects a text that has a controlled sight word vocabulary.
2. She introduces sight words for the story by presenting them in isolation, supplemented by oral context and/or pictures.
3. The teacher reviews the words by placing words on cards and flashing the words in various orders (see "Word Cards" in this chapter). If the student cannot recall the words, a meaning or semantic prompt is used. If the student cannot recall the word *dog,* the teacher might prompt him by saying, "It rained cats and _____."
4. The student reads the story that contains the words. (The teacher uses the format for directed reading activity or directed reading-thinking activity to direct discussion.)
5. The teacher reinforces sight words by using cloze exercises, games with the word cards, and repetitive reading of stories with the controlled vocabulary.
6. After the student can recognize selected words at sight, the teacher uses an analytic phonics (see "Analytic Phonics") to introduce how to decode new words by using analogies to known sight words. For example, the teacher might write *green, grass,* and *grow* on the board. She might then ask the students the following series of questions (the appropriate student answers are supplied in parentheses): "How are they alike? (They have *gr* letters.) What can we say about the *gr* sound? (It goes *gr-r-r.*) The next time you see *gr,* what sound are you going to try? *(gr-r-r.)*"

Further Diagnostic Applications

Basic View of Reading.   Reading is an interactive process where the reader learns words by associating them with meaning. Therefore, learning to read is a process of accumulating enough words recognized at sight that a student can decode new words in a story by using the written context and decoding analogies to known words. Initially, this approach places a high demand on visual feature analysis and phonemic segmentation.

Patterns of Strengths and Strategies.   The sight word approach is most appropriate for students who have developed a systematic way of analyzing the key visual features of words. At the readiness level, this strength is often indicated by letter naming.

Learner Patterns That Produce a High Success Rate

1. A simultaneous learner who attends to the key features of words. He notices what visual features are alike and what visual features are different.
2. The average learner who exhibits no divergent processing characteristics.

Using the Technique as a Diagnostic Teaching Lesson.   For sight word approach to be effective, a majority of the following statements must be answered in the affirmative.

Yes   No

_____ _____ 1. The student easily remembers the sight words taught.
_____ _____ 2. The student analyzes the words, noticing visual differences among words.
_____ _____ 3. The student can segment sounds so that applying decoding analogies is easy.

For Further Reading

Anderson, R. C., Hiebert, E. H., Scott, J. A., & Wilkinson, I. A. G. (1985). *Becoming a nation of readers: The report of the commission on reading.* Washington, DC: National Institute of Education.

Aukerman, R. C. (1984). *Approaches to beginning reading* (2nd ed.) (368–371). New York: John Wiley & Sons.

Ray, D. D. (1971). Specificity in remediation. In B. Batemen (Ed.), *Learning disorders* (pp. 180–192). Seattle, WA: Special Child Publications.

SQ3R

Description.   SQ3R is a procedure for studying content area text that includes the five steps of *survey, question, read, recite,* and *review.* It is designed as a procedure for students to use to monitor their comprehension and learning as they read and study expository text.

Targeted Reading Levels: 5–12

Text: Expository

Predominant Focus of Instruction

1. Processing focus: meaning
2. Instructional phase: before and after reading
3. Response mode emphasized: oral discussion
4. Strategy emphasized: elaboration and prediction
5. Skill emphasized: study skills

6. Source of information: text-based
7. Type of instruction: explicit, but lacks modeling
8. Type of cognitive processing: successive

Procedure

1. The teacher selects a content-area text at an appropriate reading level.
2. She introduces the five steps in a short minilesson.
3. *S—Survey.* The teacher explains how to skim (briefly read) the entire passage to construct an overall framework for the information. She directs the student to use the paragraph headings as key information in understanding the overall framework.
4. *Q—Question.* After surveying the text, the teacher directs the student to develop questions that he thinks will be answered in the passage. The teacher helps the student focus on the key concepts of the text as he develops the questions. She directs the student to use paragraph headings and italics to form the questions for each *section.*
5. *R—Read.* The student reads the text section by section to answer the questions posed at the beginning of each section. After a section has been read, the student proceeds to the next step.
6. *R—Recite.* The teacher explains that the student now is to answer the questions he posed for the section just read. The teacher encourages the student to construct an answer rather than read word for word from the text. At this point, the student may need to write down his answer to facilitate recall.
7. The three steps (question, read, and recite) are repeated for each section.
8. *R—Review.* After the last section is read, the student reviews the questions and answers for the entire text. At this time, the student tries to relate the information into an overall framework that will facilitate recall.

Further Diagnostic Applications

Basic View of Reading. Reading comprehension is a bottom-up process where information from the text forms the framework for learning and recalling facts and concepts in content-area texts.

Patterns of Strengths and Strategies. SQ3R is most appropriate for students who have facility with word recognition and comprehension but lack an overall method for organizing factual information in a content-area text. For these students, the approach provides a systematic method for studying the information.

Learner Patterns That Produce a High Success Rate

1. A passive learner who can use the steps to develop a procedure for studying and remembering text. This gives him a tool for active reading.
2. A successive learner who asks questions but forgets to look for the answers. This gives him a tool for finding answers to the important questions in the text.
3. A successive learner who questions and recalls facts without using an organizational framework so that facts can be conceptually related. The survey and review steps provide a means for relating information into an overall framework.

4. The student who develops self-control easily. This technique gives him the steps to manage his own learning.

Using the Technique as a Diagnostic Teaching Lesson. For SQ3R to be effective, a majority of the following statements must be answered in the affirmative.

Yes No

____ ____ 1. The student identifies important textual information.

____ ____ 2. The student can construct questions from the subtopics.

____ ____ 3. The student follows the procedures and easily incorporates the steps.

For Further Reading

Adams, A., Carnine, D., & Gersten, R. (1982). Instructional strategies for studying content area texts in the intermediate grades. *Reading Research Quarterly, 18,* 27–55.

Pauk, W. (1974). *How to study in college* (2nd ed.). Boston: Houghton, Mifflin.

Robinson, F. P. (1946). *Effective study.* New York: Harper and Bros.

STORY DRAMA

Description. Story drama is a method for developing reading comprehension by using the natural dramatic abilities of students. The student thinks about how a story will end by role playing scenes from the story. By taking the roles of the various characters, the student uses his knowledge of similar experiences, his affective response to the characters, and key information to act out his interpretation of the story (Walker, 1985).

Targeted Reading Levels: 2 –6

Text: Various kinds of literature. Picture storybooks and adventure stories with an intriguing plot lend themselves to dramatic interpretation.

Predominant Focus of Instruction

1. Processing focus: meaning
2. Instructional phase: during reading
3. Response mode emphasized: oral discussion
4. Strategy emphasized: prediction and monitoring
5. Skill emphasized: non-literal comprehension
6. Source of information: reader-based
7. Type of instruction: implicit
8. Type of cognitive processing: simultaneous

Procedure

1. The teacher selects a story with an intriguing plot.
2. The teacher or the students read until there is enough information about the characters to role play the story.

3. The teacher assigns the students the character roles from the story.
4. The teacher uses key props to engage the students in the drama in a concrete way.
5. The teacher and the students begin the drama at the point of interruption.
6. The students dramatize their predictions through role playing.
7. In the process of the dramatization, the teacher may stop the drama and have students exchange roles.
8. The students discuss their predictions and the information used to make the predictions.
9. After the dramatization, the students write an ending for the story.
10. Finally, the students finish reading the story.
11. The students discuss and compare both the drama and the story ending.
12. The teacher and the students discuss their personal interpretations evidenced in the drama and how their individual viewpoints influence those interpretations.

Further Diagnostic Applications

Basic View of Reading.   Reading is a top-down process where the reader's personal interpretation focuses comprehension. Reading requires a personal identification with the story's characters, problems, and events; therefore, the affective purposes of the reader and situational variables influence his model of meaning.

Patterns of Strengths and Strategies.   Story drama is most appropriate for students who are extremely expressive, divergent, and simultaneous when thinking. For these students, the powerful influence of personal, kinesthetic imagery is used to analyze the constructive comprehension process. This strategy encourages active involvement in analyzing not only the story line and character development but also the effect that personal identification with story characters has on comprehension.

Learner Patterns That Produce a High Success Rate

1. A nonverbal student who uses dramatic expression and body language to communicate. Story drama uses this strength to aid the student in verbally communicating his ideas about the story.
2. A passive learner who needs to engage in active interpretation of the story line. Story drama concretely demonstrates how to be actively involved in a story.
*3. A simultaneous learner who relies too heavily on personal identification with story characters and has difficulty establishing a sense of distance when reading. Story drama helps him analyze how his personal identification affects his interpretation.
*4. The dramatic, impulsive learner who needs to attend to the important information in the text. Story drama focuses his attention on character traits and story theme in order to portray a character.

Using the Technique as a Diagnostic Teaching Lesson.   For story drama to be effective, a majority of the following statements must be answered in the affirmative.

Yes   No

_____   _____   1. The student enjoys a dramatic presentation and can easily portray characters.

_____   _____   2. The student makes predictions as a result of the drama.

_____ _____ 3. The student analyzes his personal identification with characters more objectively.

For Further Reading

Galda, L. (1982). Playing about a story: Its impact on comprehension. *Reading Teacher, 36,* 52–58.

Miller, G. M., & Mason, G. E. (1983). Dramatic improvisation: Risk-free role playing for improving reading performance. *Reading Teacher, 37,* 128–131.

Pellegrini, A. D., & Galda, L. (1982). The effects of thematic fantasy play training on the development of children's story comprehension. *American Educational Research Journal, 19,* 443–452.

Walker, B. J. (1985). Right-brained strategies for teaching comprehension. *Academic Therapy, 21,* 133–141.

STORY MAPS

Description.   Story maps are visual representations of the logical sequence of events in a narrative text. The elements of setting, problem, goal, events, and resolution are recorded visually on a sheet of paper (Beck & McKeown, 1981; Pearson, 1982).

Targeted Reading Levels: 1–8

Text: Any narrative text with a fairly coherent story line

Predominant Focus of Instruction

1. Processing focus: meaning
2. Instructional phase: during or after reading
3. Response mode emphasized: written
4. Strategy emphasized: monitoring and elaboration
5. Skill emphasized: literal comprehension
6. Source of information: text-based
7. Type of instruction: explicit
8. Type of cognitive processing: successive, but has a visual arrangement (simultaneous)

Procedure

1. The teacher selects a narrative passage of sufficient length to have a cohesive story line.
2. The teacher prepares questions to lead students through the story map.
3. The teacher discusses the organization of a story by explaining that every story has a beginning, middle, and an end.
   a. The beginning tells the place and who the characters are.
   b. During the middle of the story, the central character has a problem and makes a plan to solve it. Certain events in the story lead to solving the problem.
   c. The end of the story tells how the character(s) solved the problem.

4. The teacher explains the visual story map (see example on page 235) and relates it to story organization.
5. The students read the story.
6. The teacher and the students fill out the map together. The teacher uses the prepared questions to guide the completion of the map.
7. The teacher and the students compare this story with other stories that they have read.

Further Diagnostic Applications

Basic View of Reading. Reading is an interactive process where the reader's understanding of the elements of a story affects reading comprehension.

Patterns of Strengths and Strategies. Story mapping is most appropriate for the learner who profits from a visual representation of story organization in order to develop adequate comprehension. Often the abundance of facts overwhelms the young reader, who needs a simple structure like a story map to apply to stories to help him organize and remember events.

Learner Patterns That Produce a High Success Rate

1. A simultaneous learner who has difficulty organizing sequential events of the story and remembering factual detail. The story map uses his visual strengths to develop the text-based skill of story development.
2. The passive learner who has difficulty retelling the story and often leaves out key events or characters in the retelling. The story map gives a structure to the retelling and reasons for the facts to be remembered.
*3. The fact-bound learner who lacks a cohesive sense of story. The map provides him with an overall view of the story.

Using the Technique as a Diagnostic Teaching Lesson. For story maps to be effective, a majority of the following statements must be answered in the affirmative.

Yes   No

____ ____ 1. The student understands the story map elements.
____ ____ 2. The student improves his ability to retell the story.
____ ____ 3. The student improves the number of questions about story events he can answer.

For Further Reading

Beck, I. L., & McKeown, M. G. (1981). Developing questions that promote comprehension: The story map. *Language Arts, 58,* 913–918.

Fowler, G. L., & Davis, M. (1985). The story frame approach: A tool for improving reading comprehension of EMR children. *Teaching Exceptional Children, 17,* 296–298.

Pearson, P. D. (1982). *Asking questions about stories* (Ginn Occasional Papers No. 15). Lexington, MA: Silver Burdett & Ginn.

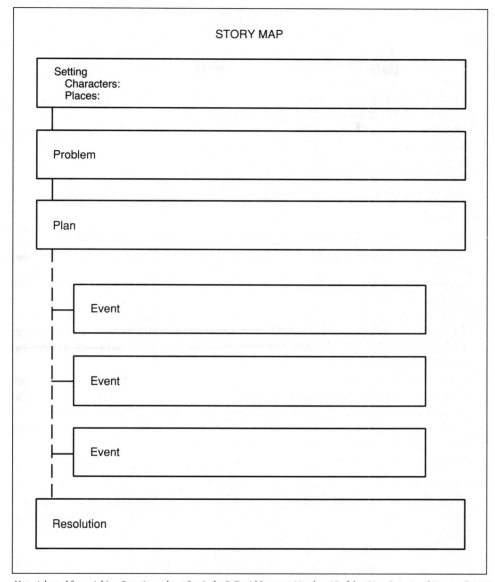

STORY MAP

Setting
   Characters:
   Places:

Problem

Plan

Event

Event

Event

Resolution

Note. Adapted from *Asking Questions about Stories* by P. David Pearson, Number 15 of the Ginn Occasional Papers, © 1982 by Ginn and Company. Used by permission of Silver, Burdett & Ginn Inc.

Figure 9–5
Story map

STORY WRITING APPROACH

Description.   Story writing is an instructional format for teaching narrative writing that includes three stages: prewriting, writing, and evaluating. By writing their own stories, students increase their awareness of story parts.

Targeted Reading Levels: 3 – 6, but can be used at all levels

Text: Student's own writing

Predominant Focus of Instruction

1. Processing focus: meaning
2. Instructional phase: after reading
3. Response mode emphasized: written discourse
4. Strategy emphasized: elaboration
5. Skill emphasized: non-literal comprehension
6. Source of information: reader-based
7. Type of instruction: implicit
8. Type of cognitive processing: simultaneous

Procedure

1. The teacher introduces the structure of a story. Stories have a beginning (the characters and place), middle (problems and the events), and an end (solution of the problem).
2. The teacher and the students brainstorm ideas to select a topic and information that might go into the story.
3. Using the information collected, the students write their stories. The teacher emphasizes that the story needs to flow from one idea to the next and make sense.
4. The teacher has the students reread their stories to see if they make sense. She uses the following questions.
   a. Does the story make sense?
   b. Do I have all the story parts?
   c. Have I left out any information that the reader might need to know in order to understand my story?
5. The students revise any unclear information.
6. The students make a final copy of their stories.

Modifications

1. Prewriting can use a visual story map to form the outline of the story.
2. For the student who has a great deal of difficulty, the teacher might use a story frame with only minimal ideas deleted.
3. Guided imagery journeys may be used as a prewriting activity.
4. A story can be composed by a small group of students. Each person writes a segment of the story and then passes the text to the next person. Each student's contribution to the story line must build upon prior information and make sense.
5. Pairs of students can read and edit each other's stories.
6. Instead of step 4, the students can take their stories to the author's circle where students provide input on the three questions (see Harste, Short, and Burke, 1988, for complete description).

Further Diagnostic Applications

Basic View of Reading.   Reading is a top-down process where the reader interprets the author's intended meaning. An author writes a text that allows a clear interpretation by the reader but assumes that a certain amount of inferencing will occur on the part of the reader.

Patterns of Strengths and Strategies.   The story writing approach is most appropriate for students who need to write in order to experience how a story is organized so that it makes sense. This approach emphasizes the constructive nature of reading and that the text needs to "make sense."

Learner Patterns That Produce a High Success Rate

1. The simultaneous learner who writes and reads for self-understanding and meaning but does not realize that a story is a contractual agreement between reader and writer. This technique helps him think about what the author wants him to understand.
2. The passive learner who does not understand story organization. By writing his own parts of a story, he learns to attend to these story features when he reads.
*3. The reader who relies on his own background knowledge to interpret text and does not attend to sentence meaning. By writing his own stories and listening to others interpret them, he becomes more sensitive to the function that text structure has in developing meaning.

Using the Technique as a Diagnostic Teaching Lesson.   For story writing to be effective, a majority of the following statements must be answered in the affirmative.

Yes   No

_____ _____ 1. The student prefers to write what he thinks rather than contribute to a discussion.
_____ _____ 2. The student writes fluently and can construct text that makes sense.
_____ _____ 3. The student understands the parts of a story well enough to be able to construct a coherent story.

For Further Reading

Aulls, M. (1982). *Developing readers in today's elementary school.* Boston: Allyn & Bacon.

Glazer, S. M., & Searfoss, L. W. (1988). *Reading diagnosis and instruction: a C-A-L-M approach.* Englewood Cliffs, NJ: Prentice Hall.

Tiedt, I. M., Bruemmer, S. S., Lane, S., Stelwagon, P., Watanabe, K. O., & Williams, M. Y. (1983). *Teaching writing in K–8 classrooms.* Englewood Cliffs, NJ: Prentice-Hall.

STRATEGY INSTRUCTION

Description.   Strategy Instruction is an instructional format designed to teach procedures related to print and meaning processing. In these lessons, teachers model their own thinking related to an unfamiliar task and then ask students to think out loud about how they are completing the task. This instruction is followed by coaching students to ensure self-regulated learning.

Targeted Reading Levels: All levels

Text: Authentic text

Predominant Focus of Instruction

1. Processing focus: print or meaning
2. Instructional phase: before, during and after reading
3. Response mode emphasized: oral discussion
4. Strategy emphasized: monitoring and elaboration
5. Skill emphasized: all reading tasks
6. Source of information: text and reader-based
7. Type of instruction: explicit phasing to self-directed learning
8. Type of cognitive processing: successive quickly phasing to simultaneous

Procedure

1. The teacher selects the new procedure to be learned.
2. The teacher talks about what the strategy is, what it is like, and gives some examples.
3. The teacher explains why the strategy works when reading.
4. The teacher models the new strategy in authentic texts. This means she talks out loud about how she reads the text paying particular attention to the targeted strategy.
5. The students use the targeted strategy in authentic texts. They talk out loud about their problem-solving strategies.
6. The teacher supports the "strategic thinking" of the readers. She phases in to coach thinking and phases out to let students use strategies independently.
7. After reading, the students and teacher discuss the strategies they used for text interpretation.
8. Students are asked to assess their strategy deployment and how it affected their text interpretation.
9. The teacher explains when to use the strategy and what to do if its use is not effective.

Further Diagnostic Applications

Basic View of Reading.   Reading is a strategic, interactive process where the reader strategically implements the strategies and skills he knows to solve problems when interpreting texts.

Patterns of Strengths and Strategies.   The strategy instruction format is most appropriate when teaching unfamiliar reading procedures or when students lack particular reading strategies.

Learner Patterns That Produce a High Success Rate:

1. This format can be used to teach unfamiliar strategies to active readers. It helps them consolidate strategies.
2. This format is designed for the student who needs a teacher to model the reading process. By following the teacher's model, the student develops more strategic reading.

*3. This format has been used with passive readers who read words without constructing meaning. The modeling and coaching help passive readers use active reacting strategies.

Using the Technique as a Diagnostic Teaching Lesson. For Strategy Instruction to be effective, a majority of the following statements must be answered in the affirmative:

Yes   No

_____ _____ 1. The student can imitate the teacher's model.
_____ _____ 2. The student profits from oral discussion of strategic reading.
_____ _____ 3. The student can assess his own strategy use.

For Further Reading

Palincsar, A. S., & Brown, A. L. (1989). Instruction for self-regulated reading. In L. B. Resnick & L. E. Klopfer (Eds.), *Toward the thinking curriculum: Current cognitive research* (pp. 19–40). Alexandria, VA: Association for Supervision and Curriculum Development.

Walker, B. J. (1990b). *What research says to the teacher: Remedial reading.* Washington, DC: National Education Association.

SUMMARIZATION

Description. Summarization teaches the student how to write summaries of what he reads. He is shown how to delete unimportant information, group similar ideas, decide on or invent topic sentences, and list supporting details. These procedures culminate in a short paragraph that reflects the most important information.

Targeted Reading Levels: 6–12

Text: Most appropriate for expository text

Predominant Focus of Instruction

1. Processing focus: meaning
2. Instructional phase: after reading
3. Response mode emphasized: written discourse
4. Strategy emphasized: elaboration
5. Skill emphasized: literal comprehension and study skills
6. Source of information: text-based to reader-based
7. Type of instruction: explicit
8. Type of cognitive processing: simultaneous

Procedure

1. The teacher selects an expository text.
2. She describes a summary as a short version of the text that contains all the important information.

3. The teacher explains that the purpose of writing summaries is to put all the important information together so it can be remembered better.
4. The students read a short selection.
5. The students reread the selection and ask themselves, "What is this mainly about?"
6. The teacher reads her summary of the selection and presents it on the overhead.
7. Each student finds the summary statement in the original text. The student marks the information that each statement represents.
8. The teacher talks about the rules for writing summaries by telling the students how she wrote her summary.
9. The teacher demonstrates the rule of deleting trivial information. She points out that many writers tell us interesting information that is not a key idea. She tells them to ignore this information when writing a summary.
10. The teacher demonstrates the rule for deleting repeated information. She explains that many writers repeat information to make their point. When writing a summary, students should use this idea only once and ignore repeated information.
11. The teacher demonstrates the rule for combining details into a generalization. When possible, students should combine details that fit into the same category and rename that category with a bigger category. For example, *pigs, horses, cows,* and *chickens* can be renamed to *farm animals.*
12. The teacher demonstrates how to select the topic sentence. She points out that the topic sentence is the author's one sentence summary. It usually comes at the beginning or the end of the paragraph.
13. The teacher demonstrates how to invent a topic sentence when there is not a summary sentence. In this case, she shows how to organize all the important information into one category. Then she writes a sentence that tells what it is mainly about. She shows how to think about how the important information relates.
14. The students write a summary for the demonstration selection and check their summaries individually with the rules.
15. The students compare their summaries in small groups.
16. The students write a summary for another selection.
17. When they have finished, the students describe how they constructed their summaries.
18. The teacher shows them her summary and talks about how she constructed it.
19. The students write summaries for several more selections on their own.

Further Diagnostic Applications

Basic View of Reading.   Reading is an interactive process where the reader decides what is important about the text in order to summarize and remember what it says.

Patterns of Strengths and Strategies.   Summarization is most appropriate for students who like to think about what a text mainly says but have difficulty remembering the facts that support this decision. The approach helps this student focus on relating all the textual information that is important to the key idea.

Learner Patterns That Produce a High Success Rate

1. A passive reader who needs to be actively engaged in interpreting the text. This gives him a written record of what he thinks and how his strategies work when he reads.

*2. A successive reader who cannot tie important information together in order to remember information. Summarization helps him decide on general categories that relate details.

*3. A successive reader who thinks everything in the text is important to remember. Summarization helps him learn to delete unimportant and repeated information.

Using the Technique as a Diagnostic Teaching Lesson.   For summarization to be effective, a majority of the following statements must be answered in the affirmative.

Yes   No

_____ _____ 1. The student can write fairly fluently; therefore, writing the words on paper does not interfere with the task.

_____ _____ 2. The student learns to distinguish what is important and what is unimportant fairly easily.

_____ _____ 3. The student learns to group individual information of like categories easily.

For Further Reading

Hare, V. C., & Borchardt, K. M. (1984). Direct instruction of summarization skills. *Reading Research Quarterly, 20,* 62–78.

King, J. R., Biggs, S., & Lipsky, S. (1984). Students' self-questioning and summarizing as reading study strategies. *Journal of Reading Behavior, 16,* 205–218.

SUSTAINED SILENT READING

Description.   Sustained silent reading (SSR) is the designation of an uninterrupted time where both the students and the teacher read self-selected reading materials for their own purposes. The teacher models her own enjoyment of reading. In turn, the students begin to define their interests and read for their own enjoyment.

Targeted Reading Levels: All levels

Text: Self-selected

Predominant Focus of Instruction

1. Processing focus: meaning
2. Instructional phase: during reading
3. Response mode emphasized: some oral discussion
4. Strategy emphasized: depends on student
5. Skill emphasized: fluency and non-literal comprehension
6. Source of information: reader-based

7. Type of instruction: implicit
8. Type of cognitive processing: depends on student

Procedures

1. Before beginning SSR, the teacher collects a variety of reading materials that represent a wide range of reading levels and text types (magazines, newspapers, novels, and informational texts).
2. Next, the teacher reads aloud favorite parts of books or talks about books other students have enjoyed to stimulate students' interest.
3. The teacher designates a specific time for reading each day. (After lunch is a good time; students select their books before lunch so they can be ready to read as soon as lunch is over. Another good time is at the end of the day.)
4. The students select their books prior to the designated time.
5. The teacher explains the "rule of thumb," which aids in book selection. According to this rule, the student selects a book and reads a page at random. When he reaches the first word he does not know, he places his little finger on it. On the next difficult word, he places the next finger, and so on. If he reaches his thumb before the end of the page, the book is too difficult and he must find another book.
6. The students do not browse and select books during the designated time span.
7. Initially, the teacher sets aside a short time period (5 to 10 minutes) and then increases the amount of time each day.
8. The teacher uses a timer to monitor the time so everyone is free to read.
9. The students read silently for the time period.
10. The teacher and anyone else in the room read silently for the time period.
11. The teacher does not keep records or have students make reports on what they read. The students are in control of what and how much they read.
12. Initially, the teacher allows pretend reading, browsing through books, and looking at pictures. She also initially provides a narrow range of selection choices.
13. The teacher reiterates some key principles of sustained silent reading.
    a. Read what you want.
    b. Getting all the words right is not necessary.
    c. If it meets your needs, skipping pages is OK.

COMMENT: Although this technique is more effective for some children than others, it is recommended as part of the diagnostic teaching session because it allows students to read for their own purpose, practice their reading skills, and experience "wanting to read."

Further Diagnostic Applications

Basic View of Reading.   Reading is a top-down process where the readers' personal interpretations and enjoyment are the focus of reading. By the teacher's modeling her own enjoyment of literature, she shares "wanting to read."

Patterns of Strengths and Strategies.   Sustained silent reading is most appropriate for the active, independent reader who enjoys reading for his own purposes rather than the teacher's purposes. In this technique, personal enjoyment is gained while reading for individual purposes.

Learner Patterns That Produce a High Success Rate

1. A successive learner who needs to identify his own reasons for reading. Sustained silent reading allows him to identify his own interests and reasons for reading.
*2. An inattentive reader who cannot read long sections of text silently. This technique allows him to increase his attention during silent reading.
*3. A passive reader who views himself as a failure when reading. This technique allows him to feel success when reading because he controls the reasons for reading.

Using the Technique as a Diagnostic Teaching Lesson. For SSR to be effective, a majority of the following statements must be answered in the affirmative.

Yes   No

____ ____ 1. The student selects books he wants to read.
____ ____ 2. The student observes the rules of silent reading and is not disruptive during that time.
____ ____ 3. The student increases his own task reading time and asks for longer time for sustained silent reading.

CAUTION: Be persistent in expecting success. Even though some students will pretend to be reading, it is the model and message that they can read what they like that is important.

For Further Reading

Berglund, R. L., & Johns, J. L. (1983). A primer on uninterrupted sustained silent reading. *Reading Teacher, 36,* 534–539.
Trelease, J. (1985). *The read-aloud handbook.* New York: Penguin Books.

SYNTHETIC PHONICS APPROACH

Description. Synthetic phonics teaches sound-symbol relationships in words to facilitate word identification. The student is systematically instructed to say the letter sounds in words and then blend the sounds together to decode the unknown word. Rules for the phonic relationships are presented with examples. The rapid transfer of decoding principles to new words is expected as the text includes many words that follow the rule but were not presented before reading.

Targeted Reading Levels: 1–2

Text: Decodable words and some isolated drill

Predominant Focus of Instruction

1. Processing focus: print
2. Instructional phase: before reading

3. Response mode emphasized: oral discussion
4. Strategy emphasized: elaboration
5. Skill emphasized: word analysis
6. Source of information: text-based
7. Type of instruction: explicit
8. Type of cognitive processing: successive

Procedure

1. The teacher selects phonic rules to be taught.
2. She selects texts and words to illustrate the rule.
3. The teacher directly teaches the letter sounds.

> The letter *s* goes *s-s-s.*
> The letter *t* goes *t-t-t.*
> The letter *n* goes *n-n-n.*
> The letter *m* goes *m-m-m.*

> In short words that have a consonant at the beginning and the end and an *a* in the middle, the letter *a* says *ă-ă-ă*

4. The student blends the sounds together to form words.

> *S-ă-m* says *Sam.*
> *S-ă-t* says *sat.*

5. The student reads the words in a text that uses the sound-symbol relationships that the teacher has introduced.

> Sam is on the mat.
> The man is on the mat.
> Sam sat on the man on the mat.

6. The teacher facilitates the transfer of rules to new words. She teaches the sounds for *d, h,* and *c.* Then she asks the student to read the following story:

> The man has a hat. The hat is in the sand.
> The man sat on the mat in the sand.
> Dan sat on the mat in the sand.
> Sam is a cat. Sam ran in the sand.
> Sam ran to Dan. Sam ran to the man.
> Sam ran in the sand. Sam sat in the sand.
> Sam sat on the man's hat.
> The man is mad at Sam. Sam ran.

Further Diagnostic Applications

Basic View of Reading.   Reading is a bottom-up process where effective reading is based on accurate decoding of words. Learning sounds of letters and sounding out words precedes reading stories; therefore, decoding precedes comprehension.

Patterns of Strengths and Strategies.   Synthetic phonics is a process of successive blending of sounds requiring the child to hold a sequence of sounds in his memory while synthesizing them to form a word. Young children who have facility with sound blending and can hold oral sequences in memory will have the greatest success with this method.

Learner Patterns That Produce a High Success Rate

1. A successive learner who can rapidly and flexibly apply the rules to new words in new contexts. This technique allows him to apply phonic rules to the stories that he reads.
2. A successive learner who has facility with language so that the systematic decoding of words becomes a tool rather than an end by itself. For this reader, the phonics facilitates word identification without interfering with fluency.
3. A passive learner who can blend sounds and profits from direct instruction in the sound system. This technique directly shows him how to decode new words as well as directs his attention to individual letters.
4. The successive learner who can blend sounds but has no visual memory. (The student can always decode the word he has forgotten.) The Distar program allows for this.
5. The successive learner who needs many repetitions before the word becomes part of his sight vocabulary. The Distar phonics program provides many repetitions of new words before they are expected to be learned.

Using the Technique as a Diagnostic Teaching Lesson.   For synthetic phonics to be effective, a majority of the following statements must be answered in the affirmative.

Yes   No

____ ____ 1. The student can blend sounds.
____ ____ 2. The student can segment sounds.
____ ____ 3. The student can hold a sequence of letter sounds in memory long enough to blend the sounds to form a word.

For Further Reading

Aukerman, R. C. (1984). *Approaches to beginning reading* (2nd ed.). New York: John Wiley & Sons, 368–371.

Bereiter, C., & Englemann, S. (1970). *The Distar reading program.* Chicago: Science Research Associates.

Ray, D. D. (1971). Specificity in remediation. In B. Bateman (Ed.), *Learning disorders* (pp. 180–191). Seattle, WA: Special Child Publications.

TALKING BOOKS

Description.   The talking books method uses tape-recorded readings of selected stories to increase word recognition and reading fluency. The student repeatedly reads along with a tape until he can read the text fluently with comprehension (Carbo, 1978).

Targeted Reading Levels: K – 5

Text: Stories with specially prepared tape recordings

Predominant Focus of Instruction

1. Processing focus: print
2. Instructional phase: during reading
3. Response mode emphasized: oral
4. Strategy emphasized: prediction
5. Skill emphasized: word identification and fluency
6. Source of information: reader-based
7. Type of instruction: implicit
8. Type of cognitive processing: simultaneous

Procedure

1. The student selects a text that is interesting to him.
2. The teacher secures or makes a tape recording of the story.
3. If she makes a tape, she includes the following:
   a. She segments the story so that the student can easily finish a tape in one sitting.
   b. She cues the page numbers so the student can easily find the page.
   c. She records the text using the natural phrases of language.
4. The student follows the line of print with his finger.
5. The student listens to the tape recording to develop an overall understanding of the story.
6. Then the student listens and reads along with the tape as many times as necessary until he can read the text fluently.
7. The student rehearses the text by himself.
8. The student reads the text to the teacher.
9. The teacher evaluates fluency and comprehension.
10. If he reads the passage fluently with comprehension, the student listens and reads the next segment of the story or another story.

Further Diagnostic Applications

Basic View of Reading.   Reading is a top-down process where the reader's personal understanding of the story drives the word recognition process. By repeatedly listening to the story, the reader gains an understanding of the story meaning, story structure, and sentence structure. He uses this understanding to facilitate recognizing the words in the story.

Patterns of Strengths and Strategies.   The talking books technique is most appropriate for the beginning reader or the nonfluent reader who easily memorizes stories. This memorization facilitates fluent reading of text and allows the student to attend to both meaning and print simultaneously. By memorizing stories, the student is exposed to lots of words in context, enabling him to apply phonic knowledge, recognize sight words, and self-correct as he meaningfully reads text.

Learner Patterns That Produce a High Success Rate

1. A simultaneous learner who relies too heavily on background knowledge when orally reading; therefore, he does not self-correct using graphic cues. This

technique develops word identification by using the overall textual meaning (a strength) to identify words.

2. A nonfluent reader who has had an overemphasis of synthetic or explicit phonic instruction and, therefore, has become word-bound. This technique develops reading in meaningful phrases.

3. A passive reader who reads word by word without attention to meaning. This technique restores reading for meaning by learning to read whole stories with expression and allows the student to experience success.

*4. A slow reader who has not developed either decoding skills or a recognition vocabulary. Talking books use memorizing whole stories so that the student can read lots of words before developing either phonic knowledge or a sight word vocabulary.

Using the Technique as a Diagnostic Teaching Lesson. For talking books to be effective, a majority of the following statements must be answered in the affirmative.

Yes   No

____ ____ 1. The student is sufficiently interested in the text to listen and read the story repeatedly.

____ ____ 2. The student memorizes the story fairly easily, requiring only a minimal number of listen-and-read sessions.
(More than a week on the same story is too long.)

____ ____ 3. As the story is read, the student follows the text and associates the words he hears with the words on the page.

For Further Reading

Carbo, M. (1978). Teaching reading with talking books. *Reading Teacher, 32,* 267–273.

Chomsky, C. (1978). When you still can't read in third grade: After decoding what?" In J. Samuels (Ed.), *What research has to say about reading instruction* (pp. 13–30). Newark, DE: International Reading Association.

THEMATIC EXPERIENCE APPROACH

Description. The Thematic Experience Approach is a technique to develop an indepth knowledge of a particular topic through integrating reading and writing activities (Davis, 1990).

Targeted Reading Levels: 4 – 12

Text: Particularly suited for expository text, but can be used with all types.

Predominant Focus of Instruction

1. Processing focus: meaning
2. Instructional phase: before and after reading
3. Response mode emphasized: oral discussion and written responses

4. Strategy emphasized: elaboration
5. Skill emphasized: literal and non-literal comprehension
6. Source of information: text-based leading to reader-based
7. Type of instruction: implicit
8. Type of cognitive processing: simultaneous

Procedure:

1. The teacher and students select a topic to be studied.
2. The teacher creates experiences to engage students in a general understanding of the topic.
3. The teacher and students then discuss what they are learning and already know about the topic.
4. The teacher and students brainstorm possible research topics while the teacher records these on a chart or chalkboard.
5. The students select a possible research topic and discuss this topic in a small group.
6. The teacher discusses research focus with each student elaborating ideas and suggesting possible reference sources.
7. Each student independently researches his special focus related to the topic.
8. Each student takes notes on his special focus area.
9. Each student prepares a presentation on his special focus to share with the class. This presentation can take many response modes: graphic organizer, video, written report, etc.
10. The teacher and students evaluate their learning.

Further Diagnostic Applications

Basic View of Reading.   Reading is a process where students build topic knowledge using what they know. What they know is usually related to their individual interests.

Patterns of Strengths and Strategies.   The thematic experience approach is appropriate for students who build a background of experiences by pursuing their own interests. In researching their interests, these students build a network of new concepts.

Learner Patterns That Produce a High Success Rate

1. Simultaneous readers who prefer to independently research topics to expand their knowledge. The thematic experience approach allows them to build their own theories and concepts.
*2. Readers who have little prior knowledge about a topic. The thematic experience approach begins by using interest to build a network of ideas on an unknown topic.
*3. Bilingual readers who need to build a network of language to express concepts. The thematic experience approach allows them to make connections in both language codes during the experience.

Using the Technique as a Diagnostic Teaching Lesson.   For thematic experience approach to be effective, a majority of the following statements must be answered in the affirmative:

Yes   No

—— —— 1. The student can easily decide what interests him.
—— —— 2. The student likes to work independently researching information about a particular topic.
—— —— 3. The student can share the information with a group of students.

For Further Reading

Davis, S. J. (1990). Breaking the cycle of failure through Thematic Experience Approach. *Journal of Reading, 33*(6), 420–423.

Harste, J. C., Short, K. G., & Burke, C. (1988). *Creating classrooms for authors* (336–339). Portsmouth, NH: Heinemann.

TRIPLE READ OUTLINE

Description.   Triple read outline is the rereading of expository text to develop an organizational framework of main ideas and supporting details. By reading the information three times, the student focuses on different purposes for organizing information during each reading.

Targeted Reading Levels: 7–12

Text: Expository

Predominant Focus of Instruction

1. Processing focus: meaning
2. Instructional phase: during reading
3. Response mode emphasized: written discourse
4. Strategy emphasized: monitoring and elaboration
5. Skill emphasized: study skills
6. Source of information: reader-based and text-based
7. Type of instruction: explicit
8. Type of cognitive processing: simultaneous, but interrupted reading (successive)

Procedure

1. The teacher selects a short expository passage to demonstrate the triple read outline.
2. She makes an overhead of the passage and copies for the students.
3. The teacher states the purpose for the first reading—identify the main idea—and models the step by reading a paragraph out loud and identifying the main idea. Then she writes or illustrates the main idea in the paragraph margins. She

continues the procedure for the entire passage, identifying the main idea of each paragraph in the passage.

4. The teacher models the second procedure—identify supporting details—by talking out loud as she rereads the entire passage and underlining the key details that support the main idea for the first paragraph. She continues the procedure for each paragraph in the entire passage.

5. On the third reading, the teacher models the third step—organize the information into an outline. She puts the notes that she wrote in the margins and the key details into an outline of the passage. Some of the key ideas will not fit into the overall outline. She writes those on a separate page.

6. The teacher writes a summary of the passage. She uses the main idea as the topic sentence and puts in the details that support the main idea. She leaves out information that is not important.

7. Next the teacher distributes copies of a passage from the textbook to be read.

8. This time the students read the passage, looking for the main idea of each paragraph and writing the main idea in the margin. She tells them that some paragraphs will not have a main idea.

9. The students compare their margin "main ideas" with the teacher's margin "main ideas."

10. The students revise the information as necessary.

11. The students read the passage again, looking for and underlining the supporting details for the main ideas in the margin.

12. The students compare the facts they underlined with the facts the teacher underlined.

13. The students revise the underlining as necessary.

14. The students read the passage a third time to organize the information into an outline of main ideas and supporting details. Unimportant information is to be forgotten.

15. The students compare their outlines with the teacher's outline. They discuss the differences and similarities.

16. If the students have left out important information, the teacher models her thinking about why something is important enough to leave in the outline.

17. Using the outline, the students write a three- to four-sentence summary of passage.*

Further Diagnostic Applications

Basic View of Reading.   Reading is an interactive process that requires the reader to select information and organize this information so it can be remembered. Organizing the information into a logical structure facilitates recall, as does rereading the text with different purposes for selecting information.

---

*Note: From *The Triple Read Method for Expository Text* by P. D. Pearson, 1985. Seminar presentation, Eastern Montana College, Billings, MT. Adapted by permission.

Patterns of Strengths and Strategies.   The triple read outline is most appropriate for students who read expository text rapidly and fluently but remember very little of the information when they have finished. Frequently these students do not understand how the author organized the information, so they passively read the words without a reason for gaining information. They think that good readers read the text once rapidly and are somehow able to remember an enormous amount of facts with this simple strategy.

Learner Patterns That Produce a High Success Rate

1. The simultaneous reader who remembers main ideas but forgets the facts. This gives the student a strategy for remembering facts within an overall framework.
2. The passive reader who lacks the strategy to read for different purposes as he is reading. This shows him how to read information for different purposes and the results of these rereadings.
*3. The successive reader who verbalizes the words, remembers some facts, but does not organize the facts by relating them to the key ideas. This gives him a tool for organizing information.

Using the Technique as a Diagnostic Teaching Lesson.   For the triple read outline to be effective, a majority of the following statements must be answered in the affirmative.

Yes   No

_____ _____ 1. The student is able to read the passage rapidly enough that the technique is not too time-consuming.
_____ _____ 2. The student learns how to find a main idea rather easily.
_____ _____ 3. The student learns how to find the supporting details for each main idea without much difficulty.

For Further Reading

Giordano, G. (1982). Outlining techniques that help disabled readers. *Academic Therapy, 17,* 517–522.

Santa, C., Danner, M., Nelson, M., Havens, L., Scalf, J., & Scalf, L. (1986). *Content reading in secondary school: Learning across the curriculum.* Unpublished manuscript, Kalispell School District No. 5, Kalispell, MT.

VISUALIZATION

Description.   Visualization is an approach for improving comprehension by suggesting to children that they form a mental image of the setting and characters as they are reading. It is used to develop word meaning by asking the students to form mental images of words, relating descriptors with the new word.

Targeted Reading Levels: All levels

Text: Isolated words, narrative text, or expository text

Predominant Focus of Instruction

1. Processing focus: meaning
2. Instructional phase: before reading
3. Response mode emphasized: non-verbal responses and oral discussion
4. Strategy emphasized: elaboration
5. Skill emphasized: word meaning
6. Source of information: reader-based
7. Type of instruction: implicit
8. Type of cognitive processing: simultaneous

Procedure for Word Meaning

1. The teacher selects target words for developing meanings.
2. The students look at the word and then close their eyes.
3. The teacher reads a definition and *like a* statements and asks the students to form a mental picture of the word. For example, if the target word is *geyser,* the teacher could say, "Think about a geyser as a large whistling teapot just about to boil. The water is bubbling and the pressure is mounting. When enough pressure builds up, the teapot begins to whistle and blow steam into the air. The geyser is a large teapot in the ground."
4. The teacher and the students discuss their mental pictures.
5. In some cases, the students draw their images.
6. The students read text that uses and elaborates the targeted words.

Procedure for Comprehension

1. The teacher selects the text.
2. The teacher tells the students that forming pictures in their minds can increase their understanding of the text. These mind pictures are like illustrations within the text that can help the reader remember the text.
3. The teacher introduces the story setting.
4. The students close their eyes and imagine what the story is going to be about by using the title and the story setting.
5. The students read the selection up to a designated turning point.
6. The students and the teacher discuss both images and story line.
7. The students close their eyes and imagine what is going to happen next.
8. The students finish reading the selection.
9. The students and the teacher compare and contrast images and what the text said.
10. The teacher uses these questions to guide discussion: How did the characters resolve the problem in the story? How is their resolution like what you imagined? How is it different?

Further Diagnostic Applications

Basic View of Reading.   Reading is an interactive process where information is stored in images as well as words. Reading involves inferencing from the text by using words and images that are stored in memory.

Patterns of Strengths and Strategies. Visualization is most appropriate for the highly visual, simultaneous learner who initially searches visual images to comprehend text. This approach activates these students' strength in representing knowledge in its visual-spatial relationships and encourages them to relate this information to verbal comprehension.

Learner Patterns That Produce a High Success Rate

1. The passive reader who does not check his past experiences to see if what he is reading makes sense. Visualization enhances his active comprehension and monitoring as he learns to check his interpretation with his images.
2. The extremely nonverbal student who codes information in images rather than words. Visualization links his visual images to verbal descriptions.
*3. The highly successive learner who needs to relate text to past experiences. Visualization offers him a tool to connect textual information with prior knowledge.

Using the Technique as a Diagnostic Teaching Lesson. For visualization to be effective, a majority of the following statements must be answered in the affirmative.

Yes   No

_____ _____ 1. The student sees pictures in his mind and uses these to elaborate his interpretation.

_____ _____ 2. The student has difficulty verbalizing ideas and the visualization helps him connect words and images.

For Further Reading

Gambrell, L. B., & Bales, R. J. (1986). Mental imagery and the comprehension-monitoring performance of fourth and fifth grade poor readers. *Reading Research Quarterly, 21,* 454–465.

McNeil, J. D. (1987). *Reading comprehension: New directions for classroom practice* (2nd ed.). Glenview, IL: Scott, Foresman.

Peters, E., & Levin, J. R. (1986). Effects of a mnemonic imagery strategy on good and poor readers' prose recall. *Reading Research Quarterly, 21,* 179–192.

VOCABULARY MAPS

Description. This is a technique for developing word meanings by visually mapping the relationships among words. The target vocabulary word is placed in the center of the map. Related words and concepts are arranged around this word to show relationships between what the student already knows and the new word (Johnson & Pearson, 1984).

Targeted Reading Levels: All levels

Text: Key vocabulary words. (Often this technique is used to introduce vocabulary words for a story.)

Predominant Focus of Instruction

1. Processing focus: meaning
2. Instructional phase: before or after reading
3. Response mode emphasized: oral discussion and written responses
4. Strategy emphasized: elaboration
5. Skill emphasized: word meaning
6. Source of information: reader-based
7. Type of instruction: implicit
8. Type of cognitive processing: simultaneous

Procedure

1. The teacher chooses a word or concept that is a key element of what is to be read.
2. She places the word inside a circle in the middle of a blank page or chalkboard.
3. The students and the teacher brainstorm what is already known about this word and place the information in conceptual relationships, making a visual array of the relationships.
4. The teacher adds each new word that describes the central word to the map by drawing lines and new circles that indicate their relationships to the words. For the word *image,* for example, some relationships involve similes of what an image is like, some suggest the composition of an image, and others look at how an image might be useful.
5. The students read the story.
6. The students and the teacher add additional story information to the map.
7. The students and the teacher discuss new meanings to known words and new relationships among the words that were gained by reading the story.

Modification.   For the student who needs to build a meaning vocabulary, vocabulary cards can be made with vocabulary maps on one side of the card and the word in a sentence on the reverse side. These words are then reviewed periodically for comprehension (see Figure 9–6).

Further Diagnostic Applications

Basic View of Reading.   Reading is an interactive process where readers use their background knowledge to map relationships between word knowledge (verbal labels) and world knowledge (concepts).

Patterns of Strengths and Strategies.   Vocabulary mapping encourages the student to use his experiential knowledge to expand his definitional knowledge; therefore, it is most appropriate for the student who tends to think visually about the relationship of information without describing these relationships in words. This strategy facilitates learning for this student because it begins by showing the visual relationships and then uses words to explain that relationship.

Learner Patterns That Produce a High Success Rate

1. A simultaneous thinker who perceives visual-spatial relationships rather than definitional relationships. This technique helps the student use his visual understanding of relationships to increase his understanding of what words mean.

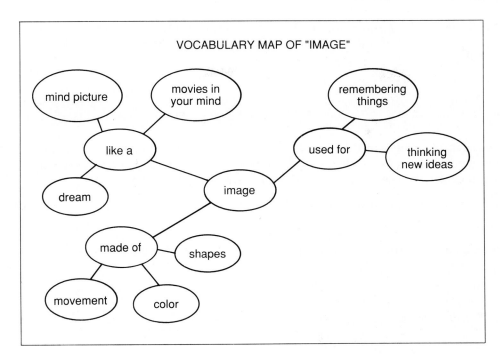

Figure 9–6
Vocabulary Map

2. A bilingual student who has a well-developed conceptual base but nonspecific word usage. The visual mapping of words and relationships helps him make specific comparisons between the events of his life and the words that are commonly used to express them.

*3. A student with verbal weaknesses who needs to develop word knowledge in order to read and understand. This technique helps him develop conceptual relationships among words as well as the verbal labels used to express those relationships.

Using the Technique as a Diagnostic Teaching Lesson.   For vocabulary maps to be effective, a majority of the following statements must be answered in the affirmative.

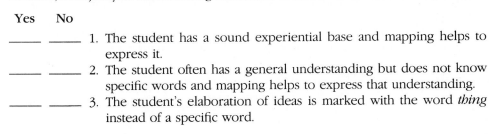

Yes   No

_____ _____ 1. The student has a sound experiential base and mapping helps to express it.

_____ _____ 2. The student often has a general understanding but does not know specific words and mapping helps to express that understanding.

_____ _____ 3. The student's elaboration of ideas is marked with the word *thing* instead of a specific word.

For Further Reading

Heimlich, J. E., & Pittleman, S. D. (1986). *Semantic mapping: Classroom applications*. Newark, DE: International Reading Association.

Johnson, D. D., & Pearson, P. D. (1984). *Teaching reading vocabulary* (2nd ed.). New York: Holt, Rinehart & Winston.

Sinatra, R. C., Berg, D., & Dunn, R. (1985). Semantic mapping improves reading comprehension of learning disabled students. *Teaching Exceptional Children, 17,* 310–314.

WORD CARDS

Description. The word card technique is a systematic recording of sight words introduced during the reading lesson. These words are placed on individual cards so that they may be used to review and reinforce a recognition vocabulary.

Targeted Reading Levels: PP – 2

Text: Isolated words

Predominant Focus of Instruction

1. Processing focus: print
2. Instructional phase: after reading
3. Response mode emphasized: oral
4. Strategy emphasized: elaboration
5. Skill emphasized: word identification
6. Source of information: text-based
7. Type of instruction: implicit
8. Type of cognitive processing: successive, because it is only part of the meaning

Procedure

1. The teacher selects target sight words (including easy words too) for each lesson. (CAUTION: Word cards are most effective when concrete words are selected.)
2. She writes these words on 3″ × 5″ cards.
3. On the back of the card, she places the word in a sentence taken from the child's own vocabulary or the story.
4. To reinforce sight word recognition, the teacher flashes the word cards with a semantic cue from the story. For example, when the target word *play* is forgotten, the teacher uses the semantic cue, "We like to run and _____ ."
5. The teacher counts the correct word cards and records the student's responses on a graph (see the example) so that the student can monitor his progress.

JANE'S PROGRESS					
Word	*M*	*T*	*W*	*Th*	*F*
door	✔	✔	✔	✔	✔
window			✔		✔
shade		✔	✔	✔	✔
visitor				✔	✔

6. The teacher keeps two file boxes of cards. One box is for those words that are mastered; it can be used to construct activities that reinforce learning and as a spelling dictionary for creative writing. The other box is for those words that need to be reinforced through repetition.

Modifications.   A multitude of ideas are available for using word cards to reinforce and stimulate word learning. These are a few of the most popular.

1. The teacher uses the word cards to form a word bank that can be used to write and combine sentences. This bank becomes a spelling dictionary of known words for writing during uninterrupted sustained silent writing.
2. The teacher uses word cards to construct games to reinforce learning.
3. Students classify the word cards according to categories and make a feature analysis grid (see "Feature Analysis Grid" in this chapter).

Further Diagnostic Applications

Basic View of Reading.   Reading is a bottom-up process where the reader initially masters a set of words that are automatically recognized "at sight." These sight words are mastered in isolation, then read in sentences, and finally read in stories.

Patterns of Strengths and Strategies.   Word cards are most appropriate for the young reader who is developing a recognition vocabulary. For these students, the isolated drill of sight words draws attention to the key visual features of words. This reinforces the learning of word features and aids the automatic recognition of words.

Learner Patterns That Produce a High Success Rate

1. A simultaneous learner who needs more than the average contextual repetitions before a word is mastered. Presenting the word card with a semantic cue helps the student focus on meaning and visual cues at the same time.
2. An inattentive learner who attends more to the pictures and context when reading stories than the important features of the words. Word cards isolate the word so the student can identify and remember the key visual features.
*3. A passive learner who needs direct instruction in how to select the key features so he can remember what the words look like. Word cards provide a tool for the teacher to talk about what words look like.

Using the Technique as a Diagnostic Teaching Lesson.   For the word card technique to be effective, a majority of the following statements must be answered in the affirmative.

Yes   No

____ ____ 1. The student can remember the words flashed.
____ ____ 2. The student needs a minimal number of trials to remember the word visually.
____ ____ 3. The student needs a minimal amount of prompting when the word is flashed.

For Further Reading

Stauffer, R. (1970). *The language experience approach to teaching of reading.* New York: Harper & Row.

Wilson, R. M., & Cleland, C. J. (1985). *Diagnostic and remedial reading for classroom and clinic* (5th ed.) (pp. 233–234). Columbus, OH: Merrill.

Epilogue

This text has included the means that effective teachers have used to adapt instruction to individual student needs. Intuitively, teachers have always changed their instruction as they encountered problems in teaching. Diagnostic teaching recognizes this decision-making power and places assessment in the hands of effective teachers.

SOME POINTS FOR ASSESSMENT

Although different from the traditional forms of assessment, diagnostic teaching produces practical, efficient, and valid information about the learner.

1. It is practical because suggestions for instruction can be incorporated immediately into the instructional program.
2. It is efficient because reading instruction and learning do not stop in order to test; instead they become an integral part of assessment.
3. It is valid because diagnostic teaching assesses reading in the same kind of instructional situation that is used throughout the student's educational plan.

SOME FINAL POINTS ON INSTRUCTION

1. Selecting techniques from the tables should be considered tentative and subject to confirmation through teaching.
2. The student's response to instructional techniques changes as she learns.
3. The student's response to instruction is an interaction among instructional variables in the reading event. Every event has a different set of interactions.
4. Instructional placement is based not only on how the student performs with aided instruction (mediated level) but also on the degree of task modification and teacher investment. The basic premise for placement is this: "If I can find a way to teach easily what the student needs to know, I can place the student at a higher reading level."

Administering an Informal Reading Assessment

1. Select texts that sample a range of reading levels, or use a published informal reading inventory.
2. Establish the readability of the text, if necessary.
3. Prepare questions that focus on important information, coherent textual structure, and key concepts. If you use a published informal reading inventory, be sure to check the questions for coherence and importance.
4. Establish rapport quickly and begin assessment.
5. If necessary, use a word recognition list to establish a beginning level for assessment.
6. Start with a passage that you think will be at the independent level of difficulty.

Substitutions or mispronunciations (the replacement of one word for another): Mark the mispronounced word by drawing a line through it and writing the substitution above the word.

want
"The man ~~went~~ to the store," said Ann.

Omissions (leaving out words): Circle the word omitted.

"The man to (the) store," said Ann.

Insertions (adding extra words): Draw a caret and write the inserted word above it.

away
"The man went ^ to the store," said Ann.

Transpositions (changing the word order): Mark with a ⌐‾‾‾‾ .

"The man went to the store," said Ann.⌐

Prompted words (words that have to be prompted or supplied by the teacher): Write the letter *P* above these words.

P
"The man went to the store," said Ann.

Table A–1
Scoreable Errors
(to be used in
computing error
rate)

Repetitions (words or phrases that are repeated more than once): Draw a line over the word and write the letter *R* over the line.

R
''The man ~~went~~ to the store,'' said Ann.

Repeated repetitions (words or phrases that are repeated several times): Draw a line over the word or phrase and mark it with a *2R* over the line.

2 R
''The man ~~went~~ to the store,'' said Ann.

Self-correction: If the child corrects an error, a line is drawn through the previously marked error and the letter *C* is written at the end of the line.

~~went~~ C
''The man ~~went~~ to the store,'' said Ann.

Pauses: Long pauses that are used to gain meaning are marked with slashes.

''The man//went to the store,'' said Ann.

Punctuation errors (ignoring punctuation symbols): Draw a circle around the omitted punctuation mark.

''The man went to the store,'' said Ann. ''Then he went home.''

7. Have the student read the passage orally.
8. Using the coding system in Table A–1 (p. 261) and Table A–2, record the student's performance as he reads. Both scoreable errors (Table A–1) and recordable errors (Table A–2) are coded. Scoreable errors determine whether a passage was read at the independent, instructional, or frustration level. Recordable errors are additional errors used to evaluate a reader's strategies but are not computed in the error rate.
9. Assess comprehension by asking the prepared questions.
10. Find the oral accuracy score by calculating the error rate (Table A–3) or the percentage of oral accuracy (Table A–4).
11. Compute the comprehension percentage score for the passage by (a) dividing the number of questions answered correctly by the total number of questions asked and (b) multiplying the resulting decimal number by 100. Example: Brian answered 8 of 10 questions correctly.

    (a) $\frac{.80}{10)\overline{8.00}}$

    (b) $.80 \times 100 = 80\%$

1. Determine the number of scoreable errors per passage read.

   Example: Brian made 4 scoreable errors.

2. Estimate the total number of words in the passage read.

   Example: Brian read 86 words.

3. Divide the total number of words by the number of scoreable errors. Round off the quotient to the nearest whole number.

   Example: $\dfrac{21 \text{ r } 2}{4\,)\,86} = 21$

4. The quotient determined in Step 3 becomes the denominator in the error rate and the number 1 becomes the numerator.

   Example: Brian read the passage with 1 error every 21 running words; the error rate is 1/21.

Table A–3
Calculating Error
Rate

1. Estimate the number of words read.

   Example: Brian read 80 words.

2. Count the number of scoreable errors.

   Example: Brian made 4 errors.

3. Subtract the number of scoreable errors from the number of words read.

   Example: 80 words – 4 errors = 76 words

4. Divide the number of words read correctly by the number of words read.

   Example: $\dfrac{.95}{80\,)\,76.00}$

5. Multiply the resulting decimal number by 100 to find the percentage of oral accuracy.

   .95 × 100 = 95%

Table A–4
Calculating
Percentage of
Oral Accuracy

12. Administer another passage on the same level. Have the student read the paragraph silently.
13. Assess comprehension by an oral retelling followed by direct questioning.
14. Decide the level of performance for each passage the student read. Use either Powell's criteria (1978) from Table A–5 or Betts' criteria (1946) from Table A–6.

Table A–5
Scoring Criteria
by Performance
Grade Level Sug-
gested by W. R.
Powell (1978)

Reading Level	*Word Recognition Error Rate*	*Comprehension Percentage*
Independent		
1–2	1/17 +	80 +
3–5	1/27 +	85 +
6 +	1/35 +	90 +
Instructional		
1–2	1/8–1/16	55–80
3–5	1/13–1/26	60–84
6 +	1/18–1/35	65–90
Frustration		
1–2	1/7 –	55 –
3–5	1/12 –	60 –
6 +	1/17 –	65 –

Note. From *The Finger Count System for Monitoring Reading Behavior* (pp. 7–11) by W. R. Powell, 1981, unpublished paper. Adapted by permission.

Table A–6
Scoring Criteria
Suggested by
Betts (1946)

Reading Level	*Word Recognition*	*Comprehension*
Independent	99% +	90% +
Instructional	95%	75%
Frustration	90% –	50% –

15. Using the information from Step 14, decide how to continue the assessment.
    a. If the student is reading at an independent level, move him up to the next level.
    b. If the student is reading at an instructional level, move him down to the next level to establish independent reading.
    c. If the student is reading at a frustrational level, consider moving him down two levels to establish independent and then instructional reading experiences.
16. Continue using this procedure, alternating between oral and silent reading at each level until a passage is read at the frustration reading level for both oral and silent reading.
17. Summarize the results using the Informal Reading Inventory (IRI) Summary Sheet reproduced in Table A–7.

Student's Name _____ Age _____ Grade _____

Examiner _____ Date _____

IRI Used _____ Form _____

Levels of Performance   Oral   Silent

Independent Level   _____   _____
Instructional Level   _____   _____
Frustration Level   _____   _____

Level	Scoreable Errors (Error Rate)	Percentage of Comprehension Oral	Silent
pp			
p			
1			
2			
3			
4			
5			
6			
7			
8			
9			
10			
11			
12			

Table A–7
Informal Reading
Inventory Sum-
mary Sheet

Bibliography

Adams, A., Carnine, D., & Gersten, R. (1982). Instructional strategies for studying content area texts in the intermediate grades. *Reading Research Quarterly, 18,* 27–55.

Allington, R. L. (1977). If they don't read much how they ever gonna get good? *Journal of Reading, 21,* 57–61.

Allington, R. L. (1980). Teacher interruption behaviors during primary grade oral reading. *Journal of Educational Psychology, 72,* 371–377.

Allington, R. L. (1983). Fluency: The neglected reading goal. *Reading Teacher, 36,* 566–561.

Allington, R. L. (1984a). Content coverage and contextual reading in reading groups. *Journal of Reading Behavior, 16*(2), 85–96.

Allington, R. L. (1984b). Oral reading. In P. D. Pearson (Ed.), *Handbook of reading research* (pp. 829–864). New York: Longman.

Alvermann, D. E. (1989). Effects of spontaneous and induced lookbacks on self-preceived high- and low-ability comprehenders. *Journal of Educational Research, 81,* 325–331.

Anders, P., Bos, C., & Filip, D. (1984). The effects of semantic feature analysis on the reading comprehension of learning disabled students. In J. Niles & L. Harris (Eds.), *Changing perspectives on research in reading/language processing and instruction* (pp. 162–166). Rochester, NY: National Reading Conference.

Anderson, R. C., Hiebert, E. H., Scott, J. A., & Wilkinson, I. A. G. (1985). *Becoming a nation of readers: The report of the commission on reading.* Washington, DC: National Institute of Education.

Andre, M., & Anderson, T. H. (1978–1979). The development and evaluation of a self-questioning study technique. *Reading Research Quarterly, 14,* 605–623.

Andrews, N. (1977). Six case studies in learning to read. (Doctoral dissertation, Indiana University, 1976). *Dissertation Abstracts International, 37,* 4838A.

Armbruster, B. (1985). Content area textbooks: A research perspective. In J. Osborn, P. T. Wilson, & R. C. Anderson (Eds.), *Reading education: Foundations for a literate America* (pp. 47–60). Lexington, MA: D. C. Heath & Co.

Au, K. (1979). Using the experience-text-relationship method with minority children. *Reading Teacher, 32,* 677–679.

August, D., Flavell, J., & Clift, R. (1984). Comparison of comprehension monitoring of skilled and less skilled readers. *Reading Research Quarterly, 20,* 39–54.

Aukerman, R. C. (1984). *Approaches to beginning reading* (2nd ed.). New York: John Wiley & Sons.

Aulls, M. (1982). *Developing readers in today's elementary school.* Boston: Allyn and Bacon.

Baker, L., & Brown, A. (1984). Metacognitive skills and reading. In P. D. Pearson (Ed.), *Handbook of reading research* (pp. 353–394). New York: Longman.

Barr, R. (1972). The influence of instructional conditions on word recognition errors. *Reading Research Quarterly, 7,* 509–579.

Barr, R. (1974–1975). The effect of instruction on pupil reading strategies. *Reading Research Quarterly, 10,* 555–582.

Barr, R., & Sadow, M. (1985). *Reading diagnosis for teachers.* White Plains, NY: Longman.

Barr, R., Sadow, M., & Blachowicz, C. (1990). *Reading diagnosis for teachers: An instructional approach.* New York: Longman.

Beck, I. L. (1981). Reading problems and instructional practices. In G. E. Mackinnon & T. G. Waller (Eds.). *Reading research: Advances in theory and practice. Vol. 2.* New York: Academic Press.

Beck, I. L., & McKeown, M. G. (1981). Developing questions that promote comprehension: The story map. *Language Arts, 58,* 913–918.

Beck, I. L., Omanson, R. C., & McKeown, M. G. (1982). An instructional redesign of reading lessons: Effects on comprehension. *Reading Research Quarterly, 17,* 462–481.

Beck, I. L., McKeown, M. G., Omanson, R. C., & Pople, M. T. (1984). Improving the comprehensibility of stories: The effects of revisions that improve coherence. *Reading Research Quarterly, 19,* 263–277.

Bereiter, C., & Englemann, S. (1966). *Teaching disadvantaged children in the preschool.* Englewood Cliffs, NJ: Prentice-Hall.

Bereiter, C., & Englemann, S. (1970). *The Distar reading program.* Chicago: Science Research Associates.

Berglund, R. L., & Johns, J. L. (1983). A primer on uninterrupted sustained silent reading. *Reading Teacher, 36,* 534–539.

Berliner, D. C. (1981). Academic learning time and reading achievement. In J. T. Guthrie (Ed.), *Comprehension and teaching: Research reviews* (pp. 203–226). Newark, DE: International Reading Association.

Betts, E. A. (1946). *Foundations of reading instruction.* New York: American Book.

Bloome, D., & Green, J. (1984). Directions in the sociolinguistic study of reading. In P. D. Pearson (Ed.), *Handbook of reading research* (pp. 395–421). New York: Longman.

Bloomfield, L., & Barnhart, C. (1961). *Let's read: A linguistic approach.* Detroit: Wayne State Press.

Bond, G. L., & Dykstra, R. (1967). The cooperative research program in first-grade reading instruction. *Reading Research Quarterly, 2,* 1–142.

Brennan, A. D., Bridge, C. A., & Winograd, P. N. (1986). The effects of structural variation on children's recall of basal reader stories. *Reading Research Quarterly, 21,* 91–104.

Bristow, P. S. (1985). Are poor readers passive readers? Some evidence, possible explanations, and potential solutions. *Reading Teacher, 39,* 318–329.

Brophy, J. (1984). The teacher as thinker: Implementing instruction. In G. Duffy, L. Roehler, & J. Mason (Eds.), *Comprehension instruction: Perspectives and suggestions* (pp. 71–92). New York: Longman.

Brown, A. L., & Campione, J. C. (1986). Psychological theory and the study of learning disabilities. *American Psychologist, 41,* 1059–1068.

Brown, C. S., & Lytle, S. L. (1989). Merging assessment and instruction: Protocols in the classroom. In S. M. Glazer, L. W. Searfoss, & L. M. Gentile (Eds.), *Reexamining reading diagnosis: New trends and procedures* (pp. 128–149). Newark, DE: International Reading Association.

Carbo, M. (1978). Teaching reading with talking books. *Reading Teacher, 32,* 267–273.

Carr, E., & Ogle, D. (1987). K-W-L plus: A strategy for comprehension and summarization. *Journal of Reading, 30,* 626–631.

Casale, U. (1985). Motor imaging: A reading-vocabulary strategy. *Journal of Reading, 28,* 619–621.

Cazden, C. B. (1981). Social context of learning to read. In J. T. Guthrie (Ed.), *Comprehension and teaching: Research reviews* (pp. 118–139). Newark, DE: International Reading Association.

Chall, J. (1985). Afterword. In R. C. Anderson, E. H. Hiebert, J. A. Scott, & I. A. G. Wilkinson, *Becoming a nation of readers: The report of the commission on reading* (pp. 123–125). Washington, DC: National Institute of Education.

Chomsky, C. (1978). When you still can't read in third grade: After decoding what? In J. Samuels (Ed.), *What research has to say about reading instruction* (pp. 13–30). Newark, DE: International Reading Association.

Cioffi, G., & Carney, J. J. (1983). Dynamic assessment of reading disabilities. *Reading Teacher, 36,* 764–768.

Clay, M. M. (1969). Reading errors and self-correction behavior. *British Journal of Educational Psychology, 39,* 47–56.

Clay, M. (1985). *The early detection of reading difficulties* (2nd ed.). Portsmouth, NH: Heinemann.

Cohen, R. (1983). Self-generated questions as an aid to reading comprehension. *Reading Teacher, 36,* 770–775.

Collins, A., Brown, F. S., & Larkin, K. M. (1980). Inference in text understanding. In R. F. Spiro, B. C. Bruce, & N. F. Brewer (Eds.), *Theoretical issues in reading comprehension* (pp. 385–410). Hillsdale, NJ: Lawrence Erlbaum Associates.

Collins, A., & Smith, E. (1980). *Teaching the process of reading comprehension.* (Technical Report No. 182). Urbana, IL: University of Illinois, Center for the Study of Reading. (ERIC Document Reproduction Service No. ED 193 616)

Combs, W. (1980). Sentence-combining practice aids in reading comprehension. In D. Sawyer (Ed.), *Disabled readers—Insight, assessment, instruction* (pp. 104–112). Newark, DE: International Reading Association.

Dale, E. (1969). *Audiovisual methods in teaching* (3rd ed.). New York: Holt, Rinehart & Winston.

Dank, M. (1977). What effect do reading programs have on the oral reading behavior of children? *Reading Improvement, 14,* 66–99.

Das, J. P., Kirby, J. R., & Jarman, R. F. (1979). *Simultaneous and successive cognitive processes.* New York: Academic Press.

Davis, S. J. (1990). Breaking the cycle of failure through Thematic Experience Approach. *Journal of Reading, 33*(6), 420–423.

Deford, D. E. (1985). Validating the construct of theoretical orientation in reading instruction. *Reading Research Quarterly, 20,* 351–367.

Delain, M. T., Pearson, P. D., & Anderson, R. C. (1985). Reading comprehension and creativity in black language use: You stand to gain by playing the sounding game! *American Educational Research Journal, 22,* 155–173.

Dowhower, S. (1989). Repeated reading: Research into practice. *The Reading Teacher, 42,* 502–507.

Duffy, G. G., & Roehler, L. R. (1986). *Improving classroom reading instruction.* New York: Random House.

Duffy, G. G., & Roehler, L. R. (1987). Teaching reading skills as strategies. *Reading Teacher, 40,* 414–418.

Durkin, D. (1978–1979). What classroom observations reveal about reading comprehension instruction. *Reading Research Quarterly, 14,* 481–533.

Dybdahl, C. S. (1983, October). *Comprehension strategies and practices.* Paper presented at the Annual Conference of the College Reading Association, Atlanta, GA.

Dybdahl, C. S., & Walker, B. J. (1986). *Predictions strategies and comprehension instruction.* Unpublished paper, Eastern Montana College, Billings, MT.

Ekwall, E. E., & Shanker, J. L. (1983). *Diagnosis and remediation of the disabled reader.* (2nd ed.). Boston: Allyn and Bacon.

Elkind, D. (1983). Stress and learning disabilities. In D. Carnine, D. Elkind, A. D. Hendrickson, D. Meichenbaum, R. Sieben, & F. Smith (Eds.), *Interdisciplinary voices in learning disabilities and remedial education* (pp. 67–80). Austin, TX: Pro-ed.

Faas, L. A. (1980). *Children with learning problems: A handbook for teachers.* Boston: Houghton Mifflin.

Fernald, G. (1943). *Remedial techniques in basic school subjects.* New York: McGraw-Hill.

Feuerstein, R. (1979). *The dynamic assessment of retarded performers: The learning potential assessment device, theory, instruments, and techniques.* Baltimore: University Park Press.

Finn, P. J. (1985). *Helping children learn to read.* New York: Random House.

Fitzgerald, J. (1989). Research on stories: Implications for teachers. In K. D. Muth (Ed.), *Children's comprehension of text* (pp. 2–36). Newark, DE: International Reading Association.

Fowler, G. L., & Davis, M. (1985). The story frame approach: A tool for improving reading comprehension of EMR children. *Teaching Exceptional Children, 17,* 296–298.

Galda, L. (1982). Playing about a story: Its impact on comprehension. *Reading Teacher, 36,* 52–58.

Gambrell, L. B. (1985). Dialogue journals: Reading-writing interaction. *Reading Teacher, 38,* 512–515.

Gambrell, L. B., & Bales, R. J. (1986). Mental imagery and the comprehension-monitoring performance of fourth and fifth grade poor readers. *Reading Research Quarterly, 21,* 454–465.

Gambrell, L. B., Wilson, R. M., & Gantt, W. N. (1981). Classroom observations of task-attending behavior of good and poor readers. *Journal of Educational Research, 74,* 376–381.

Garcia, G. E., & Pearson, P. D. (1990). *Modifying reading instruction to maximize its effectiveness for all students* (Technical Report No. 489). Champaign, IL: University of Illinois, Center for the Study of Reading.

Garner, R., Alexander, P., Slater, W., Hare, V. C., Smith, T., & Reis, R. (1986). Children's knowledge of structural properties of expository text. *Journal of Educational Psychology, 78,* 411–416.

Gentile, L. M. (1983). Lance M. Gentile's comments. In D. Carnine, D. Elkind, A. D. Hendrickson, D. Meichenbaum, R. Sieben, & F. Smith (Eds.), *Interdisciplinary voices in learning disabilities and remedial education* (pp. 81–85). Austin, TX: Pro-ed.

Gentile, L., & McMillan, M. (1987). *Stress and reading difficulties.* Newark, DE: International Reading Association.

Gillet, J. W., & Temple, C. (1986). *Understanding reading problems* (2nd ed.). Boston: Little, Brown.

Giordano, G. (1982). Outlining techniques that help disabled readers. *Academic Therapy, 17,* 517–522.

Gipe, J. P. (1978–1979). Investigating techniques for teaching word meanings. *Reading Research Quarterly, 14,* 624–644.

Glass, G. (1973). *Teaching decoding as separate from reading.* Garden City, NY: Adelphi University Press.

Glass, G., & Burton, E. (1973). How do they decode: Verbalization and observed behaviors of successful decoders. *Education, 94,* 58–63.

Glazer, S. M. (1984). Liberating students to write. *Early Years, 15*(1), 67–69.

Glazer, S. M., & Searfoss, L. W. (1988). *Reading diagnosis and instruction: a C-A-L-M approach.* Englewood Cliffs, NJ: Prentice-Hall.

Goodman, K. S. (1967). Reading: A psycholinguistic guessing game. *Journal of the Reading Specialist, 6,* 126–135.

Goodman, Y. M., & Burke, C. (1980). *Reading strategies: Focus on comprehension.* New York: Holt, Rinehart & Winston.

Graves, M. (1986, January). *Prereading, reading, and postreading activities to foster comprehension and enjoyment of difficult selections.* Paper presented at Seventh Rocky Mountain Regional Conference of the International Reading Association, Colorado Springs, CO.

Grimmett, P. P. (1988). Introduction. In P. P. Grimmett & G. L. Erickson (Eds.), *Reflection in teacher education.* New York: Teachers College Press.

Guszak, F. J. (1967). Teacher questioning and reading. *Reading Teacher, 21,* 227–234.

Guszak, F. J. (1985). *Diagnostic reading instruction in the elementary school.* New York: Harper & Row.

Hare, V. C., & Borchardt, K. M. (1984). Direct instruction of summarization skills. *Reading Research Quarterly, 20,* 62–78.

Hare, V. C., Rabinowitz, M., & Schieble, K. M. (1989). Text effects of selected text features on main idea comprehension. *Reading Research Quarterly, 24,* 72–88.

Harris, A. J. (1977). Ten years of progress in remedial reading. *Reading Teacher, 31,* 29–35.

Harris, A. J. (1984). The diagnosis of reading disabilities. In A. Harris & E. Sipay (Eds.), *Readings on reading instruction* (pp. 416–426). New York: Longman.

Harris, A. J., & Sipay, E. R. (1985). *How to increase reading ability.* New York: Longman.

Harste, J., Burke, C., & Woodward, V. (1982). Children's language and world: Initial encounters with print. In J. Langer & M. Smith-Burke (Eds.), *Reader meets author/bridging the gap: A psycholinguistic and sociolinguistic perspective* (pp. 105–132.). Newark, DE: International Reading Association.

Harste, J. C., Short, K. G., & Burke, C. (1988). *Creating classrooms for authors* (pp. 336–339). Portsmouth, NH: Heinemann.

Harste, J., Woodward, V., & Burke, C. (1984). *Language stories and literacy lessons.* Portsmouth, NH: Heinemann Educational Books.

Haussler, M. M. (1985). A young child's developing concepts of print. In A. Jagger & M. T. Smith-Burke (Eds.), *Observing the language learner* (pp. 73–81). New York: International Reading Association & National Council of Teachers of English.

Heckelman, R. G. (1969). A neurological-impress method of remedial reading instruction. *Academic Therapy, 4,* 277–282.

Heimlich, J. E., & Pittleman, S. D. (1986). *Semantic mapping: Classroom applications.* Newark, DE: International Reading Association.

Helfeldt, J. P., & Lalik, R. (1979). Reciprocal student-teacher questioning. In C. Pennock (Ed.), *Reading comprehension at four linguistic levels* (pp. 74–80). Newark, DE: International Reading Association.

Herber, H. L. (1978). *Teaching reading in content areas* (2nd ed.). Englewood Cliffs, NJ: Prentice-Hall.

Hoffman, J. V. (1988). *Understanding reading instruction: A guide of field-based experiences in reading education.* Boston, MA: Allyn & Bacon.

Hric, K. A., Wixson, K. K., Kunji, M., & Bosky, A. (1988). Individual variability among less able readers. *Reading, Writing, and Learning Disabilities, 4,* 49–87.

Jaggar, A. (1989). Teacher as learner: Implications for staff development. In G. S. Pinnell & M. L. Matlin (Eds.), *Teachers and research: Language learning in the classroom* (pp. 66–80). Newark, DE: International Reading Association.

Johns, J. L. (1981). *Basic reading inventory* (2nd ed.). Dubuque, Iowa: Kendall/Hunt Publishing Company.

Johnson, D. D. (1982). *Three sound strategies for vocabulary development* (Ginn Occasional Papers, No. 3). Lexington, MA: Silver-Burdett & Ginn.

Johnson, D. D., & Pearson, P. D. (1984). *Teaching reading vocabulary* (2nd ed.). New York: Holt, Rinehart & Winston.

Johnston, P. H. (1983). *Reading comprehension assessment: A cognitive basis.* Newark, DE: International Reading Association.

Johnston, P. H. (1984). Assessment in reading. In P. D. Pearson (Ed.), *Handbook of reading research* (pp. 147–182). New York: Longman.

Johnston, P. H., & Pearson, P. D. (1982). Assessment: Response to exposition. In A. Berger & H. A. Robinson (Eds.), *Secondary school reading—What research reveals for classroom practice* (pp. 127–142). Urbana, IL: ERIC Clearinghouse on Reading and Communication Skills and National Conference on Research in English.

Johnston, P. H., & Winograd, P. N. (1985). Passive failure in reading. *Journal of Reading Behavior, 16,* 279–302.

Jongsma, E. A. (1980). *Cloze instruction research: A second look.* Newark, DE: International Reading Association.

Jordan, Andrea (1989). Diagnostic Narrative. Unpublished journals of lessons. Eastern Montana College.

Juel, C. (1984). An evolving model of reading acquisition. In J. Niles (Ed.), *Changing perspectives on research in reading/language processing and instruction.* (pp. 294–297). Rochester, NY: National Reading Conference.

Juel, C. (1988). Learning to read and write: A longitudinal study of 54 children from first through fourth grades. *Journal of Educational Psychology, 80,* 437–447.

Kahn, R. (1983). The method of repeated readings: Expanding the neurological impress method for use with disabled readers. *Journal of Learning Disabilities, 16,* 90–92.

Kaufman, A. S., & Kaufman, N. L. (1983). *K∗ABC Kaufman assessment battery for children: Interpretive manual.* Circle Pines, MN: American Guidance Services.

King, J. R., Biggs, S., & Lipsky, S. (1984). Students' self-questioning and summarizing as reading study strategies. *Journal of Reading Behavior, 16,* 205–218.

Kogan, N. (1971). Educational implications of cognitive styles. In G. S. Lesser (Ed.), *Psychology and educational practice* (pp. 242–292). Glenview, IL: Scott, Foresman.

Labov, W. (1972). *Language in the inner city.* Philadelphia: University of Pennsylvania Press.

Langer, J. A. (1982). The reading processes. In A. Berger & H. A. Robinson (Eds.), *Secondary school reading* (pp. 39–52). Urbana, IL: ERIC Clearinghouse on Reading and Communication Skills and the National Conference on Research in English.

Leu, D. J., DeGroff, L. C., & Simons, H. D. (1986). Predictable texts and interactive-compensatory hypotheses: Evaluating individual differences in reading ability, context use, and comprehension. *Journal of Educational Psychology, 78,* 347–352.

Lipson, M. Y. (1983). The influence of religious affiliation on children's memory for text information. *Reading Research Quarterly, 18,* 448–457.

Luria, A. R. (1973). *The working brain,* London: Penguin.

Manzo, A. V. (1969). The request procedure. *Journal of Reading, 2,* 123–126.

Manzo, A., & Manzo, U. (1990). *Content area reading: A heuristic approach* (pp. 160–163). Columbus, OH: Merrill.

Maria, K., & MacGinitie, W. H. (1982). Reading comprehension disabilities: Knowledge structures and non-accommodating text processing strategies. *Annals of Dyslexia, 32,* 33–59.

Mason, J. M., & Au, K. H. (1990). *Reading instruction for today* (2nd ed.). Glenview, IL: Scott, Foresman.

May, F. (1986). *Reading as communication: An interactive approach* (2nd ed.). Columbus, OH: Merrill.

McClure, A. A. (1985). Predictable books: Another way to teach reading to learning disabled children. *Teaching Exceptional Children, 17,* 267–273.

McKeown, M. (1985). The acquisition of word meaning from context by children of high and low ability. *Reading Research Quarterly, 20,* 482–496.

McNeil, J. D. (1987). *Reading comprehension: New directions for classroom practice* (2nd ed.). Glenview, IL: Scott, Foresman.

Meichenbaum, D. (1977). *Cognitive-behavior modification: An integrative approach.* New York: Plenum Press.

Meichenbaum, D. (1983). Teaching thinking: A cognitive-behavioral approach. In D. Carnine, D. Elkind, A. D. Hendrickson, D. Meichenbaum, R. Sieben, & F. Smith (Eds.), *Interdisciplinary voices in learning disabilities and remedial education* (pp. 127–142). Austin, TX: Pro-ed.

Memory, D. M. (1981). The impress method: A status report of a new remedial reading technique. *Journal of Research and Development in Education, 14,* 102–114.

Miller, G. M., & Mason, G. E. (1983). Dramatic improvisation: Risk-free role playing for improving reading performance. *Reading Teacher, 37,* 128–131.

Mills, R. E. (1956). An evaluation of techniques for teaching word recognition. *Elementary School Journal, 56,* 221–225.

Moore, D., & Cunningham, J. (1984). Task clarity and sixth-grade students' main idea statements. In J. Niles (Ed.), *Changing perspectives on research in reading language processing and instruction* (pp. 90–94). Rochester, NY: The National Reading Conference.

Morrow, L. M. (1989). Retelling stories as a diagnostic tool. In S. M. Glazer, L. W. Searfoss, & L. M. Gentile (Eds.), *Reexamining reading diagnosis: New trends and procedures* (pp. 128–149). Newark, DE: International Reading Association.

Moyer, S. B. (1982). Repeated reading. *Journal of Learning Disabilities, 15,* 619–623.

Newell, G., Suszynski, K., & Weingart, R. (1989). The effects of writing in a reader-based and text-based mode of students' understanding of two short stories. *Journal of Reading Behavior, 21,* 37–57.

Ogle, D. (1986). K–W–L: A teaching model that develops active reading of expository text. *The Reading Teacher, 39,* 564–570.

Ogle, D. (1989). The know, want to know, learn strategy. In K. D. Muth (Ed.), *Children's comprehension of text* (pp. 205–223). Newark, DE: International Reading Association.

O'Hare, F. (1973). *Sentence-combining* (NCTE Report No. 15). Urbana, IL: National Council of Teachers of English.

Olson, G. M., Duffy, S. A., & Mack, R. L. (1984). Thinking-out-loud as a method for studying real-time comprehension processes. In D. E. Kieras & M. A. Just (Eds.), *New methods in reading comprehension research* (pp. 253–285). Hillsdale, NJ: Lawrence Erlbaum Associates.

Orton, J. (1966). The Orton-Gillingham approach. In J. Money (Ed.), *The disabled reader* (pp. 119–146). Baltimore: Johns Hopkins University Press.

Palincsar, A. S., & Brown, A. L. (1984). Reciprocal teaching of comprehension-fostering and comprehension-monitoring activities. *Cognition and Instruction, 1,* 117–175.

Palincsar, A. S., & Brown, A. L. (1989). Instruction for self-regulated reading. In L. B. Resnick & L. E. Klopfer (Eds.), *Toward the thinking curriculum: Current cognitive research* (pp. 19–40). Alexandria, VA: Association for Supervision and Curriculum Development.

Paris, S. G., & Myers, M. (1981). Comprehension monitoring, memory, and study strategies of good and poor readers. *Journal of Reading Behavior, 13,* 5–22.

Paris, S. G., & Oka, E. R. (1989). Strategies for comprehending text and coping with reading difficulties. *Learning Disability Quarterly, 12,* 32–42.

Park, B. (1982). The big book trend—A discussion with Don Holdaway. *Language Arts, 59,* 815–821.

Pauk, W. (1974). *How to study in college* (2nd ed.). Boston: Houghton, Mifflin.

Pearson, P. D. (1982). *Asking questions about stories* (Ginn Occasional Papers No. 15). Lexington, MA: Silver-Burdett & Ginn.

Pearson, P. D. (1983). A critique of F. J. Guszak's study: Teacher questioning and reading. In L. Gentile, M. Kamil, & J. Blanchard (Eds.), *Reading research revisited* (pp. 271–281). Columbus, OH: Merrill.

Pearson, P. D. (1985a). Changing the face of reading comprehension instruction. *Reading Teacher, 38,* 724–738.

Pearson, P. D. (1985b, July). *The triple read method for expository text.* Seminar presentation, Eastern Montana College, Billings, MT.

Pearson, P. D., Hansen, J., & Gordon, C. (1979). The effect of background knowledge on young children's comprehension of explicit and implicit information. *Journal of Reading Behavior, 11,* 201–209.

Pearson, P. D., & Johnson, D. D. (1978). *Teaching reading comprehension.* New York: Holt, Rinehart & Winston.

Pearson, P. D., & Raphael, T. E. (1985). Increasing student's awareness of sources of information for answering questions. *American Educational Research Journal, 22,* 217–235.

Pearson, P. D., & Spiro, R. J. (1980). Toward a theory of reading comprehension instruction. *Topics in Language Disorders, 1,* 71–88.

Pellegrini, A. D., & Galda, L. (1982). The effects of thematic fantasy play training on the development of children's story comprehension. *American Educational Research Journal, 19,* 443–452.

Peters, E., & Levin, J. R. (1986). Effects of a mnemonic imagery strategy on good and poor readers' prose recall. *Reading Research Quarterly, 21,* 179–192.

Pichert, J. W. (1979). *Sensitivity to what is important in prose.* (Technical Report No. 149). Champaign, IL: University of Illinois, Center for the Study of Reading. (Eric Document Reproduction Service No. ED 179 946)

Pinnell, G. S., Deford, D. E., & Lyons, C. A. (1988). *Reading recovery: Early intervention for at-risk first grader.* Arlington, VA: Educational Research Service.

Pinnell, G. S., Fried, M. D., & Estice, R. M. (1990). Reading recovery: Learning how to make a difference. *Reading Teacher, 43,* 282–295.

Powell, W. R. (1973). Acquisition of a reading repertoire. *Library Trends, 21,* 177–195.

Powell, W. R. (1978, May). *Measuring reading informally.* Paper presented at the International Reading Association, Houston, TX.

Powell, W. R. (1984). Mediated (emergent) reading levels: A construct. In J. Niles (Ed.), *Changing perspectives on research in reading language processing and instruction* (pp. 247–251). Rochester, NY: The National Reading Conference.

Powell, W. R. (1986, December). *Emergent (mediated) reading levels: A new construct for placement from a Vygotskian view.* Paper presented at the National Reading Conference, Austin, TX.

Raffini, J. P. (1988). *Student apathy: The protection of self-worth.* Washington, DC: National Education Association.

Raphael, T. E. (1982). Question-answering strategies for children. *Reading Teacher, 36,* 186–190.

Raphael, T. (1986). Teaching question answer relationships, revisited. *The Reading Teacher, 39,* 526–522.

Rasinski, T. V. (1985). *A study of factors involved in reader-text interactions that contribute to fluency in reading.* Unpublished doctoral dissertation. Columbus, OH: The Ohio University.

Rasinski, T. V., & Deford, D. E. (1988). First graders' conception of literacy: A matter of schooling. *Theory into Practice, 27,* 53–61.

Ray, D. D. (1970). *Ray reading methods test* (Experimental ed.). Stillwater, OK: RRMT Publications.

Ray, D. D. (1971). Specificity in remediation. In B. Batemen (Ed.), *Learning disorders* (pp. 180–191). Seattle, WA: Special Child Publications.

Readence, J. E., Baldwin, R. S., & Rickelman, R. J. (1983). Instructional insights into metaphors and similes. *Journal of Reading, 27,* 109–112.

Reynolds, R. D. (1980). The effect of attention on the learning and recall of important text elements (Doctoral dissertation, University of Illinois, 1979). *Dissertation Abstracts International, 40,* 5380A.

Robinson, F. P. (1946). *Effective study.* New York: Harper and Bros.

Routman, R. (1988). *Transitions: From literature to literacy.* Portsmouth, NH: Heinemann.

Rowe, D. & Harste, J. (1986). Reading and writing in a system of knowing: Curriculum implications. In M. R. Sampson (Ed.), *The pursuit of literacy: Early reading and writing* (pp. 126–144). Dubuque, IA: Kendall/Hunt Publishing Company.

Rowe, M. B. (1973). *Teaching science as continuous inquiry.* New York: McGraw-Hill.

Rupley, W. H., & Blair, T. R. (1978). Characteristics of effective reading instruction. *Educational Leadership, 36,* 171–173.

Samuels, S. J. (1979). The method of repeated readings. *Reading Teacher, 32,* 403–408.

Samuels, S. J. (1980). The age-old controversy between holistic and subskill approaches to beginning reading instruction revisited. In C. McCullough (Ed.), *Persistent problems in reading education* (pp. 202–221). Newark, DE: International Reading Association.

Santa, C. M., Dailey, S. C., & Nelson, M. (1985). Free-response and opinion-proof: A reading and writing strategy for middle grade and secondary teachers. *Journal of Reading, 28,* 346–352.

Santa, C., Danner, M., Nelson, M., Havens, L., Scalf, J., & Scalf, L. (1986). *Content reading in secondary school: Learning across the curriculum.* Unpublished manuscript, Kalispell School District No. 5, Kalispell, MT.

Schneider, E. J. (1979). Researchers discover formula for success in student learning. *Educational Research and Development Report, 2,* 1–6.

Schon, D. A. (1988). Coaching reflective teaching. In P. P. Grimmett & G. L. Erickson (Eds.), *Reflection in teacher education* (pp. 19–30). New York: Teachers College Press.

Schunk, D. J., & Rice, J. M. (1987). Enhancing comprehension skill and self-efficacy with strategy value information. *Journal of Reading Behavior, 19,* 285–302.

Sinatra, R. C., Berg, D., & Dunn, R. (1985). Semantic mapping improves reading comprehension of learning disabled students. *Teaching Exceptional Children, 17,* 310–314.

Singer, H. (1989). An instructional model for reading and learning from text in the classroom. In R. A. Thompson (Ed.), *Classroom reading instruction* (pp. 3–12). Dubuque, IA: Kendall/Hunt.

Singer, H., & Donlan, D. (1982). Active comprehension: Problem-solving schema with question generation for comprehension of complex short stories. *Reading Research Quarterly, 17,* 166–185.

Slater, W. H. (1986, December), *Expository text features which influence comprehensibility.* Paper presented at the National Reading Conference, Austin, TX.

Sloyer, S. (1982). *Readers theatre: Story dramatization in the classroom.* Urbana, IL: National Council of Teachers of English.

Smith, F. (1978). *Reading without nonsense.* New York: Teachers College Press.

Smith-Burke, M. T. (1982). Extending concepts through language activities. In J. Langer & M. T. Smith-Burke (Eds.), *Reader meets author/bridging the gap: A psycholinguistic and sociolinguistic perspective* (pp. 163–180). Newark, DE: International Reading Association.

Spiro, R. J., (1979). *Etiology of reading comprehension style.* (Tech. Rep. No. 124). Champaign, IL: University of Illinois, Center for the Study of Reading.

Spiro, R. J., & Myers, A. (1984). Individual differences and underlying cognitive process. In P. D. Pearson (Ed.), *Handbook of reading research* (pp. 471–504). New York: Longman.

Stanovich, K. E. (1980). Toward an interactive-compensatory model of individual differences in the development of reading fluency. *Reading Research Quarterly, 16,* 32–71.

Stanovich, K. E. (1981). Attentional and automatic context effects in reading. In A. M. Lesgold & C. A. Perfetti (Eds.), *Interactive processes in reading* (pp. 241–262). Hillsdale, NJ: Lawrence Erlbaum Associates.

Stauffer, R. (1970). *The language experience approach to the teaching of reading.* New York: Harper & Row.

Stauffer, R. (1975). *Directing the reading-thinking process.* New York: Harper & Row.

Stein, N. L., & Trabasso, T. (1982). What's in a story: An approach to comprehension and instruction. In R. Glaser (Ed.), *Advances in instructional psychology* (Vol. 2, pp. 213–254). Hillsdale, NJ: Erlbaum.

Strange, M. (1980). Instructional implications of a conceptual theory of reading comprehension. *Reading Teacher, 33,* 391–397.

Straw, S. B., & Schreiner, R. (1982). The effect of sentence manipulation on subsequent measures of reading and listening comprehension. *Reading Research Quarterly, 17,* 339–352.

Tannen, D. (1982). Spoken and written language. In D. Tannen (Ed.), *Exploring orality and literacy.* Norwood, NJ: Ablex Publishing Corporation.

Taylor, B. (1985). Toward an understanding of factors contributing to children's difficulty summarizing textbook material. In J. A. Niles & R. V. Lalik (Eds.), *Issue in literacy: A research perspective* (pp. 125–132). Thirty-fourth Yearbook of the National Reading Conference, Rochester, NY: National Reading Conference.

Tiedt, I. M., Bruemmer, S. S., Lane, S., Stelwagon, P., Watanabe, K. O., & Williams, M. Y. (1983). *Teaching writing in K–9 classrooms.* Englewood Cliffs, NJ: Prentice-Hall.

Tierney, R. J. (1982). Learning from text. In A. Berger & H. A. Robinson (Eds.), *Secondary school reading—What research reveals for classroom practice.* Urbana, IL: National Conference on Research in English and ERIC Clearinghouse on Reading and Communication Skills.

Tierney, R. J., & Cunningham, J. (1984). Research on teaching reading comprehension. In P. D. Pearson (Ed.), *Handbook of reading research* (pp. 609–656). New York: Longman.

Tierney, R. J., & Pearson, P. D. (1983). Toward a composing model of reading. *Language Arts, 60,* 568–580.

Tierney, R. J., Readence, J. E., & Dishner, E. K. (1990). *Reading strategies and practices: A compendium* (3rd ed.). Boston, MA: Allyn & Bacon.

Trelease, J. (1985). *The read-aloud handbook.* New York: Penguin Books.

Vacca, R., & Vacca, J. (1986). *Content area reading* (2nd ed.). Boston: Little, Brown.

Vygotsky, L. S. (1978). *Mind in society.* Cambridge, MA: Harvard University Press.

Walker, B. J. (1982). A new approach to language experience. *Journal of Language Experience, 5,* 25–30.

Walker, B. J. (1985a). Right-brained strategies for teaching comprehension. *Academic Therapy, 21,* 133–141.

Walker, B. J. (1985b). *Using guided fantasy to teach reading.* Paper presented at the Second Rupertsland Regional Reading Conference of the International Reading Association, Regina, Saskatchewan, Canada. (ERIC Document Reproduction Service No. ED 253 850)

Walker, B. J. (1989). Classroom strategies for learner differences in reading. In R. A. Thompson (Ed.), *Classroom reading instruction* (pp. 91–102). Dubuque, IA: Kendall/Hunt.

Walker, B. J. (1990a). A model for diagnostic narratives in teacher education. In N. Padak, T. Rasinski, & J. Logan (Eds.), *Challenges in reading* (pp. 1–10). Kent, OH: College Reading Association.

Walker, B. J. (1990b). *What research says to the teacher: Remedial reading.* Washington, DC: National Education Association.

Walker, B. J., & Mohr, T. (1985). *The effects of self-questioning on reading comprehension*. Paper presented at the Washington Organization for Reading Development—Research Conference, Seattle, WA. (ERIC Document Reproduction Service No. ED 262 392)

Watson, D. (1985). Watching and listening to children read. In A. Jaggar & M. T. Smith-Burke (Eds.), *Observing the language learner* (pp. 115–129). Newark, DE: International Reading Association and National Council of Teachers of English.

Weaver, G. C. (1979). Using the cloze procedure as a teaching technique. *Reading Teacher, 32,* 632–636.

Wertheimer, A. (1974). Story dramatization in the reading center. *English Journal, 64,* 85–87.

Wilson, R. M., & Cleland, C. J. (1985). *Diagnostic and remedial reading for classroom and clinic* (5th ed.). Columbus, OH: Merrill.

Winograd, P. (1984). Strategic difficulties in summarizing texts. *Reading Research Quarterly, 19,* 404–425.

Witkin, H. A., Moore, C. A., Goodenough, D. R., & Cox, P. W. (1977). Field-dependent and field-independent cognitive styles and their educational implications. *Review of Educational Research, 47*(1), 1–64.

Wixson, K. K., & Lipson, M. Y. (1986). Reading (dis)abilities: An interactionist perspective. In T. E. Raphael (Ed.), *Contexts of school-base literacy* (pp. 131–146). NY: Random House.

Zutell, J. (May, 1988). Developing a procedure for assessing oral reading fluency: Establishing validity and reliability. Paper presented at 33rd Annual Convention, International Reading Association, Toronto, Canada.

Zutell, J. (1989). Developing a procedure for assessing oral reading fluency: Establishing validity and reliability. Paper presented at the National Reading Conference, Tucson, Arizona.

Index

Reading Disabilities

① Reading by Eye

written Lang

letters composed of lines → VIS. An.

↓

Vis. Wd. Recogn. (code in brain pattern)

↓

sd wd. picture → Meaning

↓

Speech Prod. (correct wd)

↓

Spoken Lang.

(Direct Model)

---

② Rd by Ear

Spoken Lang.

↓

Acoustic anal

↓

Acous. code ← letter to Sound Conversion ← graphic code

↓

Aud. wd Recog.

↓

meaning

S. Lang

↓

A A

↓

AC

↓

AWR

Direct Road Wr. Lang.

↓

V A

↓

generaling Surface GC Indirect Route

can't comprehend

notice earlier

STEK for steak

Vis. Wd. Recog

— meaning —

Speech Prod.

Spoken Lang.

× Phonological sight vocab

struc sound symbol

L to S Conv.

---

written Lang.

↓

Vis. Analysis

↓

graphic code

The Author

Barbara J. Walker is professor and chair of the Department of Special Education and Reading at Eastern Montana College, where she also coordinates the Reading Clinic. Dr. Walker was a distinguished finalist for the International Reading Association's 1991 Albert J. Harris Award, and was the 1987 recipient of the Eastern Montana College Faculty Achievement Award for scholarship and creativity. She received her Ed.D from Oklahoma State University in Curriculum and Instruction specializing in reading disabilities. Her research interests focus on individual assessment, learning styles, and imagery instruction. Before entering college teaching, Dr. Walker was a reading specialist in the elementary schools of Stillwater, Oklahoma; organized and taught in the college reading program at Vernon Regional Junior College in Vernon, Texas; and coordinated the educational program at the Hogar Paul Harris in Cochabamba, Bolivia.

Dr. Walker is a frequent presenter at state, regional, and national reading conferences, where she speaks on individual differences in the acquisition of literacy. She is active in various professional organizations, including the Montana State Reading Council (where she is editor of the *Montana Reading Journal*), the International Reading Association, the College Reading Association, and the National Reading Conference.

[handwritten notes:]

Dyslexia = bk. down of one or more cogn. areas
Obstical bH Graphic code + visur.

PL 94 142
1 Def
2 Symptoms
3 Synonyms
4 exclusion

1986
1 Ref
2 Symp incl.
3 Symptoms
4 Excl.
5 Eligi.

fail, fail, fail

(4) Surveys:

* if at 50%ile you are taller than 50% shorter than 50%

* if at 90%ile you are taller than 90% or 9 out of 10 people

50% (average)

<23%ile

7 78%ile

below

above

mean median = largest #

100% of group

Why?

* provides a quick indication of student attitudes toward reading.

* very pos. to very neg. } Garfield ranked against a Nat'l. Sample

Score $\rightarrow$ 4pts 3pts 2pts 1pt

Recreational: (ie) 92%ile → in the top 10% of how he feels about reading

Academic: (ie) 13%ile doesn't feel great 83% feel better!

Total (Full): (ie) 48% → close to average (Total) look at Rec. + acad. to evaluate.

Acquired Dyslexia = due to brain injury

Devel. Dyslexia = not related to brain injury

Bottom up = Print driven.
TOP Down = meaning driven
Interactive = Both

Readability → most general task to matching

* reasonable to talk about text as being easy or difficult

Scale ↑ usually based on grade level
IRI ≈ ex. passages

5 approaches to assessing

① Eyeball = you look at it & say yes 3rd grade. (Experience)
* most common
* Adv = fast, easy
* Disadv = relies on exp.

② Informal Testing
(a) IRI = a student who is an average reader have them open a book & read from it
text → reader

(b) CLOZE = eliminate a blank out words
* Inside the head factors (not the text) (Predict)

③ Readability formulas (Quant. approach)
* ave. sentence length ① Fry's (59)
* word length ② Rauygor graph (60)
* comparing wd. lists
* heavy emphasis on linguistic variables

④ Reading Scales (not quantitative)
* more structured than eyeball
* Series of graded passages
* lay book on one side, wd. list on another
* internal & external factors
- Printed materials (external)
external added to eyeball read. outside the head

⑤ Readability Nomograph (61)
* similar to readability formula along w/ task of vocabulary & background knowledge
(a) inside the head = background, interests
(b) outside " " = text itself
(syntactic, ave. wd. length, abstract)
* highlights readability for student & broader sense (classroom) (S.S. Book)
quantitative

① Fry's = counting Ling. variables
(59) ① ave. wd. length
② ave. sentence length Syllables count/100 wd.
② Rauygor = more popular
length of wd. more than 6 letters

CLOZE (Mad Libs)

* gives context, but no support for choosing type of wd.

* may be placed as a 20% closed task (every 5th wd. blank)

adaption: * may adapt; by giving first letter & blanks

Easier * MAZE TASK = have mult. choice/select wd.
(pg. 63)

* must fill in same wd, not a wd that is diff. but means the same.

Ⓐ CLOZE (assessment)

3 Related Roles
① Readability of text (text → cloze → STUDENT (both ways))
② reading level of students
③ match materials & students (Reader → Text)

Ⓑ CLOZE for (Instruction)
① Look @ wds. & make sure wd. your deleting has clues scattered throughout text.
② Using Cloze w/ material

Reading level	Cloze %	Diff. level	Solution
IND	61+	too easy	Supplement no IND research more diff. tex.
INST	40-60	adequate	structured reading teacher guidance
FRS	39-	too diff.	Struct. List Easier text

Baumann IND 58-100   MAZE IND ≥ 85
INS 44-57   INS 60-75
FRS 0-43   FRS ≤ 50

Louis Chong
if NCE 7 △ NCE = overachiever

* important to identify students for
  special services, not always approp.

① Norm Ref. =

* interpretation of scores
* compare students to others based
  on normally dist. scores

* helps identify expectations for children

② Criterion Ref. =

* ~~prior~~
   prior curricular areas

* What accept as student competence
  in this area

NP Nat'l % = % of students in the norm
   group ~~both~~ that your student did as
   well as or better. 1-99% (50% = norm)
   below ave. = <23-24% / above = >78%

NS = national Stanine based on normal curve (1-9)
      1-3 below, 4-6 average, 7-9 (above)

GE = Grade Equiv = X . Y
          year/grade ← month of school yr.

NCE addresses problem w/ % scores
     diff. b/t 50 & 55 & 90 & 95
            ↓ when on the scale you are

    ① don't correspond to raw scores
NCE ② make it constant (5 pt. eg. = 5 pt. eg.)

AANCE = Anticipated Norm Curve Equiv.
           level you expect student to perform

CSI = 100 = the mean = like IQ
         * measure ability
         * estimate where student should perform

Check discrepancy b/t ability + achievement